P9-CET-999

BY BEN RHODES

The World as It Is

After the Fall

After the Fall

AFTER THE FALL

Being American in the World We've Made

BEN RHODES

RANDOM HOUSE
New York

Published in the United States by Random House, an imprint and division of Penguin Random House LLC, New York.

Random House and the House colophon are registered trademarks of Penguin Random House LLC.

LIBRARY OF CONGRESS CATALOGING-IN-PUBLICATION DATA
Names: Rhodes, Benjamin, author.
Title: After the fall : being American in the world we've made / Ben Rhodes.
Other titles: Being American in the world we've made
Description: New York : Random House, [2021] | Includes index.
Identifiers: LCCN 2020056623 (print) | LCCN 2020056624 (ebook) |
ISBN 9781984856050 (hardback) | ISBN 9781984856067 (ebook)
Subjects: LCSH: World politics—21st century. | Globalization—Political aspects—United States. | United States—Politics and government—2017– | Nationalism—United States—History—21st century. | Political corruption—Hungary—History—21st century. | Political corruption—Russia (Federation)—History—21st century. | Political corruption—China—History—21st century. | Global Financial Crisis, 2008–2009.
Classification: LCC D863 .R48 2021 (print) | LCC D863 (ebook) |
DDC 909.83/1—dc23
LC record available at https://lccn.loc.gov/2020056623
LC ebook record available at https://lccn.loc.gov/2020056624

Printed in the United States of America on acid-free paper

randomhousebooks.com

2 4 6 8 9 7 5 3 1

First Edition

Book design by Fritz Metsch

For my family, and for people battling authoritarianism everywhere

The final takeover does not happen with one spectacular Reichstag conflagration, but is instead an excruciating, years-long process of many scattered, seemingly insignificant little fires that smolder without flames.

—ECE TEMELKURAN

Contents

PART III: THE CHINESE DREAM

PART IV: WHO WE ARE: BEING AMERICAN

Prologue

ONCE THERE WAS a nation that ascended to a position of preeminence unparalleled in history. This nation held within its hands the capacity to destroy, shape, and enlighten all human life on earth. Its position of preeminence was reached after what seemed like an inexorable rise: born in revolution, built in part by the toil of those who suffered the lash of the whip, preserved through the crucible of Civil War, populated by immigrants from everywhere, enlarged through the brutal conquest of a continental frontier, enhanced by great feats of engineering and ingenuity, validated by the defeat of fascist ideologies that subjugated people half a world away and the extension of civil rights at home.

The expansion of this nation's influence was for a time contained by the barrier of an alternative form of human organization: communism. When the wall that symbolized this barrier came down, it was as if a dam had broken, allowing a great flood to water the soil on the other side. New markets would create wealth that people had been denied. Unmatched military strength would maintain peace among nations. Technological innovation would raise standards of living and make all human knowledge accessible to people everywhere. The people themselves would live in the freedom guaranteed by democracy, the uncorrupted government of, by, and for the people: the inevitable endpoint of history.

To be born American in the late twentieth century was to take the fact of a particular kind of American exceptionalism as granted—a state of nature arrived at after all else had failed.

In the span of just thirty years, this assumption would come crashing down. Ironically, once they were unbridled, the very forces that enabled this nation's rise would accelerate its descent. The globalized spread of profit-seeking capitalism accelerated inequality, assaulted people's sense of traditional identity, and seeded a corruption that allowed those with power to consolidate control. After the attacks of September 11, 2001, this nation's sense of purpose was channeled into a forever war that hemorrhaged resources, propagated a politics of Us versus Them, and offered a template and justification for autocratic leaders who represented an older form of nationalism. This nation's new technologies proliferated like an uncontrolled virus before we understood their impact, transforming the way that human beings consume information; at first hopeful, the unifying allure of the Internet and social media segmented people back into lonely tribes where they could be more easily manipulated by propaganda, disinformation, and conspiracy theory. Somehow, after three decades of unchecked American capitalism, military power, and technological innovation, the currents of history had turned against democracy itself, bringing back those older forms of nationalism and social control in new packaging.

To be American in 2020 was to live in a country diminished in the world, unwilling to control the spread of disease or face up to our racism, and looking over the precipice of abandoning the very democracy that was supposed to be the solid core of our national identity.

Understanding how that happened is the starting point to figuring out how to move forward. America itself is a nation that encompasses the multitudes of humanity, a country populated with all of humanity's contradictions, hypocrisies, and opposing impulses. Having been humbled by our own excesses and salvaged by the narrow escape of the 2020 election, America has an opportunity to step back into history as a nation with a new understanding of how to improve upon the world we made. To do so, we have to re-create an identity that draws on our better history as a nation of outsiders, reflexively distrustful of power, joined together to do big things, united by a set of principles that allows each of us to be whoever we want to be regardless of tribe. That is what we owe the world, and ourselves.

After the fall, we must determine what it means to be American again.

I SET OUT to write this book in the wake of the Obama presidency so that I could understand what happened to the world, my country, and myself. After working for eight years at the height of American political power, I felt like an exile in my own country. It was a newly disorienting reality, and one that lent itself to questioning every assumption I had as an American.

Travel was the most comforting and illuminating escape I could make from the political chaos back home. I took every opportunity I could to go overseas, and I found myself seeking out the kind of people I never really had the opportunity to fully *know* when I was in government: dissidents, activists, oppositionists—anyone, really, who looked at power from the perspective of an outsider. What an opportunity—to learn the stories of individuals who lived the political trends that I had watched from the exalted distance of the White House. Unburdened by being American themselves, they experienced no difficulty of politeness or discomfort that prevented them from seeing the Trump years for what they were: an American experiment with fascism, albeit of a particularly incompetent and corrupt kind. But there was also a similarly obvious reality: The forces that produced a Trump presidency long predated it and would still be there after it was over. Indeed, a new model of nationalist authoritarian politics is a defining reality of our world today.

The more I investigated this phenomenon, trying to work it out for myself, the more I saw the fingerprints of the era of American hegemony on what was shaping the lives of people all around me. How the 2008 financial crisis had collapsed not only the global economy, but also confidence in the very fact of American-led globalization, opening the door to deeply familiar nationalist appeals. How the post-9/11 wars had also discredited American leadership while opening the door to a hypersecuritized politics of Us versus Them, one that could easily be repurposed to target an available Other in country after country. How the spread of social media had unleashed a flood of disinformation that undermined democracy while offering autocrats ever more powerful tools of social and political control.

I saw this most clearly in three countries that were Communist throughout the Cold War and are at the center of the political forces remaking the world today. In Hungary, where the anticommunist liberal turned reactionary nationalist Viktor Orban took advantage of the 2008 financial crisis to create a model of authoritarian politics that is strikingly similar to the playbook that the Republican Party has run in America. In Russia, where Vladimir Putin capitalized upon the humiliations of the end of the Cold War to build a cabal anchored in corruption and nationalism and then set out to turn the United States into a mirror image with American social media as his most potent offensive weapon. And in China, where Xi Jinping is building the model for a new world order on the pillars of state-controlled capitalism, national sovereignty, and totalitarian technology. Remove any democratic values, and you get the shift from the recent American model to the emerging Chinese one.

This is a book of stories, based on the instinct that it is best to see global events through the perspective of individual lives. The Hungarian opposition searching for a democratic identity capable of overcoming the blood-and-soil nationalism of the past and the failure of globalization to deliver on its promise. The Russians who have been victimized by violence and are still insisting on a politics cleansed of corruption, anchored in the truth. The Hong Kong protesters who saw a freedomless capitalist techno-totalitarian future encroaching upon their city and launched a movement that should be heard as a cry of warning. Collectively, their stories allowed me to see more clearly what had happened in their countries and why, as well as to see the myriad ways that the era of American hegemony had contributed to it. That, in turn, allowed me to see America more clearly—through the eyes of outsiders in other countries, and through my own experience of being an outsider at home.

Ultimately, this book is my story. My journey from the wake of a historic presidency to a world that looked at America and saw that presidency's opposite. My effort to relearn what it means to be an American in a world gone wrong. While I was writing this book, a Russian who is a leading character in it was poisoned and nearly killed, the Hong Kong protests I immersed myself in were snuffed out, the world went on lockdown in the face of a pandemic, and an American autocrat was voted out of office and sought to overturn the result. Through these dramatic developments, the currents of history that I was feeling around me remained constant; if anything, the picture became clearer and clearer, like a landscape from which fog is lifting.

Because this book represents my own experience of these things, it is inevitably incomplete. We are all inherently limited in our perspective, shaped by our own history. But by recognizing ourselves in others, we can expand our own lens of vision. Perhaps we can also see our own shortcomings more clearly. For me, the experience of looking into the eye of where America has gone wrong has only made me love more fiercely what America is supposed to be.

That is the starting point of my present journey.

Part I

THE AUTHORITARIAN PLAYBOOK

We can never start a new life.
We can only continue the old one.
—IMRE KERTESZ

I

The Currents of History

FROM THE MOMENT I was deposited back into civilian life after the Trump inauguration, I felt compelled to get away from what was happening in America. To emerge bleary-eyed from some international flight, change currency in the baggage claim, and walk into blinding sunlight and the cacophony of voices speaking another language along the curbside—men smoking in soccer jerseys, clustered around a metal pole—was to be reminded that life went on despite the sense of hostage taking that afflicted my homeland. It was a form of self-imposed exile. And yet, in each locale, there was the discovery that the same thing was happening everywhere.

In March 2017, I went to Myanmar to help the government there prepare for peace negotiations with a patchwork of provincial ethnic groups who had been waging civil war for decades. Diplomacy, it turned out, was privatized like everything else. I would be an independent contractor for a British-based nongovernmental organization (NGO) led by Jonathan Powell, who had served as chief of staff for Tony Blair. Powell had led the negotiations to secure the Good Friday Accords that secured peace in Northern Ireland in the late nineties. Ever since, he'd become something of a globe-trotting private peacemaker from Africa to Latin America to Southeast Asia, a figure out of a Graham Greene novel meeting rebels in jungles and deserts, seeking to recapture the accomplishment of his career's high-water mark. Perhaps because I was newly admitted into the ranks of former officials, it seemed no surprise to Powell or his staff that I wanted to get to Burma a little early to unwind. We were trying to help end wars, but we were also dealing with our own private ones.

For a couple of days, I walked aimlessly around the sprawling city of Yangon, a blanket of heavy heat over me, buying knock-off Nikes for a few bucks to make it easier on my feet. I went to a pagoda and sat staring at a Buddha, waiting to feel something. I walked into a U.S.-government-funded library where I'd been a guest of honor a couple of years before, now anonymous to young Burmese buried in books and screens. Then I conducted workshops in the capital city of Naypyidaw to help the Myanmar negotiating team prepare, sharing lessons I'd learned while negotiating reconciliation between the United States and Cuba. The civilians took earnest, copious notes. The stern-faced military men in drab green uniforms wrote nothing down. Afterward, I joined a meeting with Aung San Suu Kyi, dissident turned state councilor, at her residence. For the first time in my several meetings with her, we were asked to take off our shoes inside the Buddhist home, a reminder of the Burmese Buddhist nationalism that had become more predominant in recent years.

Within a matter of months, the Burmese military that had once imprisoned Suu Kyi would pursue a campaign of ethnic cleansing against a Muslim minority, the Rohingya. A million people were driven into neighboring Bangladesh. Through it all, Suu Kyi would remain silent. People wondered at her fall from Nobel Peace laureate of the early nineties to international pariah. But it made a certain kind of sad sense to me. A survivor from a country on the periphery of power in the world, she once surfed the wave of democracy that accompanied the end of the Cold War. She rocketed to international attention in 1989, the year that the Berlin Wall came down, by leading a democratic movement protesting the military government. By 2017, she was doing what she felt she needed to do to survive in a world where nationalism ran amok. Her own journey—from democracy icon to tacit collaborator in brutality fueled by Buddhist nationalism and rampant anti-Rohingya disinformation on Facebook—didn't cut against the currents of history, it drifted in the wake of events in the wider world.

In April 2017, I went to Milan with Barack Obama. He was there to speak about climate change a few weeks after Donald Trump pulled out of the Paris Climate Agreement. The rhythm of the trip felt familiar: a private plane, a block of hotel rooms, Secret Service agents. But the plane was a fraction the size of Air Force One, there were only a handful of hotel rooms and agents, and unlike the crush of responsibilities that used to follow me, I had very little to *do*. I accompanied Obama on a private tour of Leonardo da Vinci's drawings, peering down at bold lines that improbably anticipated the machines of the future—helicopters and missiles, the machinery of war that we'd presided over for eight years. Dusty volumes hundreds of years old lined the walls of the library. From human creations like this the Renaissance had emerged, paving the way for the pursuit of scientific inquiry and cultivation of a more enlightened Western civilization that now felt under assault. Back at the hotel, throngs of Italians waited outside Obama's hotel. I told him that he remained the most popular politician in the world. "No," he corrected me, "I'm one of the biggest *celebrities* in the world now." He didn't mean it as a good thing—progressive change relegated to cultural celebrity.

In July 2017, I went to Cuba. I stayed at the sprawling Hotel Nacional in the heart of Havana. Black-and-white photos of the Castros with visiting dignitaries and celebrities, vestiges of Cold War history, hung in the lobby. I met a friend from the American embassy for drinks at the outdoor bar, the kind of place that you assume has been populated by revolutionaries and spies for the last several decades. In a hushed voice, my friend told me about a mysterious illness that had struck employees of the embassy. There were theories about "sonic attacks," but the source would never be firmly established. It felt to us like something the Russians might do—people who wanted to sow conflict, drive others apart, put America and Cuba back into the Cold War that I thought we had ended.

A couple of days later, I flew to Santiago, where the Cuban Revolution had begun. I felt sicker than I could remember ever having been—a throbbing headache, ringing in the ears, repeatedly (and not always successfully) suppressing the urge to vomit. Was it food poisoning, or something else? I was shown around the revolutionary sites by an eager guide. A museum that documented the crimes of the prerevolutionary, U.S.-backed Batista government felt several historical epochs out of date, and so did the Cuban Revolution. I was driven into the countryside, almost two hours on roads at times blocked by mangy herds of animals, my stomach doing flips with every bump. We came to a secluded cemetery in the mountains, the place where the revolutionaries had become guerrillas. It was lush and peaceful, the only sounds coming from the birds and the breeze through the trees. An old man who'd fought with the Castros showed me around, his tour culminating at the site where Raúl Castro would be buried. I looked at the tomb with Raul's name already etched into it; this was a man who wanted to be remembered in the place where he had been young, when it was all still a cause uncorrupted by power and the passage of time.

Back at the Nacional the next day, I lay on my bed staring at the ceiling and having a conversation in my head. Had we misled all of these people, from the Cubans who wanted to move beyond the past, to the Europeans who saw America as a guarantor of democracy, to the Burmese who wanted democracy for themselves? People who had trusted us, only to be burned. Or were we always pushing against inexorable forces, the hard-line Cubans who clung to power with Russian backers, the nationalists trying to unravel the European Union, the Burmese military who wanted a nation for Buddhists? Was the dark turn I sensed everywhere I went a cause of America's nationalist, authoritarian turn, or was America merely following the same turn happening everywhere, caught in the current of history like a piece of driftwood?

This question continued to roll around in my head, from continent to continent. In Kenya, an American diplomat told me the Chinese were methodically supplanting American influence—buying up businesses and media, courting the students who no longer felt welcome in the United States. In Singapore, a senior government official told me casually over drinks that Asia had moved on from America—speaking as if this gleaming capitalist construction had almost been seamlessly handed off to the Chinese. In Amsterdam, Obama and I toured the empty Anne Frank house at night, peering into the small rooms where she'd penned her diary, the absence of tourists lending the place a feeling of having been forgotten.

In country after country, people asked me searching questions about how Trump could have happened. In Europe, Trump was often tied to the British vote for Brexit and the refugee crisis of 2015, the fears of Muslim hordes invading our open societies. But this theory, I felt certain, was wrong. It diminished the more structural, consequential forces at work everywhere I went, forces that had been building for a long time. No, this wasn't some black swan event, easily explained by a couple of years' worth of scary headlines. It ignored the lived reality of the eight years that I worked in the White House, the feeling that a cancer was metastasizing everywhere despite our efforts to treat it. It conveniently elided the ways in which decades of American capitalism, technology, and the politicized pursuit of national security had ripened so many people in the United States and around the world for crude nationalist appeals.

Then, on an early 2018 trip to Berlin for an Obama town hall with European youth, I met a young Hungarian named Sandor Lederer. We talked in an empty room of what was once the headquarters of the German Democratic Republic (GDR), a Soviet-backed nation that doesn't exist anymore. The building was built in the drab style of 1960s Communist architecture. The exterior was gray and imposing, the interior filled with mosaics depicting idealized scenes of Germans in factories, farms, and mines contrasted with images of book burning and the persecution of workers under the Nazis. For more than three decades, the men who ruled the GDR with access to the Stasi's files on the private lives of other East German citizens came to work in this building. It has since become one of Germany's leading business schools, the European School of Management and Technology (ESMT), a name that encapsulates the technocratic ethos of globalization that shaped the beginning of the twenty-first century. A monument to Communist power turned into a place to train capitalists. A reminder that history never ends.

Not yet forty, Sandor had knowing, sunken eyes and a mop of black hair flecked with gray, as if he carried around his country's post–Cold War journey like a weight. I asked him to walk me through how his country's prime minister, Viktor Orban, had transformed Hungary from an open democracy to a largely authoritarian system in the span of a decade. It took him only a few minutes. Win elections through right-wing populism that taps into people's outrage over the corruption and inequities wrought by unbridled globalization. Enrich corrupt oligarchs who in turn fund your politics. Create a vast partisan propaganda machine. Redraw parliamentary districts to entrench your party in power. Pack the courts with right-wing judges and erode the independence of the rule of law. Keep big business on your side with low taxes and favorable treatment. Demonize your political opponents through social media disinformation. Attack civil society as a tool of George Soros. Cast yourself as the sole legitimate defender of national security. Wrap the whole project in a Christian nationalist message that taps into the longing for a great past. Offer a sense of belonging for the disaffected masses. Relentlessly attack the Other: immigrants, Muslims, liberal elites.

It struck me that Sandor could have been describing America instead of Hungary.

I saw more clearly what had been stirring in me since Trump's inauguration: America wasn't at risk of being transformed into a semiauthoritarian nation by Trump; we were already well along that spectrum, and the damage could not be undone by any single election. And sitting in the old headquarters of the GDR, this monument to the world that America transformed with the end of the Cold War, I began to see the outlines of how America's own actions over the last thirty years made this transformation possible—in our own country and in others.

This is the world we made.

2

Freedom's High-Water Mark

SANDOR LEDERER WAS six years old when the Berlin Wall was torn down in 1989. His father was a foreign correspondent based in East Berlin, and Sandor remembers the energy of the people in the streets, the excited conversations at the dinner table, the sense that something important was happening all around him even if he was too young to fully grasp it. After experiencing the euphoria of Berlin's reunification, his family returned to Budapest to find it transforming. "As a child," he told me, "you see the visuals. Visuals in terms of statues that you see on the streets, street names, cars on the street, billboard advertising, and also what you see on TV—several political parties discussing things." Gone were the traces of Soviet-sponsored totalitarianism, with its stale sameness, Communist iconography, and anointed heroes. In its place, suddenly, was the promise of an open society—the freedom to choose what news you watched, what products you aspired to buy, which political parties you joined. The freedom to choose who you were.

Viktor Orban was just twenty-five years old when he made his first impression on Hungarians at a rally in Budapest five months before the Wall came down. The purpose of the rally was to rebury the corpse of the martyred Imre Nagy, the man who led Hungary during its 1956 uprising against Soviet rule. Nagy, the Communist prime minister, had embraced the uprising, called for multiparty democracy, declared Hungary's neutrality in the Cold War, and demanded an end to Soviet military occupation. In a scene analogous to that in

Tiananmen Square a few decades later, Soviet tanks rolled into Budapest, crushing the uprising, killing thousands and displacing hundreds of thousands more. Nagy was hanged, his body discarded in a prisoner's grave.

At the time of the 1989 rally, Orban was a young beneficiary of the wealthy Hungarian-American émigré George Soros. As the leader of the Federation of Young Democrats, Orban represented the demands of Hungarian youth. Tieless, his dark hair in the style of a 1980s lead singer, he stood in front of four microphones and a crowd of a hundred thousand people. Orban paid tribute to the fact that Nagy "identified himself with the wishes of the Hungarian nation to put an end to the Communist taboos, blind obedience to the Russian Empire, and the dictatorship of a single party." Orban himself was strident and uncompromising in his own defiance.

"Orban was a very popular liberal politician back then," Sandor told me. Listening to him recall those days, I remembered my wonder at the images I watched on television as a twelve-year-old in New York City, of the crowds of Europeans filling the streets of fallen imperial capitals. I believed that what they wanted was simple: They wanted freedom, and that meant that America—in my young boy's mind—was winning. *The winds of change.*

This was freedom's high-water mark. In a dizzying few years, the Communist regimes of Eastern Europe collapsed, followed by the Soviet Union. Nelson Mandela strode out of a South African prison. Right-wing dictatorships tumbled from South America to Southeast Asia, no longer a useful extension of American anticommunism. The organizing principle of American politics disappeared as well: the Cold War, which had driven everything from our ascent to the moon, to the structure of our government, to the pop culture that shaped my worldview through osmosis. Bill Clinton was elected, the first American president born after World War II, who melded together center-left policies with accommodation to the unregulated, wealth-creating markets unleashed by the collapse of the Iron Curtain.

When the Cold War ended, Orban was in some ways an American creation—an underdog and vessel for the same arguments American presidents had been making for decades, a beneficiary of the American policy of containment that compressed the Communist bloc into a pressure cooker overheated by its own corruption and hypocrisy. Today, the anticorruption organization that Sandor leads, along with many other civil society organizations, has been deemed an "enemy of the state" by the government of Prime Minister Viktor Orban. Meanwhile, Orban has become what he once railed against: obedient to Russia, the corrupt beneficiary of the dark money that courses through the veins of global markets, leader of what increasingly resembles a dictatorship by a single party. The story of how that happened is the story of how the period after that high-water mark of freedom failed to reconcile the wounds of the past or offer people a sense of purpose for the future. It's a story that shaped the lives of Hungarians like Viktor Orban and Sandor Lederer in very different ways.

AT THE TIME, the fall of the Berlin Wall seemed to end the historical epoch that had begun with the rise of fascism and Communism. The carnage of World War II had morphed into the competition between capitalist democracy and Communist autocracy, and now that battle was over. As an American, I believed we had all emerged into a new consensus, the benevolent cocoon of American-led globalization. But within Europe, the early-twentieth-century clashes over identity cast long shadows; after the Iron Curtain was lifted, the shadows were still there within nations, communities, and individual lives.

Sandor is a half-Jewish Hungarian whose family circle encompasses the various conflicts and contradictions of the twentieth century. He was born in a country that suffered under the rule of Nazi-backed Hungarian fascists during World War II and Russian-backed Communists during the Cold War. His Jewish grandparents on his father's side met in exile, in Turkey, during World War II. During the war, Sandor's grandmother—who was born in the Ukrainian city of Odessa—

worked for Soviet intelligence. Sandor's grandfather—horrified by what was happening in Europe—worked for the British secret services. After the war, Sandor's grandparents moved to Budapest, where they were generally loyal to the new Soviet-backed system. "For them," Sandor said, "I think the Communist rule was a safeguard that Nazism could not come back. Politics was a question of red or brown"—Communist or Nazi.

As a child, Sandor was preoccupied with the Holocaust. He wasn't religious, but he was acutely aware that he would have been marked for the death camps. "It's still a lesson from history that shapes my thinking," he said. "How such a tragedy can happen in a civilized world as Europe was in the first half of the twentieth century." During his time in Germany as a child, Sandor used to take a particular interest in the older buildings, whose timelessness seemed to represent something sturdy and lasting from the past. He'd look around and wonder how it was that a country that was in many ways the center of Western civilization could produce such evil, supported explicitly or implicitly by the people who'd lived in those old buildings. As I am half-Jewish and secular myself, it's not surprising that this question used to gnaw at my American mind as a child as well, even though I was insulated by the distance of an ocean.

Sandor grew up wary of the dark places that charismatic political leaders can take nations, so his heroes were not politicians, but ordinary people—Victor Kugler and Johannes Kleinman, the two Dutch men who helped hide Anne Frank and her family in that small annex to an apartment during the Nazi occupation of Holland. "I never really liked authority and celebrities and stars and these kinds of heroes," Sandor told me. "And for me these two guys were powerful examples of risking their own lives, risking their own well-being, to protect a family that was in danger because they were Jewish." It made no difference that none of the people in this drama were Hungarian. "What we need in society are such people," he said.

Yet as Sandor moved through school in 1990s Budapest, he noticed how Hungarians avoided the minefields of the twentieth century.

Some Hungarians had supported the Nazi-collaborating government that sent hundreds of thousands of Jews to their death. Others, like Sandor's family, had supported the Communists who kept a tight lid on Hungary for more than four decades. "We did not really deal with it," he said. "Teachers were afraid to touch these topics, or speak out on this, because immediately students brought up their family stories. Because every family could look back on this—we were victims of the Nazis, we were benefiting from the Communists, we were benefiting from the Nazis taking flats from the Jews. So instead of having these debates, the teachers I think always wanted to share the minimum—the dates and people involved, and just to have a timeline of history but not really the interesting stuff."

In this way, instead of forging a renewed sense of national identity after the experience of the Cold War, one that exorcised its ghosts and replaced them with something different, the newly free Hungary avoided the matter of identity, what it meant to be Hungarian in the political sense. That was something private, tied to the painful past. Globalization was the new identity on offer from the American victors of the Cold War: expanding markets, opening societies, and liberal democracy washing over Eastern Europe like the rushing water of a breaking wave before it recedes.

AS SANDOR MOVED through school, Viktor Orban began his transformation from liberal firebrand to reactionary. There was a crowded slate of parties on the left, and Orban's own party—Fidesz—performed poorly in elections. So he pulled his party to the right, embracing—at first—a conventional form of center-right politics: smaller government, market-friendly, socially conservative. He served an unremarkable term as prime minister from 1998 to 2002 and was then voted out.

Over the next eight years, Orban turned his political party into a social movement, organizing "civic circles" across the country. The civic circles were small gatherings of people, often centered in churches, that cemented a longing for a traditional set of values rooted in a lost Hungarian identity: a Hungary that was Christian, a

Hungary with an ancient past, a brotherhood rooted in patriotism and shared grievances. Orban reached back to the time before the Cold War and even before World War II. He highlighted the historic humiliation of the Treaty of Trianon, which dismembered Hungary at the end of World War I, costing it two thirds of its territory and stranding millions of ethnic Hungarians beyond newly drawn borders. Here was a history that many Hungarians could agree upon. But it was also the same blood-and-soil form of European nationalism that had ravaged the continent during World War II and killed hundreds of thousands of people in the Balkan wars of the 1990s, a nationalism that implicitly excused the ideology of fascism while rebuking the more recent evil of Communism.

Orban's politics didn't always fit neatly on the West's left-right spectrum. Many of his supporters from the civic circles joined the global protests against the Iraq War in 2003, embracing antiwar rhetoric that rightly cast the American occupation of an Arab country as a form of imperialism that discredited the entire American-led international order. As the decade marched on toward the financial crisis of 2008, Orban attacked amoral multinational corporations and the neoliberalism that fueled their profits, along with widening inequality between individuals and nations. In this way, Orban's identity-based nationalism drew upon resentment of two fundamental pillars of the post–Cold War American order: the unequal wealth creation of open markets, and the unchecked excesses of American military power. At the same time, Orban began to expropriate themes from the Republican Party's culture wars within American society: fidelity to Christian values, opposition to abortion and LGBT rights, antipathy to crass popular culture, and resentment of the political correctness of elites.

To many Hungarians, the first two decades after the fall of the Berlin Wall had been disorienting and disappointing. The nation was wealthier, but that wealth was still far behind that of its Western European neighbors, and it was concentrated more in the hands of faceless corporations and a small elite than in those of individual

Hungarians. The nation was a member of clubs like NATO and the European Union, but it lacked the clout to have a voice on foolish American projects like the invasion of Iraq. The nation was free, but to many, the liberated culture seemed designed to offend more traditional Christian sensibilities. In response, Orban wasn't just leading a political party, he was building a movement rooted in a deeper sense of national identity, offering a seawall of protection against the encroaching tides of globalization. To do that, he planted a foot on one side of that unresolved divide between red and brown—Communism and fascism—in Hungarian history. He was a nationalist, and he was poised to make Hungary great again.

AROUND THE SAME time, in the mid-2000s, Sandor had a very different kind of political awakening. He was finishing university with plans to be a diplomat when he noticed that one of his favorite parts of Budapest was being systematically destroyed—the 7th District, a neighborhood of pleasantly worn-in nineteenth-century buildings with balconies and long courtyards, housing a teeming mix of people from different classes, backgrounds, and ethnicities. It was also Hungary's old Jewish quarter, the neighborhood where Jews had been pushed into ghettos toward the end of Nazi dominance. That distinctive charm and resonant history, he noticed, was being replaced by new buildings without any character—the stale sameness not of Communism but of utilitarian capitalism. "Ugly, irrelevant buildings," Sandor told me, "that could be anywhere in the world."

It was not hard for me to understand why Sandor might have a visceral reaction to this cultural erasure. Like Sandor's, my Jewish roots are in the Eastern European countries where pogroms drove people deep into the Jewish quarters of the grand cities. A good chunk of my family came to America early, decades before German nationalism lit the fires that fueled the Holocaust, while some stayed behind, destined to be surrounded by walls. Growing up in New York City, I did not feel my Jewishness as a religious identity; history was something we had escaped from. Our rabbis were writers—

Roth, Bellow, Singer—who told stories from the residue of nation-states, the assertion of the individual. Our temples were the apartment buildings, courtyards, and fire escapes of Manhattan, where every life contained multitudes. As unbridled capitalism washed across New York at the same time that it remade Budapest, I had felt Sandor's sense of loss as I watched characterless glass towers erase those old apartment buildings and with them the stories they held.

While Orban was starting his civic circles, Sandor decided to investigate what was remaking this neighborhood he cared about. It wasn't hard to find a paper trail around the real estate transactions, or to figure out the larger context. The people kicked out of their old apartments received little compensation. The developers made a lot of money putting up these larger, uglier buildings. The politicians funded their campaigns—and probably made something on the side—from the developers. "It was not simply ignorance or a lack of culture," he told me, "it was mainly corruption. Very typical. I think you have these stories all around the world."

When Sandor graduated from university, he decided to do something about it. Together with two friends, he started K-Monitor, an organization dedicated to combating corruption and promoting transparency and accountability in politics. They had no money. They worked, Sandor said, like a garage band out of a worn-down house that one of his friends' parents owned on the outskirts of Budapest. They collected data and created a database mapping corruption across the country. The Internet was essential to their work. Ultimately, their database grew to include more than fifty thousand articles. They began to raise funds and receive grants. In keeping with the grassroots, egalitarian ethos of the organization, Sandor insisted on paying each employee the same amount, himself included.

In their different ways, Orban and Sandor were both reacting to a sense in the broader society that the economy and politics were increasingly corrupted. And there was ample evidence to justify that feeling. At the same time that K-Monitor was formed in 2006, confidence in the center-left government collapsed when the recently reelected prime minister, Ferenc Gyurcsány, was secretly recorded giving a speech to party elites in which he acknowledged, "obviously we lied throughout the last year and a half, two years . . . we lied morning, noon and night." He was referring, in part, to a refusal to tell the truth in the last campaign about austerity measures that would be needed because of the excess government spending that seemed to have benefited mostly those at the top. "If there is a scandal in the society," he lamented, "it's the fact that the upper ten thousand are building themselves up again using public money." As if anticipating the coming direction of events, he implored the left "that it doesn't have to hang its head in this fucking country. That we shouldn't shit ourselves in fear of Viktor Orban and the right."

The prime minister had committed the political sin of stating the truth, confirming a sense in the country that the government was dishonest, corrupt, and powerless against the forces of globalization shaping life in Hungary. The streets exploded in protest. There were riots at the national television station and in front of the parliament building. Sandor recalls being unsettled by the instability. He could understand the anger, but it seemed that Orban was inciting the protests, the far right was taking over the streets, and the police did little to assert control. "You see the police cars in the neighboring street and you see some policemen coming up, but they are just pushed away by the crowds—the far-right crowds, there were many skinheads and right-wing radicals. And somehow the government is unable to stop it." From his perch as leader of Fidesz, Orban fueled this dynamic with provocative talk about who was a "real Hungarian" and who was not. The competition between red and brown that had gone unresolved in Sandor's classroom was now being pursued in the streets.

Meanwhile, in those early years of K-Monitor, Sandor told me they learned a basic truth: "Political corruption is very much connected to political finance." In the post-Soviet bloc, the financing of politics was poorly regulated. "If I want to put it in a nice way," Sandor said, "it made politicians become corrupt because they do this to be able to fund campaigns. They had to get the money from somewhere." Once parties like Fidesz won elections at the local level, they also started funneling public money into their campaigns.

K-Monitor saw some results in its anticorruption work—local politicians were shamed, and national corruption scandals were a feature of campaigns, but nobody was vigorously prosecuted because everyone had similar clouds hanging over them. This proved corrosive to Hungarian politics and society, as ordinary Hungarians became more cynical about the whole enterprise of democracy, which was, after all, less than two decades old.

Many Hungarians recall Orban's rise by citing the Hungarian flag cockades that Fidesz members started to wear on their clothes, which recalled for me the ubiquitous American flag lapel pins that appeared on the suit jackets of American politicians after 9/11. In America, national fervor about terrorism had been marshaled by the Bush administration to replace the sense of purpose that we once had found in opposing Communism during the Cold War; in Hungary, national fervor was marshaled by Orban to fill the chasm that had opened up after the end of the Cold War, only the enemies were the forces of globalization encroaching from abroad and his political opponents at home.

In 2008, the bottom fell out of the global economy after American-made financial schemes triggered the financial crisis. Hungary was hit particularly hard, with one of the most open economies in Europe and without the deep reserves of capital that allowed Americans to avoid collapse on a similar scale. Because of foreign debts and its swollen budget deficits, Hungary was forced to turn to the International Monetary Fund to stabilize its finances—a dynamic that added humiliation to the economic injury. The already discredited government had no levers to pull to stimulate growth. Banks wouldn't lend. Investment dried up. People couldn't pay their debts. Jobs were lost. Wages stagnated. The ads on billboards showed things that people couldn't afford, the unattainable spoils of liberal democracy. The political parties on television were helpless to deliver them. The people lost confidence in the entire system of the post–Cold War world: democracy and capitalism, globalization and the American-led order, which now appeared as corrupted as an old neighborhood being wrecked for a dubious real estate deal or a politician admitting to lies in a secret recording, a soulless exercise that created wealth for the wealthy with no anchor in morality. Perhaps the post–Cold War system was no better than what came before, a pyramid scheme to protect the interests of the powerful.

Orban was ready for that moment. He was already the leading opposition figure, and as Hungary plunged into a debt spiral and people lost their savings, he swept to a massive electoral victory in 2010. Orban had completed his transformation from a young, liberal politician to a far-right nationalist with a political project rooted in Hungary's older history. "It's definitely a cut between 1989 and 2010," Sandor told me. Beginning in 2010, Orban would set about remaking Hungary, claiming as a mandate the failure of the period that went before. "The economic crisis was a main driver that change could happen. So 2010 was more than a change in government."

Viktor Orban and Sandor Lederer both formed their political identities in response to the shortcomings of the post–Cold War era, the failure of the American-led order to replace the ghosts of the past with a tangible sense of meaning. Both of them lamented globalization's bloodless encroachment on certain aspects of Hungarian identity. Both of them found a foil in a government that had become too comfortable with the soiled compromises of corrupted democratic governance. Orban's instinct was to pursue power by directing people to the currents of national identity and historical grievance left dormant and unaddressed beneath the surface of Hungarian life, like an underground river—the politics of red or brown. Sandor's impulse was to protect something he loved in his community and to search for ways to hold those in power accountable like the ordinary people who'd been his heroes. Both of them were defending things from the past that needed to be protected. But whereas Sandor was pursuing activism against the unjust use of political and economic power, Orban was methodically pursuing political and economic power. What he did when he attained it not only transformed Hungary, it joined a wave of right-wing nationalism that would reshape the world.

3

"Take Our Country Back": From Trianon to the Tea Party

I'VE WRITTEN THOUSANDS of speeches for Barack Obama. Many were box-checking exercises to one constituency or another. But every now and then circumstances align that allow the words of a politician to speak to something bigger that is happening in the society at large, the yearning for some sense of direction. In 2008, over a few hours on laptops in hotel rooms, lobbies, and a car on darkened backroads, Jon Favreau and I wrote a speech for Obama to give after the New Hampshire primary, which we assumed he would win after his resounding victory in the Iowa caucus. The speech's crescendo would be a long riff punctuated by the declaration "Yes we can." Obama lost. He delivered the speech anyway. It worked better coming from someone who'd just lost, returned to the status of underdog. And it met the moment for an America repelled by the Bush years, turned off by the more-of-the-same odor that clouded Hillary Clinton's candidacy, and thirsting for something new. It worked because the words met a moment that had already been building and were spoken by someone who sounded authentic when he said them. Obama's speech represented his own story and the sweep of American progressive politics that made his story possible—Black people, workers, disaffected youth, anyone who ever looked at power as something that excluded them.

On July 26, 2014, Viktor Orban gave a speech about the end of liberal democracy and the ascendance of a new nationalist and illiberal movement. "What we should view as our starting point," he said, "is the great redistribution of global financial, economic, commercial, political, and military power that became obvious in 2008." It had been the starting point of a new political project, but one that was more focused on consolidating Orban's own power than remedying the inequities of the global economy. By then, the fiery young anticommunist had been replaced by a stout fifty-five-year-old man with the carefully coiffed gray hair of a banker. He was speaking at the beginning of his second consecutive term as prime minister, but he wasn't speaking in Hungary; he was addressing a meeting of ethnic Hungarians in neighboring Romania. Like the European nationalists of the early twentieth century, Orban had made the concept of a broader, ethnic Hungarian nation central to his political project, tapping into historical grievance: borders redrawn after the humiliation of World War I, Hungarians stranded within other nations. That was, quite literally, his audience.

In 2014, Orban knew that he had reached that kind of moment. He declared that his government's ascendance constituted "regime change" and had to be viewed as part of a global phenomenon. "There were three great changes in the global regime during the twentieth century," he argued. "At the end of the First World War, at the end of the Second World War, and in 1990. The joint characteristic of these is that when these changes occurred it was clear to everybody from practically one day to the next that from now on they would be living in a different world from the one they had been living in until then."

Just as Obama was the right man to defiantly proclaim "Yes we can," Orban was the right man to make the argument for global regime change from the perspective of his own country. He had been on the front lines at the end of the Cold War, only to capitalize on the failure of that moment to deliver on its promise, a failure embodied in the 2008 financial crisis. "The significance of this change is not quite so obvious," he acknowledged. "At the time of the great Western financial collapse in 2008, it was not clear that we would be living in a different world from now on. The change is not as acute as in the case of the first three great global regime changes, but it somehow effuses our minds at a slower pace, and just as the fog slowly settles on the landscape, we slowly grasp the knowledge that if we take a good look around and properly analyze everything going on around us, then this is a different world."

Standing in the heart of Europe, Orban suggested that the time of looking west for leadership was over. The future, he suggested in words that would have been unthinkable a decade earlier, belonged to "systems that are not Western, not liberal, not liberal democracies—and perhaps not even democracies." He name-checked Russia and China as two "stars" of this emerging cosmos.

Even as Orban spoke, the American Republican Party was attacking the wiring of America's own democracy as aggressively as Orban was remaking Hungary's.

HOW DID THAT happen, and what was it all about? To answer those questions, you have to understand how Orban redefined Hungary as the fog settled on the post-2008 landscape. When you do, you begin to see a mirror image of what has happened in the United States.

Orban's party didn't just win in 2010; it captured a two-thirds majority in parliament, which gave Orban free rein to mold the Hungarian polity like a lump of clay. More than a thousand laws were passed during his first few years in office, usually with little debate. Many of the most important laws were not about solving problems, but about power. This included an overhaul of the constitution in 2011. Election laws were changed. Voting rights were extended to ethnic Hungarians living beyond Hungary's borders. The number of members of parliament was cut in half and parliamentary districts were redrawn for the benefit of Orban's party, Fidesz. The courts were changed. The retirement age of judges was lowered in order to open up more slots for Orban's party to fill, and the selection of judges was handed over to a single person named by Orban to a nine-year term. Hungary's constitutional court—its version of the U.S. Supreme Court—was thus turned into a body that would reliably decide in favor of Orban's government. The distribution of economic power was changed. Instead of taming the power of big business, Orban co-opted it. Billions of dollars in economic assistance from the European Union were funneled to contracts that enriched Orban's cronies. One close friend of Orban's from his home village—Lőrinc Mészáros—went from gas fitter to billionaire. "That I have been able to come so far," he said, "God, luck, and the person of Viktor Orban have certainly played a role." The cronies who benefited from this corrupt largesse then funded Orban's politics.

To understand how a mix of state power and corrupt cronies could remake Hungarian society, you need only look at the Hungarian media. In Budapest, I sat down with Szabolcs Panyi, a dogged investigative journalist. I wanted to understand what had happened from the perspective of someone who had both covered this corruption and been on the receiving end of it. "Both Orban and his lieutenants at Fidesz were complaining for a long time," Szabolcs told me, "just like in the U.S., that the media is dominated by the leftist liberal conglomerate, that most of the mainstream outlets are just inherently hostile toward them. So they had this clear mission to balance out the media landscape." America, the country that had once been the emblem of a free press, had offered the example of the original Fox News slogan, which suggested that elevating right-wing viewpoints was an end in itself: "fair and balanced."

Orban transformed what news the Hungarian people consume and therefore what reality they live within. Some steps were straightforward. The National Communications and Media Authority, which oversaw the sector, was filled with Fidesz appointees and given broad powers to punish outlets that engaged in coverage deemed unbalanced or threatening to common morals. It became harder for independent broadcasting stations to get licenses, and the state-supported media were pulled to the right. Nearly a thousand people were forced to leave their public broadcasting jobs. "First, the public media was turned into government media: fire people, completely restructure it, they get tons of government money, and just in some years it became a really low-quality propaganda vehicle," Szabolcs said. Beyond that, Orban also saw that many Hungarian media outlets were dependent on government-associated advertising from entities ranging from the lottery to the national energy company. "So he cut off government advertising for left-wing or liberal outlets and channeled all of the money into the right-wing media."

Once his crony network was established, Orban's tactics became more aggressive. Around 2013 and 2014, Szabolcs told me, "these huge buy-ups started." At the same time that right-wing media were being given preferential treatment, "these government proxies—businessmen—bought up first the second-largest privately owned TV station, and then they went after newspapers and other TV and radio stations." Sometimes the newly purchased media entities were pulled to the right; sometimes they were simply shut down. "Since technically these were individuals buying it," Szabolcs said, "Orban and his people could say we have nothing to do with the media, these are private citizens investing, blah blah blah." One of the newspapers that was purchased and shut down was the one where Sandor Lederer's father had worked for decades. When complaints were raised about the decision, the Orban government pointed out that an Austrian company, not the Hungarian government, had bought the newspaper. Left unsaid was the fact that that company was tied to right-wing interests close to Orban.

Within just a few years, Orban could count on compliant media to tell his story. In vast swaths of Hungary, where there are only a few television stations and local newspapers, the voice of Fidesz is now omnipresent. "You have the pro-government sphere," Szabolcs said, "where most of the readers and listeners are from the countryside, where there's no alternative, for example, to local newspapers. And all of Hungary's local newspapers, print newspapers, are owned by the same right-wing conglomerate."

Szabolcs had worked at one of Hungary's largest online outlets, Index, which was recently sold to a Fidesz proxy that promptly fired much of its staff and eventually shut it down. Since 2018, Szabolcs has worked for a website called Direkt 36 (36 is Hungary's telephone code), which reaches a largely cosmopolitan Budapest elite and people outside the country. Direkt 36 relies in large part on reader donations, in part because of American creations that shape how human beings around the globe receive information. "Google, Facebook," Szabolcs said, referring to the American companies that offer the platforms where readers find online articles, "are stealing all the advertisements from online media."

Orban doesn't need to shut down these islands of independent journalism entirely, because he can largely drown them out with his propaganda machine. When I asked Szabolcs if journalists were subjected to physical intimidation or harassment, he said no—he could freely do his work. But that work was routinely attacked by the much larger, government-friendly media enterprises. "It's quite frequent that they name and shame journalists," he told me. "The goals are one—try and discredit them because there are still a lot of people listening to independent journalists because what this right-wing conglomerate is giving them is basically bullshit." The aim, Szabolcs said, is "to cast some doubt that what they are reading is also partisan, it's influenced by George Soros—you know, there's no reality, there's no facts, it's just opinion, everything is partisan."

IF THE NATION-STATE was increasingly inseparable from Orban and the media his mouthpiece, what story was he telling? After all, there was no clear ideological project at the heart of all this—no turn to Communism or militarism. There was, instead, Orban's idea of Hungarian identity—a Christian nation rooted in ethnicity, a traditional society with an assortment of triumphs and grievances. There was, above all, a sense of what Hungary was *not*—what it was *against*. To identify who the Us were, Orban focused more on the Them.

For Orban, this was a flexible target. The one constant was that They could be cast as foreign, a threat to national sovereignty and

Christian identity. He nationalized certain sectors of multinational corporations, even as he would also slash taxes and worker protections. He lambasted the European Union and its cadre of faceless bureaucrats in Brussels, even as he took the EU's money. When the refugee crisis came in 2015, he stoked fears of a Muslim invasion and built a 110-mile fence topped with barbed wire along Hungary's border with Serbia. And he zeroed in on his former patron—George Soros. A billionaire many times over, Soros had established foundations that give grants to civil society organizations in Hungary and around the world. On the heels of the refugee crisis, a ferocious media campaign was launched against all nongovernmental organizations that received foreign funding, alleging that they were the beachhead for foreign interests seeking the overthrow of the legitimate Hungarian government. Before the last Hungarian election in 2018, Fidesz campaigned on a "Stop Soros" law to restrict funding for organizations that work with migrants, and he promoted laws to force NGOs receiving funding from abroad to register as foreign agents, giving the government ambiguous powers to investigate them. Soros himself has been vilified as the leader of a global conspiracy against Hungary.

"It's a dog whistle for anti-Semitic tropes," Szabolcs told me. "The far-right conspiracy theory in the nineties was quite similar to what it is right now, but it was about Jews and especially Orthodox Jews immigrating to Hungary in masses and buying up land, buying up water resources, because Israel is a desert." In this way, Orban wasn't innovating so much as tapping older currents of anti-Semitism in Hungary and Europe. Again, the old politics of red and brown, Communist and fascist. "Throughout the twentieth century, the far right, or the right wing, associated Jews with the Communist regime, since there were some leaders who were of Jewish origin, and that was basically the basis for the conspiracy that every Jew is left-wing, all of them are Communists, they are internationalists, and they are against the national interest of Hungary."

* * *

LIKE SZABOLCS AND Sandor, Márta Pardavi was swept up in these ceaseless attacks despite posing no threat to Hungary. She helps lead the Hungarian Helsinki Committee—a post–Cold War NGO that works on issues including prisoners' rights and migrant rights. As Orban's attacks on civil society grew, she emerged as a leading voice criticizing his crackdown. The morning we met at a trendy coffee shop in a younger demographic district of Budapest, she was dragging her roller bag behind her. After our meeting, she was headed for Brussels, a regular destination for Hungarians seeking support from Europe as the walls close in around them at home. Almost exactly the same age, we exchanged small talk about the challenges of traveling for work when you have young children who are old enough to be upset that you're gone but not old enough to understand why.

Márta had left Hungary as a child in the eighties to live in the United States. Her family returned in 1989, when she was in the eighth grade, eager to be part of the transformation. She started her job as a human rights lawyer at the Helsinki Committee when she was in law school. The organization did good work, but she said that those working on behalf of human rights in Hungary made the mistake of thinking that the country's future as a liberal democracy was settled, so no effort was made to educate the public about the value of democracy itself to their own interests. "There was this false understanding that, you know, after the nineties, human rights are sort of a given. Same as democratic rules. You know, they're given. So we didn't need to reinforce that through popular support." By contrast, when Orban started his civic circles, he was "building from the bottom up." In this way, human rights activists who worked with those on the margins of society could be cast as elites, while right-wing politics funded by wealthy interests could be cast as opposition to an out-of-touch establishment.

Márta remembered the moment when Orban's attention shifted in the direction of civil society, making use of the media that he had co-opted. In August 2013, an article in a pro-Fidesz newspaper listed thirteen nongovernmental organizations that were tarred as "fake NGOs" doing the bidding of Soros. The Helsinki Committee has many donors, including Soros's Open Society Foundations, and works on many issues. In a small country like Hungary, it's not uncommon for NGOs to have foreign donors. But what followed was a steady campaign from the government and media to cast NGOs as a tool of foreign interests. This reached a fever pitch in the run-up to the 2018 national election in a campaign that was well funded by Orban's cronies. After the election, the "Stop Soros" law was passed. At that point, Márta had to sit down her staff and explain that there were lawyers prepared to fight the law in the courts and that the most onerous provisions were unlikely to be acted upon. "You know, people were thinking that the police will come and get them at five in the morning and you have to dispel this kind of fear," she said. "The chilling effect was very, very present." For many Hungarian donors, this led to a feeling that "we'd rather support the ballet because otherwise it might mean that we'll be attacked or harassed."

The Helsinki Committee sued Fidesz and refused to comply with the requirement to register as a foreign agent. They endured a circus-like atmosphere in which pro-Fidesz media camped out in front of their office, naming and shaming their staff just as they named and shamed journalists, creating a cloud of harassment and intimidation around their efforts. Like independent media, NGOs still exist, still do their work, but Orban created an information war around them—to discredit them, raise doubts about their motivations, and demoralize would-be supporters. It all adds up to an effort to breed apathy, to make people think that it's not even worth getting involved in politics or supporting NGOs trying to help people on the wrong side of the government's nationalist agenda. Márta has won some battles—court injunctions in Hungary, support from the European Union. But she acknowledged the scale of what she's up against, including Fidesz's constant polling of public opinion, which serves as a feedback loop for its propaganda campaigns. "Seven years down the line, the whole machinery of polling and assessing and measuring and surveying that helps Fidesz do its thing is extremely well funded and elaborate." In this way, Fidesz both shapes public opinion through its media and responds to it based on polling.

All of this serves the political imperative of casting Orban as the one man standing up to threats against the Hungarian nation, a message that resonates in a country so wounded by foreign powers in its past. What worries Márta is less the fate of her own NGO than what Orban is doing to the country where her children are growing up. "What I am worried about," she said, "is how this chips away at public support for this sector, for civil society, and also the basic idea of democracy. It is a hate narrative, you know—you have to hate the migrants, you have to hate the Muslims. There were attempts at getting people to hate the homeless that didn't work out, getting people to hate gay people not really working out. There's a lot of anti-gender stuff that is clearly taken from a playbook. This idea that you should hate is something that we've seen around here quite a lot. And it has worked pretty well."

On February 19, 2009, I walked into the office of White House press secretary Robert Gibbs. It was less than a month into the Obama administration, and the new president was still covered in the afterglow of his history-making election. Below clocks that showed the times in Moscow, Beijing, and Baghdad, the wall-mounted television played a clip of CNBC analyst Rick Santelli ranting about Obama. "How many of you want to pay their neighbor's mortgage that has an extra bathroom and can't pay their bills?" he vented, lamenting the government intervention to stop the financial crisis as if the treatment administered to a sick economy was more to blame than the disease. He called for a Tea Party in Obama's hometown of Chicago, evoking the Founding Fathers and declaring, "All you capitalists who want to show up to Lake Michigan, I'm going to start organizing!"

"Insane," I said.

"Rick Santelli leading an army of traders with pitchforks," Gibbs joked, but with some unease in his voice. That rant and the rallying cry of "Take our country back" would echo across the country. Over the next year and a half, the Tea Party movement built into a wave that retook the House of Representatives under a new brand of Republicans.

The Tea Party was built on the wreckage of American capitalism, American leadership, and the Republican Party—making possible everything that came next, including Trump. The nation had seemingly been riding high headed into the twenty-first century, shaping world events and spreading a gospel of unbridled capitalism and technology. Then the 9/11 attacks punctured the sense of security at the core of the global regime, revealing as misguided the belief that the darker elements of globalization could be relegated to postcolonial outposts like Afghanistan. George W. Bush had then sought to reorient America's entire national purpose to the task of fighting terrorism, a securitized turn that was pursued with a ruthlessness that undermined democracy at home and offered a justification for more authoritarian and Us versus Them politics abroad. The Iraq War, in turn, cracked open the façade that elites in the United States knew what they were doing. Instead, they had done something so stupid and self-defeating that it called into question why Americans were the stewards of world order in the first place. Then, largely because of American-made financial schemes, the global economy collapsed, wiping out trillions of dollars of value and shattering a sense of personal security for billions of people around the world.

The Tea Party offered a populism that reacted to these failures without rejecting the structural forces that caused them. It seemed like a strange movement—old white people, some dressed in colonial garb, chanting "Where are the jobs?" and excoriating Obama as a socialist while Republican politicians blamed him for the consequences of a financial crisis that he had done nothing to create. It was an American version of Orban's civic circles—a blend of bottom-up anger and top-down financing seeded by Charles and David Koch, two billionaires who were among the Republican Party's largest donors, and their innocuously named organization Americans for Prosperity. For the super-rich, it was a smart play—redirect the rage to an identity-based populism of the right instead of an economic populism of the left. For the foot soldiers of the movement, it was an easy deflection—rage against the Black president over the disruptions in your life instead of confronting the ways in which America had gone wrong. *Take our country back.*

In 2010, Republicans received an enormous boost through a 5–4 Supreme Court ruling that dismantled America's campaign finance laws, recognizing unlimited spending on political campaigns as free speech and opening the floodgates for wealthy individuals and corporations to finance American political campaigns—including through undeclared "dark money" contributions. The corruption of unchecked political finance that Sandor had remarked upon in Hungary was now the law of the land in America. In the 2010 election, powered by populist anger over the wreckage of the financial crisis and unprecedented spending from wealthy donors, Tea Party Republicans didn't just capture the House of Representatives—they won state legislatures and governorships across the country. What followed was a methodical effort to use every tool available to apply a playbook strikingly similar to Orban's.

Political corruption became normalized. Spending on midterm elections skyrocketed from around $300 million in 2010 to over $1 billion by 2018. A handful of Republican donors have spent billions of dollars on American politics. In turn, as with Orban's cronies, their personal and corporate interests have shaped core pillars of the Republican agenda: the denial of climate change, deregulation of industry, tax cuts for corporations and wealthy individuals, and limitless support for Israel's right-wing government.

The role of the media changed. Just as Republicans deepened a symbiotic relationship with political donors, they counted on cronies who controlled right-wing media. Rupert Murdoch's Fox News Channel was at the vanguard of an assortment of right-wing television, radio, and online outlets that regularly amplified Republican congressional investigations, conspiracy theories, and policy priorities. Not unlike Orban-friendly media in Hungary, the collective reach of America's right-wing media infrastructure functioned as a shadow state media for the Republican Party while also setting narratives in motion that mainstream media felt obliged to cover. The uniformity and extremity of opinion within right-wing media were turbocharged by the sharing of information on social media, chiefly Facebook, which profits off the clicks that anger and disinformation generate. Profit-driven social media algorithms, like unchecked political contributions, were treated as free speech beyond the reach of government regulation.

Election laws were changed. Like Fidesz, Republicans leveraged their 2010 victories to redraw congressional districts for their own benefit. In the decade after 2010, more than half of America's fifty states put in place restrictive voting laws—requiring certain forms of identification to register, denying the franchise to past felons, making it harder to vote. In some cases, voting rolls were simply purged. These moves were enabled by a judiciary that increasingly served a political agenda over the law, reshaped by Republican relentlessness. When Obama nominated a Supreme Court justice who could have tipped the balance of the Supreme Court from conservative to liberal, Senate Majority Leader Mitch McConnell broke from precedent by denying him not only a vote but a hearing. In Trump's four years in office, far more judges were confirmed than during Obama's eight. From the Supreme Court on down, the United States now has a right-leaning judiciary that can be expected to look favorably on Republican priorities for decades.

The brute force of these moves represented the stakes for a Republican Party that needed to ensure that it could wield power even if a majority of the country wouldn't vote for them. Obama's landslide election threatened to usher in a progressive future for a country where a soon-to-be-majority nonwhite population is insisting upon a more equitable stake. The steps taken to climb out of the financial crisis in turn exacerbated some of the same failures endemic to the American model of globalization. Trillions of dollars were transferred to some of the same banks that caused the crisis so that they could be a source of lending and investment. This helped prevent a depression, but it also left in place the basic wiring of the financial system and the inequality that made so many people angry in the first place. The few people who were rich enough to have their wealth invested in markets got richer; for everyone else, the cost of necessities from rent to transportation to education went up. Meanwhile, new technologies accelerated the disruptions that displaced workers, changed the nature of daily life, and transformed the way that human beings consume information before we were prepared for the problems that would arise when people began living in self-contained bubbles, leaving data trails of their likes and dislikes, a vast blueprint for advertisers, propagandists, and authoritarians.

All of this has created a fertile landscape for nationalists. In America, as in Hungary, the right wing has embraced a nationalism characterized by Christian identity, national sovereignty, distrust of democratic institutions, opposition to immigration, and contempt for politically correct liberal elites. Like Fidesz, Republicans have also increasingly told a national story defined in large part by what the United States is *not*—what the United States is *against*. To identify who constitutes the American Us, Republicans—like Orban—have focused more on Them. As in Hungary, They have been a shifting target. A Black president. Radical Islam. Refugees. Hispanic immigrants. The mainstream media. Socialism. China. Antifa. The Deep State. George Soros. The conduct of elections. The real Them, of course, is where America seems to be going: a country where white people are in the minority, a world that we cannot control.

None of this happened because of Donald Trump.

4

Identity Politics

IN MAY 2018, I learned that I had been spied on by a private intelligence firm of former Mossad operatives, Black Cube, which had recently gained notoriety for spying on Harvey Weinstein's accusers. *The Guardian* published a story reporting that Trump associates had hired Black Cube to dig up dirt on me and another Obama administration official, Colin Kahl, in order to discredit the Iran Nuclear Deal. The revelation was jarring even as it seemed to fit the tenor of the times. Early in the Trump presidency, allegations mushroomed on right-wing websites that I was one of the external leaders of the so-called Deep State that aimed to undermine Trump. For years, I had featured as a villain in right-wing conspiracy theories, a character of varying degrees of guilt in whatever narrative they were pushing, attacked by news outlets, flooded with vitriol on social media. The Israeli nexus wasn't particularly surprising either. There had been a blending of right-wing Israeli and American attacks on me through the fight over the Iran Deal in 2015.

Shortly after the Black Cube story broke, I was contacted by the *New Yorker* journalist Ronan Farrow. It was a weekend, and to avoid talking about being surveilled by Israeli spies in a cramped apartment with two children under four years old, I walked the fifteen minutes or so to my office. I took my usual route, cutting across a dirt path behind a tennis court. For the first time, the simple choices associated with walking to work were infused with intrigue. Was my pathway to work a subject of interest? If I saw someone sitting under a tree get up and begin to walk behind me, should I question their motivation? How many people had access to the phone that I carried in my pocket?

When I called Ronan, he told me that he'd confirmed that Black Cube had spied on me just as he'd learned that they'd spied on Weinstein's accusers. Just a few of his prompts about suspicious emails that had come to me or my wife led me back to a strange one that Ann had received a few months earlier:

Dear Mrs. Norris,
I'm reaching out on behalf of Shell-Productions, a UK based production company. We are currently working on a movie revolving around people working in the US government during a major geopolitical event, the focus is on their lives and the effects their public service has on their personnel lives with family and friends.

We are in the early stages of writing the script and are looking for individuals with the relevant background and practical experience to consult with us on it. I will be in the US for a round of meetings and was wondering if we could schedule a short meeting at the beginning of July so I could tell you more over coffee or lunch. Let me know what works best for you in terms of time/place. Attached you'll find a small summary of the project.

Regards, Eva

The attachment was unsubtly relevant to me:

The movie focuses on two major events ripped from the headlines, Nuclear negotiations with a hostile nation and the negotiations to open relations with a country that has been under embargo for the better part of a century. In between the two events we see how the busy schedules of all involved impact their personal lives and professional lives, especially when crises break out in the middle.

I had been involved in nuclear negotiations with the "hostile nation" of Iran and in the negotiations to open relations with Cuba, "a country that has been under embargo for the better part of a century." Ann had forwarded the email to me at the time, unsure what to make of it, with no intention of responding.

Ronan explained how Black Cube sets up a minimal online footprint for a cover operation ("Shell Productions," for instance, had a LinkedIn page to go along with its ironic name). Then they hope that phishing emails prompt someone to bite and share personal information. They also contact other friends and associates. Sometimes they're looking for dirt. Sometimes they may just want you to know that someone is watching you, which could explain why the outreach to Ann was so obvious: Intimidation can be the point.

By the time I hung up, I felt uneasy and vulnerable. Later that day, Ronan would have his story on the *New Yorker* website, the anti-Trump universe would have another bone to chew on for a few hours, and I would have no more answers than I had before about why this happened and who was behind it. My unease was further heightened when I spoke to a reporter who had seen a Black Cube file that had been compiled on me. It included, he said, things like a picture of the outside of my apartment building, my parents' phone number, my social media accounts, and a variety of rumors to run down. Again, it felt less like a sophisticated spying operation than an effort at intimidation, one that was advanced through its revelation rather than being undermined.

Around the same time, in anticipation of the publication of my first book, my literary agent called to express concern that "your Google is a dumpster fire." This, too, was no surprise. Enter my name and the search results were sure to offer up a menu of attacks on my honesty, intelligence, and character. *Oh, I know,* I told her. *I'm used to it.* My habitual brave face. The reality was that the attacks had backed up on me. When I was in government, I could distract myself with a multitude of responsibilities, take comfort in the fact that I was in the White House while the trolls were on the outside. Now my tormentors were the ones on the inside, wielding power. It felt like a physical weight to carry around. Sometimes, in the middle of my workday, I'd cross the street to the unkempt lawn that sloped down to Rock Creek Parkway. As trite as it sounds, I'd moved to Washington as a twenty-four-year-old who wanted to serve my country and change the world. I'd succeeded more than I ever could have imagined. And at the end of all that, here I was. I'd lie there on my back, listening to the rush of cars go by, my eyes closed to the world around me.

I talked to a guy who ran a service that cleans up your reputation online. He described how, over a period of months, the reputation clean-up people click on the better Internet content about you so that the Google algorithm thinks the good stories are more important than the negative ones. I was unsure about the whole thing. What if it got out that I paid people to fix my online reputation? My decision was made for me when I learned the price tag—reputation management is another one of those services in American life reserved for wealthy individuals and corporations. The guy wasn't surprised when I said no, but he was sympathetic. They'd looked closely at my profile. "Someone else is doing *to* you what we would do *for* you," he said. My search results, he said, were by somebody else's design. The first item was always a blog post from several years ago that called me, in the headline, an "asshole." Somewhere, a government or person was making sure that this story—and others like it—were being clicked on, so that the world thought that it was the most important information about me. Was it tied to the U.S. government? The Israeli government? Some rich right-wing guy? No one could tell me.

In the years since, I've learned how widespread the use of private intelligence is by the world's autocrats, oligarchs, and corporations. Often making use of retired American and Israeli spies and Special Forces troops, dozens of outfits like Black Cube can intimidate inconvenient adversaries, obtain sensitive information, blackmail people, or shape an online or media narrative to suit the interests of their client. Consider it a service industry for the powerful who can afford to pay those bills and have the will to do so. Just as governments and political parties like Fidesz and the Republicans use media to shape people's idea of what's true and what isn't, this private espionage service economy can shape the idea of what's true and what isn't about individual targets like me or anyone else. The message is clear and the same: It's not worth the cost of opposing the powerful, particularly those willing to respect few or no limits in exercising their power.

FOR ANN, THE Black Cube episode was a final straw. "I am done with this," she said. *"Done."* Dispirited by the dark turn that Washington had taken, I succumbed to her long-standing desire to move back to the Southern California of her youth, into a house she picked out that I'd never seen. It was, I figured, her turn to make these choices, and Los Angeles wasn't exactly a hardship. The weather is good. So is the food. The kids can play outside. Given my travel, it'd be nice for her to live near her extended family. Southern California offered a progressive enclave in which to ride out the Trump years. These were the things I told myself, and they were true. But it was a disorienting transition—sitting in cars, doing away with seasons, living in a place where the conversation rarely revolves around what's happening in the world and you've removed yourself from Washington's revolving-door waiting room for future government service. I was, I knew, sending a message of sorts to the world of high politics I'd marinated in for more than a decade: *I'm out.*

I settled myself by going for runs along the ocean. As I'd pass from crowded Venice Beach into Marina Del Rey, the crowds thinned until I'd reach a largely deserted pier at the end of a promenade. Turning right, I'd run out over the ocean. There, all of Los Angeles is in the hills behind you or curving around the coastline to the north. The smell of fish blends with the sound of seagulls circling. A fisherman or two linger. In the late afternoons, as the sun begins its plunge into the ocean, you're running into a dazzling array of colors. Atop a rock wall just beyond the pier, a large American flag flutters in the breeze—the edge of the country, the last stop before the endless ocean. From that spot, the world behind me seemed impossibly far away, a distant jangle of news reports and information wars. Sometimes, stopping out there, I'd have the eerie realization that anything in the world could be happening—a war, immigrants in camps, a collapsing economy, a pandemic—and this place would still look the same. I could feel that weight on me lifting, the bliss of not caring. Perhaps this was how fascists got away with it through history, I'd then think: There's enough normal life out there for enough people to grab on to. As Márta said, they make politics dirty and dispiriting on purpose, so people will turn away. Maybe this is what whoever was behind Black Cube wanted, anyway, with their sloppy "Shell Productions" gambit—for it to get out, for me to be worn down, one more small but inconvenient voice pushed to the margins.

In those moments, I'd look at the flag that once stirred such emotion inside me and feel absolutely nothing.

WHEN I RAN in the mornings during my time in Budapest, the wind whipped in thick icy gusts off the Danube—one of those rivers whose very names evoke images of ghostly empires and the forgotten lessons of history. Orban understood that shaping perceptions of the past can set a different direction for the future, which is why Budapest has become a microcosm of his effort to remake Hungary. Across from the place where I was staying, there was a park with a statue that had been erected to much controversy in 2014, depicting an angel reaching her arms forward while an eagle flies overhead. The angel is meant to be Hungary, the eagle Nazi Germany. The message is that Hungary's World War II–era government—a Nazi-collaborating enterprise—bore no responsibility for its crimes. In the years since, as an act of protest, the entire monument was surrounded by pictures and notes honoring those who perished in the

Holocaust. I bent over the black-and-white photos laminated in protective plastic. Female faces jumped out—black-haired Jewish faces like my own young mother's gazing back at me with dark eyes.

I walked the few hundred meters to the yawning courtyard in front of Hungary's massive nineteenth-century parliament building. Entering the square, I saw a statue honoring the overthrow of Hungary's short-lived Communist government of 1918–19, which had originally been erected by the far-right government of the 1930s. Orban had the statue reerected in 2019, taking the place of a monument to Imre Nagy, the prime minister killed by the Soviets after the 1956 uprising. Orban, who began his political career at the reburial of Nagy, had thus dispensed with the icon of protest who helped launch his meteoric rise, and replaced him with an image of the far right.

I walked closer to the Danube to find a statue of Nagy. It was smaller, less impressive, and tucked away between a busy road and some characterless structures. Nagy had been a martyr, but he was also a Communist. I thought about what Sandor had said about Budapest's transformation after the fall of the Berlin Wall: *As a child, you see the visuals. Visuals in terms of statues that you see on the streets.* In a country where politics has an underlayment of "red or brown," these decisions about history indicated which side was responsible for Hungary's defeats and which side had won. It wasn't just statues. Orban was remaking Hungary's national curriculum, elevating some writers and eliminating others, including the Nobel laureate Imre Kertész—a Jew who had chronicled Hungary's Holocaust experience.

It's a strange irony of Orban's rise that a leader who whitewashes Hungary's complicity in the murder of Jews and engages in dog-whistle anti-Semitism has been closely tied to the Israeli government of Bibi Netanyahu. Orban's 2010 campaign was aided by two of Netanyahu's top political consultants—American Republican operatives who helped conceive the attacks on Soros. Orban regularly uses his friendship with Netanyahu to beat back charges of anti-Semitism, while Netanyahu shrugs off criticism over his friendship with Orban, who is a reliable voice in the counsels of Europe defending Israel's treatment of the Palestinians. In this way, the ethnonationalism of the Jewish state finds common cause with the Hungarian flavor of ethnonationalism, which has deep roots in anti-Semitism.

This, I realized, is part of what bothered me about Black Cube and the broader information war that had been waged against me by the American and Israeli right for years. It insisted that I was an adversary of the Jewish state, which had been a source of pride in my household growing up, just as it cast me as an adversary of the American government that I had spent eight years serving. I mentioned my Black Cube experience to Sandor as he showed me around Budapest's Jewish quarter, the neighborhood whose corrupt transformation had motivated his entry into civil society. "Yes, I know this," Sandor said. Presumably, he had googled me as well. But it turned out he had his own experience with Black Cube.

Sandor explained that his cousin had been contacted by people claiming that they wanted to support Hungarian civil society. When Sandor's cousin googled the names of the people who contacted him, they had a minimal online presence associated with a think tank. The people who met with Sandor's cousin pitched him on cooperative efforts to undermine Orban. It was an attempt by Black Cube to catch Hungarian civil society on tape, validating the conspiracy theory that shadowy foreign interests were colluding with Hungarians to undermine their government. "He didn't take the bait," Sandor said, "but someone else did."

The leader of one of Soros's organizations in Europe, Balázs Dénes, went to a similar meeting in Amsterdam. There, Black Cube operatives secretly recorded Dénes talking about his efforts to get European governments to pressure Hungary to overturn its law restricting foreign financing for NGOs. That should come as no surprise; Hungarian civil society has taken the same position publicly. But when someone is caught secretly on tape, it gains a conspiratorial air. Just a few weeks before the 2018 Hungarian election, the story appeared in *The Jerusalem Post* under a headline that shouted

EXCLUSIVE: HOW A SOROS-FUNDED NGO LOBBIED ONE EU COUNTRY AGAINST ANOTHER. The article made no mention of Black Cube or how the newspaper acquired the recordings. It did say things like "Dénes's remarks show a focused effort by his organization to influence Hungarian law by leveraging German influence against the country." Orban's spokesman put out a statement declaring that the information revealed that Soros "commands a quasi-mercenary force of at least 2,000 people tasked with achieving three goals: bringing down Prime Minister Orban's government, dismantling the border fence, and promoting immigration to Hungary." Orban himself declared, "Soros's people will be installed in government. This is what 'Soros Leaks' recordings tell us." The tagline "Soros Leaks" was promoted through stories in *Breitbart,* the American right-wing media outlet. Meanwhile, Orban's lobbyist in Washington, the former Republican congressman Connie Mack, circulated a memo on Capitol Hill alleging that Soros had planted a staffer named Fiona Hill in the White House to undermine Trump and Orban. The memo read, "We must continue to shine a light on the far-reaching network of George Soros in order to continually degrade his international influence."

Márta Pardavi saw the efforts of Black Cube, which had also targeted her organization, as a simple fact of life in Orban's Hungary. She wasn't surprised that Orban and Netanyahu pursued similar autocratic methods. "It's a bit boring," she said, "how hundred percent copycat these methods are. There is a law [restricting NGOs] here, but there is in Israel something called NGO Monitor, which is monitoring the human rights NGOs in Israel. It's very right-wing. [They target] anybody who would have anything to say about Israel's policies not being the best vis-à-vis the Palestinians." I noted to Márta that Orban and Netanyahu had used the same American political consultants, just as they had similar approaches to critical NGOs. "Yeah," she answered, "of course they did."

I had not expected the Hungarians I met to have a connection to Black Cube, which made me feel they had a connection to me—as if we were all a part of some international community of underdogs that was, in some intangible way, on the losing end of power. Sandor told me the story of his cousin as we approached the largest synagogue in Europe. I struggled to wrap my mind around the absurdity of it. Here we were, two half-Jews of European descent, both our families targeted by an Israeli intelligence firm in service of a shared political agenda that pushed an anti-Semitic trope that George Soros was trying to overthrow our governments.

I told Sandor that I could at least try to see it from Netanyahu's perspective. Given the way Jews have been treated over the years, if Israel doesn't act like all the other bad actors around the world, the Jews will be screwed again. So, the thinking goes, we have to be corrupt, be nationalist, make deals with unpleasant people, take the Palestinians' land, attack and discredit opponents with lies or exaggerations, because that's what's required to defend a people who have suffered. Perhaps that is the logic of a cruel world. "The Jewish people are safer in a world where people don't act like that," Sandor countered. "If you're contributing to a world of ethnonationalism, then ultimately you risk ending up back in the conditions that you suffered under, whatever gains you might get in the short term."

I looked up at the towering synagogue, grander than any other I had seen in Europe, Hebrew letters over the entrance. Had my ancestors passed through doors like that in synagogues that dotted the shtetls and imperial outposts of Eastern Europe, before they began their long pogrom-driven journey across Europe and the Atlantic, first to the row houses of Brooklyn and ultimately all the way across the country until I was deposited at the tip of a pier in Marina Del Rey?

BUDAPEST, LIKE NEW YORK, is a city of endless stories, public and private. I could see why Sandor had been so wounded by the destruction of its old neighborhoods. They reminded me of the old majority-Jewish pockets of Manhattan—block by block, weather-worn building after building, stone courtyard after courtyard. To walk those types of streets is to feel the thrill that an archaeologist must feel when looking at an ancient tablet. How many individual stories had unfolded inside these buildings? Every time I walk such a neighborhood, I feel that frisson of both unknowing and connection.

In this way, I came to realize what was so oppressive to me about Black Cube. It wasn't simply the crude authoritarian tactics, the seamless chain of right-wing political interests, spies, and media outlets that churn out self-serving and often dishonest narratives, the impunity for these actors who pursue the large goals of shaping the politics of nations and the smaller ones of making an Internet user think that someone like me is an asshole. No, it wasn't just those things. It was the realization that I was a casualty of a war over identity—who defines it and who doesn't, what is true and what isn't, what happened and what didn't, who you are and who you aren't.

As a teenager coming of age in the American nineties, I would have said that my own two most important identities were my American citizenship and my Jewish heritage. Now I was on the wrong end of an information war that was being waged by the American government, the government of the Jewish state, and would-be dictators like Viktor Orban. In their own way, they had anointed themselves the arbiters of identity, lubricated with shared corruption, tactics, and even service organizations like Black Cube, asserting the right to dictate who can really claim the identity of being Jewish, Hungarian, or American and who poses a threat to those identities. Even the Hungarian tug-of-war between red and brown wasn't absent in America; at the same time I was in Budapest, the Republicans were gearing up a campaign based on attacking Democrats as "socialist." This argument was a proxy for who was really American and who constituted the threatening Other. For the first time in my life, I understood just a little bit what it felt like to be dumped into that category. It was no wonder that I felt most like myself when I was running away from it all, at what felt like the edge of the world.

5

Opposition

KATALIN CSEH WAS born at the end of 1988, part of a generation that grew up after the fall of the Berlin Wall and came of age as Viktor Orban began his effort to remake Hungary. The arc of her life traces Hungary's post–Cold War experience and suggests how some people are trying to define who they are, and what Hungary is, in opposition to Orban.

In the promising nineties, Katalin's father started a small printing business that soon grew into a large company. New opportunities were unfolding around her, the casual experience of freedom. People talked of a future in which Budapest would become more like the wealthy Austrian city of Vienna, the other capital of the Austro-Hungarian Empire, which had avoided Soviet domination through the Cold War. But her first political memory is of something chilling: a far-right political rally, filled with radical anti-Semites, that she witnessed in 1997. "These big muscular guys marched around the city in these heavy boots and stuff," she recalled to me. "And they were really full of hate."

Given her unease with this brand of politics, Katalin was jolted by Orban's 2002 campaign, when he turned further to the right. "Orban was basically focusing on—we are the good Hungarians, and all the others aren't even Hungarians." She didn't like that Fidesz claimed the Hungarian flag, so she wore a flag pin in protest. "I was like, don't tell me what to do. I'm wearing this pin because why not?"

In high school, Katalin was a hippie kid who went to punk rock concerts. But she also lived through those 2006 far-right protests of the socialist government. And at her conservative school, this thuggish brand of nationalism was encouraged. "I remember," she said, "one of the teachers said that those who come home from the protest with a black eye, they get an extra grade 5"—the highest grade.

To Katalin, the emergence of a nationalist right felt totally disconnected from the concerns of a teenager attuned to the world's hypocrisies. "There was this very strong image of a good Hungarian that was proposed," she said, "but it just felt fake. And also ancient. So like you are a good Hungarian if you listen to music from two hundred years ago and you only appreciate old stuff from before the war. And that was also the sentiment when Fidesz was in opposition—they were really hateful of popular culture, [saying] the stuff on television is stupid, they're all liberal."

She was on the receiving end of a culture war that she didn't know she was fighting. And her reaction sounds like that of any American teenager mystified by our early-twenty-first-century culture wars, the strange insistence that the ideal of equality and the fact of diversity were threatening to some established order. "I was just like, why hate on these shows? Why use everything as a sentiment to demonstrate that you are better than somebody else?"

THEN THE FINANCIAL crisis hit. Her dad called her at university to say that their comfortable living was gone. People's mortgages collapsed. Savings were wiped out. She was young enough to avoid the wreckage, but old enough to understand it. "This really affected a lot of folks around me. Not my generation, but the parents of my friends and those who are like ten years older than me." Orban railed against the government and the government had no answers. A university student had nowhere to look for leadership. "I felt that the country was sliding backwards, and the government had no control, and the opposition was spewing hate on top of an already bad situation."

After Orban was elected, Katalin protested his efforts to change the constitution, marching across Budapest with groups holding lanterns in silent mourning for the end of the Republic. She got involved with opposition NGOs and a political party, but after she graduated in 2014, she decided to move to the Netherlands with plans to start a life outside Orban's Hungary. When she came home for Christmas, protests broke out over a proposed tax on the Internet, an issue that particularly mobilized young people. A friend of hers was organizing a rally and needed a female speaker. So Katalin found herself—in her midtwenties—talking to thousands of people. The experience changed her plans. "I started to feel that I had a responsibility for things around me, and I could not just escape to the Netherlands and say 'You guys take care of it.'"

A friend from high school recruited Katalin to help start a political movement. At first it was just grassroots—a handful of friends meeting to discuss politics, then a few dozen people, not unlike the civic circles that Orban had mobilized a decade earlier. The momentum of these meetings grew based on a simple insight: "The folks around us who are in politics right now," Katalin recalled, "they just don't have a voice that can speak for us. So we thought that if there is no credible alternative, we should try to evolve into one." For the next year and a half, they did this "community building," which took place mostly in Budapest's "intellectual urban bubble." It was students and young professionals who shared a basic worldview, which formed the basis of an identity—a belief in social justice, anticorruption, the rule of law, free media.

In late 2016, reports started to spread that Budapest was going to bid for the Olympics. Katalin and her circle started a campaign against it, informed by fears of corruption. When Russia hosted the 2014 games in Sochi, she knew, billions of dollars were spent on stadiums and infrastructure with huge cost overruns that lined the pockets of Putin's cronies. Surely Orban was planning to spend a lot of money to host an Olympic Games so that he could similarly enrich his own cronies at the expense of the taxpayer. In Hungary, you need 150,000 signatures to hold a national referendum. So Katalin and her friends launched a petition drive. On the first day, there were long lines. The potential corruption of an Olympics was easy to understand. It also became an entry point for young people dissatisfied with politics generally, including the opposition parties. "People liked these kids who collect signatures, who look young and fresh—not like all those people who've been out there before." They got a quarter of a million signatures in a country of 10 million people. Late in the campaign, Katalin was shopping when she saw a national poll on her phone that included her movement as an option for governing Hungary, not just defeating the Olympics. "I just started to cry in the middle of the stationery shop," she remembered, "and everyone was, like, looking at me."

Once the petition drive succeeded, Orban withdrew his bid in order to avoid certain defeat. Buoyed by their victory, Katalin and her friends founded a party called Momentum, a name that represented youth and change, with a pragmatic orientation. "We just felt that the political conversation was stuck between the right and the left wing. Which in Hungary comes with these horrible historical connotations." They were animated by reforming democracy and focusing it on systemic problems that mattered to young people—"the abysmal state regarding corruption, regarding the rights of minorities, regarding the huge gaps in society." In other words, the same corruption, discrimination, and inequality weighing on countries around the world. Katalin became vice chair of the party. She was twenty-nine years old.

HEADING INTO THE 2019 European parliamentary elections, Momentum couldn't get on television because that was controlled by Fidesz. There were no debates because Fidesz avoids them. People told them they needed big donors, bigger names to run as candidates, "you need a former host of whatever television show," Katalin said. Instead, they used social media and spent six months driving around Hungary, knocking on doors and distributing leaflets. They would come into rural towns in a big truck covered in their logo, stop on the streets, and approach people. Katalin said a common greeting from those who knew about them only from Fidesz-friendly media was "Oh, you are those George Soros puppets!" They'd joke about it and make small talk. "And some people are like, 'Well, you're kind of nice, what do you stand for?' And I'd tell them and they'd be like, 'Ah, it kind of makes sense.'" To Katalin, the lesson was simple: "You can actually build a movement from ground zero."

In 2019, Momentum won seats in the European parliament, in which Katalin now serves. To Orban, Hungary's status as a small country vulnerable to the prevailing winds of globalization justified his turn toward Russia and China. Katalin made a mirror image of his argument in favor of closer ties within the European Union. "We are a small, landlocked country with ten million people, a very open trading market. If we don't have friends and allies, we are lost."

Within Hungarian politics, Momentum has joined with a collection of other opposition parties who chose to band together despite their sharp ideological divisions—a Green Party, the socialist party, and a formerly far-right party. This kind of pragmatic alliance among ideologically opposed parties is an emerging opposition tactic in countries with autocratic leaders. Katalin described herself as "very pro-coalition" even as she acknowledged her discomfort allying with, among others, one of the very same political parties that she used to protest. "However, I know that if you want to make at least a more just electoral system, you need to be in the position of power to change stuff. Once Orban is ousted, I'm really hopeful that we can get to the parliament and debate each other. But now neither of us is in power, so we cannot do anything."

KATALIN AND I talked in the suite of cluttered rooms in an old Budapest apartment building that served as the headquarters of Momentum as young people came in and out of the room. Her dark brown hair was neatly trimmed at her shoulders, and she had an easy poise, slightly weary but with the reserve of energy that I'd seen good politicians sustain through a long day. I told her that there was something familiar about her trajectory—a building sense of frustration with the status quo; a high-profile rejection of one-party rule; founding a new party; building a grassroots movement that asserts an alternative identity for the nation; fears about a small country at the mercy of larger forces.

"Orban was once sitting where you are," I said.

Instead of rejecting the analogy, Katalin pointed out the critique that Orban had gotten right, the same populist critique that resonated in America. "Let's not lie to each other," she told me. "Globalization has done a lot of bad things. There are a lot of people who are poor, who lost their jobs, who are afraid of losing their jobs, they are afraid of anybody else coming into our country that might end up taking their jobs, even if it's stirred up to a crazy extent. You know, people are just not happy, and we have to respect that. These populists are playing on the emotions of these unsatisfied, very desolate people. But if we can provide these people with a better alternative, I'm hopeful that it's just as valuable as crazy populism."

This narrative bets that disgust with Orban's corruption will be as animating to those disaffected voters as the failures of globalization, and that a government that embraces democratic institutions will be able to deliver better results. It's a narrative that has animated opposition parties in different parts of the world. Momentum is working together with a broad network of sister parties in Europe, and they now help to train others in social media and canvassing, the nuts and bolts of campaigning. Like everyone I spoke with, Katalin noted the convergence of right-wing political leaders globally and said the opponents of nationalism need a similar solidarity across borders, maintaining, "It's very important to have better coordination and communication, holding out a hand for those who are in the learning phase and giving exposure to each other." Those links can lead to tactical political cooperation, but also to the development of solutions that address more localized concerns, the concerns of those desolate people she spoke of. "What kind of money you pay for your gas bill. Who takes care of your data. Who trades with you on what terms," she said. "You have to engage with those who hate you because they're also your constituents. You can show them 'I care, I hear.'"

Listening to Katalin, you could view her as part of a wave of younger, female, more progressive politicians making breakthroughs across the West in opposition to nationalism; or you could view her as part of just another small party that would be vanquished by the likes of Orban. What was clear is that she was the product of an entirely post–Cold War Hungarian experience, forging a political identity in opposition to the post-financial-crisis populism that swept across the West, made up of young people who aren't seduced by the past, who are fed up with the present, who are worried about the future, and who don't want to toss out the democracy that America and Europe once stood for just because the project of globalization has been coming apart at the seams.

Katalin's communications adviser—another schoolmate of hers—walked me out and asked if we could grab a coffee. He was an earnest young guy who seemed to delight in his job. He'd read my book, he told me, to get a sense of what it's like to be a staffer in the rough-and-tumble world of politics. I realized that I traveled to places like Budapest and met with people like Katalin because I knew—on some level—that the success of the initiatives I'd worked on and cared about depended upon the success of people like her and her associates.

Ironically, nationalism has sorted people into borderless tribes. On the one hand, the mass of people who have responded to globalization in Hungary by turning to Orban have a lot more in common with the Americans who turned to the Tea Party and Trump than with Sandor Lederer, Szabolcs Panyi, Márta Pardavi, or Katalin Cseh. On the other hand, I have a lot more in common with these younger, more liberal Hungarians than I do with almost half of my fellow Americans. This isn't because we don't understand those who have become enthralled with nationalism. We share some of the same grievances about the inequities of globalization and the failures of global elites. My reaction to those failures has simply led me into a different tribe—one that sees the project of Orban and the Republican Party as fundamentally corrupt, and that worries about the danger of where the blend of nationalism and authoritarianism can lead.

6

The Liberal Order: An Elongated Reason Cycle?

PEOPLE LIKE ME come and go in positions of power, but money and those who manage it remain constant, both shaping and responding to politics. They can also be dispassionate in their analysis, unburdened by being participants in political debates. So over the last few years I've become intrigued by my occasional conversations with people who look at the world through the prism of markets.

In Singapore, I met a British guy who has excelled in this world. He's younger than me, well-spoken and worldly—the kind of guy who reminds you that the Brits once administered far-flung places. His employer also wanted him to remain anonymous in this book. At the end of a meeting about geopolitics in late 2018, I had said that the thing that most worried me around the world was the danger that the current nationalist trend would inexorably lead to a war. *Or something along the lines of the French Revolution,* he'd said. It wasn't the type of response I'd expected; it seemed to cut against what you'd be likely to hear from someone in finance, and we agreed to continue the conversation.

When we next spoke, the British election had just swept the pro-Brexit conservatives into power, amplifying the nationalist trend that Orban represented. He noted how unbelievable it once would have been for conservatives to win in England's mining towns. "I come from the working class," he said. "What I try to explain to globalists is that the people from my hometown—it isn't just they feel they've been left behind, they feel that the one percent did a deal to deliberately screw them." I sensed something familiar, the insider who still feels he's outside the system observing it.

I asked my British friend about the impact of the 2008 financial crisis in bringing about this dynamic, the sense of desolation it fueled, people's belief that the whole system was rigged to screw them. Instead of talking about markets or elections, he talked about gas chambers—the shock that accompanied the discovery of the extent of fascist crimes at the end of World War II. "That was so appalling," he observed, "that it created an *elongated reason cycle*, aided by the creation of the American order." A cycle in which the nations of the world bound themselves to a system of international treaties, norms, and institutions that shaped everything from the development of nuclear weapons to the rules that governed trade between nations to the expectation that human rights should be protected within them—or at least within what was known as the "free world." Perhaps, he was suggesting, it wasn't some evolution of human reason that had brought about the relative peace and progress of the postwar decades, it was the shock of fear that came from staring into the abyss of where nationalism and tribalism lead.

This was the American-led international order that prevented World War III and helped bring down the Berlin Wall. After the Cold War, it lost its organizing principle, just as the memory of blitzkrieg and gas chambers was fading. What was left behind was a momentum of hypercapitalist globalization that expanded until it was felled by its own excesses in 2008. "The model was just an implicit premise—kind of a lazy premise that everyone had—this idea that it was almost a manifest destiny belief that freedom and markets and consumerism are going to take over the world, full stop." Instead, we got the return of the old history—the grievance-fueled nationalism that has usually been a precursor to war or revolution, whichever arrives first.

FOR ME, ONE person who embodied this elongated reason cycle, and the story of Europe within it, was a family friend named Peter Karpenstein.

Peter worked as a lawyer within the European Union's vast bureaucracy and came to know my father through a Cold War–era exchange program—an EU initiative that saw the value of taking a German lawyer from Brussels and connecting him with an American lawyer from Texas so that some intangible bond could be formed. The two of them became close, and our families would see each other every few years in one place or another. Both Peter and his wife, Brigitte, were German. Both of their fathers had been members of the Nazi Party from the early days. When Peter first stepped into my parents' apartment, his eyes scanned the shelves, and he asked, with admiration, "Who owns all the Hitler books?" It was my Jewish mother, who had struggled her entire life to understand how Hitler happened. I remember my parents telling me that Peter had a boyhood recollection of his father appearing in the distance a few years after World War II ended, walking the final miles home from the eastern front, carrying a pair of shoes for his son. When I heard this story as a teenager, I had a cinematic image of the father emerging like an apparition out of the fog, a symbol of a chastened Germany, staggering toward his boy. Germans, too, had to figure out how Hitler happened.

Peter had lived outside Germany for the majority of his adult life. The reasons were never articulated to me, but seemed self-evident—he'd settled in Brussels, the home of the great post–World War II project of building peace and political union, making some amends for Germany's sins. Peter bathed in the deep pools of European civilization. He traveled to Greece to sketch ruins. He went to Paris for the sole purpose of visiting one small portion of the Louvre. He took my parents on arduous tours of World War I battlefields. The first time my father visited his house, Peter greeted him in the morning with glasses of champagne and insisted they sing Beethoven's "Ode to Joy"—in German. When he saw something he liked, he punctuated it with the French word *bonne.* He wasn't above small nationalist prejudices, but they were lighthearted—one time, we drove past a man urinating on the side of the road, and Peter stopped the car, gesturing toward the man. "You see this," he said. "Typical Belgian." You can, after all, be vigilant against the excesses of politics without being politically correct.

One night, at his house, I spent a long time absorbing his book collection and was surprised to see—on a higher shelf—a copy of *Mein Kampf.* He lived like a man who tried to carry with him all that was beautiful and true across the centuries while carefully storing away the trauma as well—close enough to be remembered, but not repeated. On the question of red or brown—Communism or fascism—he was part of that postwar generation that insisted on an enlightened moderation designed to protect people from both: Human beings, left to our own devices, are equally capable of beauty and evil, so institutions like the European Union, NATO, and the United Nations were necessary to curb our excesses, while his extravagant reverence for the beautiful was itself a form of vigilance. We can do better only if we honor our better angels.

When I was studying in Paris during my junior year in college, Peter insisted that I visit him for the purpose of seeing a single Michelangelo statue of the Virgin and Child inside a church in Bruges. If I saw it, he said over many drinks, I could achieve total clarity. The day we drove up from Brussels to see this statue had the deliberate feel of a pilgrimage. We stopped in Ghent to visit a medieval castle that included ghoulish torture chambers. Then we went to an art museum that housed works by the Dutch masters. Peter told me there was only one painting in the museum that we had to see, a work so precise that an ophthalmologist was able to diagnose what was wrong with the eyes of one of the painting's subjects who held a pair of spectacles. We stood before it, reverently, for a period of silence until Peter muttered, *"Bonne, bonne."* Finally, we filed into the dark front of the church in Bruges, where the Michelangelo did not disappoint. The young Jesus appeared to be climbing out of his mother's lap. Mary's expression was more downcast than beatific, as if she foresaw the suffering to come. Peter stood next to me, noting the excellence of the craftsmanship—the smoothness of the skin, the folds of Mary's dress, the intricacy of the hands.

I stood there imagining the hundreds of workers necessary to build the eight-hundred-year-old church we stood in, just as marvelous as Michelangelo's work. Considering this marriage of communal effort with individual genius, I had my moment of clarity and could appreciate what Europe represented when it stayed true to its better history, just as I could see how it led to darkness when it did not—from the torture chambers of Ghent to the gas chambers of Auschwitz. The elongated reason cycle that had encompassed Peter Karpenstein's time had become his life's work.

IN BUDAPEST, I told Sandor Lederer that I thought Peter Karpenstein represented the postwar vigilance against the mistakes of the past. He responded by turning to the shortcomings of the European Union, the heart of that postwar effort. "I was in Brussels yesterday," he said. "I always come back with *Oh, it's hopeless.* Because you see how slowly everything operates, you see the bad compromises." For a moment, he sounded like Orban and the nationalists who had railed against "Brussels bureaucrats" for so many years, the sense that Europe had become a faceless governing enterprise, exerting control over people's lives and incapable of solving problems. "On the other hand," he said, "I would never give up on this project. I think it's a wonderful thing. But it has to become more human in many ways. And it should not take away your identity. Europe makes lots of things very uniform, because of course there is this economic drive behind it."

There is this economic drive behind it. The phrase summed up a lot about the world America has built since the end of the Cold War as the urgency of the postwar decades and the shadow of nuclear holocaust faded. The first American presidential campaign after the Berlin Wall came down was driven by a slogan—"It's the economy, stupid"—whose very effectiveness became a trap. GDP growth. Deficits. Gas prices. The markets. The politics of wealth creation. The wealth that funds politics. The wealthy and the politicians appearing on panel discussions at international conferences to discuss vague concepts of global security, global supply chains, and global sustainability in a world where consumption has made life on earth unsustainable. Washington and Brussels, London and New York, Shanghai and Silicon Valley. The computer, laptop, phone—devices that host platforms that offer the convenience of mind-numbing, socially isolating content in exchange for vast troves of data that make you a more perfect consumer. Everything is one click away, except the things you can't afford. The voyeurism into the lives of the rich and famous, the understanding that there are totally different worlds of housing, health care, education, and justice for the haves and the have-nots. The suspicion that those with money have the power to navigate the byzantine government bureaucracies where decisions are made that determine who gets what.

Underneath it all, where do you go to find meaning, to figure out who you are in a world that has this economic drive behind it? A project like the European Union that was founded with the noble purpose of protecting nations and humanity from our own worst impulses had been gradually drained of its meaning, rendered a cog in the maintenance of an unequal system. When the money ran out and the system collapsed in 2008, there was no meaning to fall back upon, no story that held it all together, so maybe it shouldn't come as a surprise that people became more willing to toss out the liberal democracy with the liberal economics. The whole edifice of power seemed to be organized in a way to tell you, again and again: *It's the economy . . . stupid.* So some people came along and told you to put on a flag pin and find somebody else to hate—anyone, really, except yourself or the people with the real power.

Sandor believed people have to find meaning closer to their own experience. "We have to strengthen democracy," he told me, "by strengthening local communities, by creating personal identities that are challenging national identity or nationalism." Sandor's own habits draw him in directions that aren't that dissimilar from Peter Karpenstein's. He hikes. He spends evenings attending classical music concerts. He finds a sense of community with those who share his aspirations for his neighborhood, for Budapest, for Hungary, for Europe. "It's as important, if not more important, to create alternative identities in terms of more local communities—communities of chosen values, which for some people might be religion and church, and for others might be the hiking club or a sports club. What's important is that people don't feel lost. Nationalism affects mainly those who need ties, need bonds to communities, and don't have them."

I asked Katalin Cseh what it was like to represent Hungary in Brussels. She said that the differences between European identities were as important as what bound people together, the imperative that union need not make people feel like they were losing something. "I think for me," she said, "the essence of a European identity is that you can have a Hungarian, Estonian, Latvian, French, whatever identity. European identity is that we are diverse and respect each other. I don't want to make Germans speak French or the other way around, and I also don't want to ditch my heritage. But we can coexist. I think this is the difference between me and Orban, because I really think that no culture is superior to the other."

This is supposed to be what the United States stands for, the idea that different people can coexist peacefully, that you can have your own local identity and still belong to a larger whole. Of course, it was never that simple. During those post–World War II decades, the Americans who helped design the international order were nearly all white men. Concepts of equality and diversity were aspirations, stories we told ourselves and others. The decades since the end of the Cold War have tested just how far we are prepared to go in actually believing that the stories should be made real. Can you still feel "American" if your country is soon to be majority nonwhite or if the president is Black? Can Europeans hold on to their Christian heritage while treating immigrants from different faiths as equals? Can an international order built by Americans and Europeans adjust to a global politics in which nonwhite nations are going to have more influence?

Leaders like Orban don't pretend to solve the problem of a corrupt and unequal economy any more than the Republican Party does in the United States. What he does is insist that in a world that is corrupt and unequal, Hungary should at least be ruled by the "true" Hungarians—white Christians who define themselves not through coexistence but through hostility to what they are not. That, in essence, is what the Republican Party has become in the twenty-first century: the arbiters of who is a true American. It should come as no surprise that this turn has been accompanied by hostility to international law, to immigration, to a Black president.

If, like me, you were born in the twilight of the twentieth century, you have to remind yourself that the elongated reason cycle of the postwar years, and the progress it enabled—from the civil rights movement in the United States to the relative peace among nations—is not the norm in world history. You have to summon the centuries of feudal order, war, empire, slavery, revolution, counterrevolution, and ultimately Holocaust. This is what is so dangerous about Orban and his fellow travelers, including in the United States—the fact that they represent the historical norm, not the aberration, and that historical norm leads inevitably to violence and subjugation.

"Ethnicity and hatred toward other groups—I think the combination of the two is a very dangerous mix," Sandor told me. "Of course you cannot compare our days with the 1930s in the way that people live. But the talk and the rhetoric and the thinking behind it is a direct connection, and that is why I find these politicians extremely dangerous." It's easy to discount this thinking as alarmist. But there has never been a time in human history when this form of nationalism hasn't led to violence, to war, to mass destruction. Think about it: always.

Now, as values like equality are no longer the business of governments around the world, they have been left to individuals to defend.

This may account for the turn to localism—the crafting of identities at the community level, the personal decisions that are inherently political. Like Márta Pardavi, for instance, Sandor refuses to register as a foreign agent. He told me it was a personal boundary: "I will not wear this yellow star."

WHAT'S IN IT for leaders like Orban? What is the payoff for transforming yourself from a young liberal to an illiberal nationalist? Szabolcs Panyi has the cynicism of a journalist who cannot afford to look in any direction other than at the cold heart of power in the current moment. "In 2009," he told me, "Orban visited Moscow for the first time and met with Putin at the party conference of United Russia. And then they had a private conversation for like fifteen minutes, maybe twenty." The content of their conversation wasn't publicized, but when Orban returned home, he argued publicly that Russia should be contracted to build a nuclear power plant for Hungary. Szabolcs also noted that one of Orban's closest associates also met with the head of the FSB, Russia's intelligence service, around the same time. The purpose of that meeting was to begin discussions of a mutually beneficial economic relationship—not between the two nations, but between the two political parties, Fidesz and United Russia. "So Orban established his contacts both with Putin on a formal level, and the underworld—the economic underworld," Szabolcs said.

Sure enough, business picked up substantially between Hungary and Russia in the decade after Orban's election, most notably in the construction of a multibillion-dollar nuclear power plant. Putin got his payment and Orban set up a corruption scheme. Szabolcs walked me through how it could go. It's not particularly complicated. An Orban crony gets, say, the contracts to pour the concrete for part of the plant. That crony does all manner of favors for the people in government. Then the crony overcharges the government for his services. Everyone profits—Putin, Fidesz, and Orban's cronies. This isn't so different from how it works in America, of course, when wealthy interests profit from government favoritism and in turn fund political campaigns—it's just a little less subtle.

In his courtship of Russia, Orban has come full circle from his early political days when he railed against Soviet domination, in the same way that the Republican Party came full circle from its anti-Russia identity. Like Orban and the Republican Party, Putin has appealed to a particular strain of nationalism—Christianity, hostility to Muslims, subversion of the international order, the longing for an idealized past. "In the past, we Hungarians have suffered a lot under Russia," Orban told one interviewer. "Nevertheless, it needs to be recognized that Putin has made his country great again."

Orban has also courted Russia's larger and more totalitarian neighbor for similar reasons. Huawei, the Chinese telecommunications giant racing ahead to develop and sell 5G Internet technology, has its largest production base outside China in Hungary. "They are producing the 5G network equipment here," Szabolcs said, "and they distribute it not just in Europe, but also in North Africa. And they can have a 'Made in the EU' stamp." Orban was also the first European leader to sign up for China's Belt and Road Initiative, a massive infrastructure development effort to project Chinese influence and investment around the world. The Hungarian Belt and Road project is a railroad that will connect Budapest to the Serbian capital of Belgrade. The project, Szabolcs noted, involves a consortium of three companies; two are Chinese, and one is owned by Orban's childhood friend, the billionaire Mészáros. "So it's quite clear what the scheme is."

I asked Szabolcs if he thought Orban was worried about his exposure, the leverage that others might have on him given his corruption. He said that this was precisely why power was such a zero-sum game for Orban. "I think he's reached a point of no return in a sense that he's involved in so many corrupt dealings with the Chinese and Russians that there's no way back for him. He cannot turn his back because he's going to be stabbed by them. And also with his schoolmate being the richest businessman in Hungary, and his son-in-law and daughter having hundreds of millions of dollars. If there's a change of government and Hungary turns into a proper democracy, his family could go to jail. So there's no alternative, there's no turning back. He's a prisoner of this path he took."

The corruption that Szabolcs described functions like a disease within the globalization that America spread, rapidly outpacing the capacity of national regulators or law enforcement to treat it. Ill-gotten wealth can easily be laundered into undeclared shell companies, or invested in things like real estate—the developers who remake an old Budapest neighborhood, or put up glass towers in New York. It can also be used to mount disinformation campaigns against your opponents, or to hire private espionage companies to discredit them. This is the cold reality of how power and wealth interact; if there is a governing ideology in the world today, it is this crude transactionalism.

Unless he is able to do away with the veneer of democracy entirely, Orban will have to face voters in 2022. Katalin Cseh continues to argue in the European parliament that her own government's antidemocratic behavior should face consequences. Márta Pardavi continues to file lawsuits against the illegality of her own government's actions. Szabolcs Panyi continues to pursue investigative journalism even after the news outlet he used to work for was shuttered. Sandor Lederer continues to fight the corruption that is the lifeblood of the system, but he told me he's had moments when he's been forced to consider what might compel him to live elsewhere. "The point where it gets really radical or violent; people specifically targeted like in Russia," he said. "The difficult time would or will come if these governments are violent, physically violent."

Putin's Russia has served as both a model and a source of corruption for people like Orban. Russia, like Hungary, holds up its own mirror to the American-led order—through the capitalist explosion of the 1990s, the hypersecuritized 2000s, and the social media boom of the 2010s. But Putin, unlike Orban, has had the resources and will to attack that order from within, launching a counterrevolution aimed at reversing the results of the Cold War—the premise that American leadership, liberal democracy, and individual rights are in any way inevitable. They aren't—not in Russia, or even in America itself.

Part II

THE COUNTERREVOLUTION

Violence can only be concealed by a lie,
and the lie can only be maintained by violence.
—ALEXANDER SOLZHENITSYN

7

The House of Soviets

GROWING UP, RUSSIA loomed larger than any other country in my American imagination in ways that are hard to comprehend today. It was the Soviet Union then, of course, but even as a boy I felt it was a Russian empire, a sprawling landmass extending outward from Moscow. Our presidents were elected to protect us from the Russians. Every one of our wars since World War II was in some way about Russia. My textbooks told a story of American greatness and progress that led inexorably into the long twilight struggle against Communism, the chapter that I'd felt myself a part of as a child. National achievements like nuclear fusion, color television, landing on the moon, or building personal computers were measured against what the Russians were up to, a testimony to the supremacy of our "way of life." The civil rights movement was a redemptive project that made us worthy of our standing as leader of the free world. Orwell's *1984* was a warning, but not about the potential totalitarianism of a capitalist, technologist dystopia—it was a portrait of Soviet Russia, and the mustached Big Brother was Stalin. A group of amateur hockey players beating the Russians in the 1980 Olympics was the sports miracle that shaped my young consciousness, just as Rocky Balboa knocking out Ivan Drago was the movie version of the story (in these narratives, America was the underdog). I was raised to loathe Communism long before I knew what it was. Any flaw I could detect in my own country—its pockets of extreme poverty or mistreatment of Black people, for instance—could be minimized as not as bad as what happened to people within the borders of Russian domination. To be American was in some intangible way inseparable from the identity of not being Russian, of being opposed to "the way of life" that Russia represented. That was our national purpose, our sense of ourselves, our definition of the freedom we stood for: We were the best, and they were the worst. When the Berlin Wall came down, it was a validation that America was in some cosmic, exceptional way correct.

It never occurred to me as a child that Russians were raised to hold views that were the mirror image of mine. The Russian experience was so remote that I couldn't see the world through a Russian's eyes other than to assume that any right-thinking Russian must have wanted to live like an American, even if it meant submitting to some form of American supremacy.

It is not just Vladimir Putin who could not stomach that fate. Today, Putin's most potent political opponent is Alexey Navalny, a man around my age who was born and raised in one of the military towns around Moscow. His experience of those twilight years of the Cold War was one in which he was raised to have a similar sense of exceptionalism, the same certainty about his own identity that I felt in America. "I was a Soviet pioneer," he told me, recalling his boyhood. "I was absolutely sure that my country was the best, the richest, the strongest, and we were going to rule the world. We have a great culture, we have a great Army, we have great artists."

Within what—to history—is the blink of an eye, the Soviet Union was gone. So many promises that comprised Navalny's boyhood identity were revealed as lies. Instead, his father brought home rations from the West German military, that leading American proxy, the successor to the Hitler regime. Navalny took the gum from the ration boxes, but, he said, "[we felt] this sense of humiliation that other countries think we are starving and they are sending us these rations from the soldiers, and then our government, they are getting it and saying thank you very much."

Whereas Hungary represents how capitalism without meaning or restraint opened the door for a return to an older nationalism, Russia represents the disruptive force that nationalism can be in the world when hitched to a belligerent approach to national security, the worldview that domestic and international laws are always to be subjugated to the raw will to power. The corruption that seeped into Hungarian political life is but a drop in the ocean of graft upon which Russia runs. The authoritarian playbook pursued by Viktor Orban was modeled on steps that Putin had taken over the previous decade. The nostalgia for the past and ceaseless Us versus Them politics was similarly a reflection of Putin's political project, one in which greatness is defined by what you can destroy, not what you can build. And what Putin set out to destroy, above all, was the idea that was so prevalent after the Berlin Wall came down: that a new world order of democratic values and agreed-upon rules and norms was here to stay.

For much of the twenty-first century, Russia has led the counterrevolution to American domination—not by seeking to upend the global order that America constructed, but rather by disrupting it from within, turning it (and ultimately America itself) into the ugliest version of itself. I think of how Russians must have seen us Americans as I was growing up: capitalist stooges, driven entirely by a lust for profit; a militarized empire, unconcerned with the lives of the distant people harmed by our foreign policies; racist hypocrites, preaching human rights abroad and practicing systemic oppression at home. That's the America that Putin wants the world to see, and that's the America that Putin wants us to be.

Think about it. Isn't that what you would want for someone that humiliated you? For them to be revealed, before the world, as the worst version of themselves? By doing so, Putin leveled the playing field—the world is what it is, a hard place in which might makes right, capitalism is as fungible as Communism, and a ruthless Russia will always have to be treated with the respect that it was denied after the wall came crashing down.

* * *

THE CITY OF Kaliningrad is one of those oddities of history, traded back and forth between empires and nation-states, swapping languages and ethnic majorities, caught in the shifting currents of history. Nestled between Poland and Lithuania along the Baltic Sea, it used to be the German city of Königsberg even though it didn't border Germany. After its brutal conquest by the Red Army, the city was renamed, Stalin repopulated it with Russians, and Kaliningrad served as the home for the Soviet Baltic fleet during the Cold War (as well as the home for some unverifiable number of nuclear weapons). After the disintegration of the Soviet Union, the Russians hung on to Kaliningrad even as neighboring Lithuania became free, leaving the city once again cut off from its nation—a part of Russia, two hundred miles from the Russian border. It was this peculiar political identity that drew me there in the summer of 2001—a twenty-three-year-old part-time teacher and graduate student with little idea what I was going to do with the rest of my life.

Before I got to Kaliningrad, I set foot on Russian soil for the first time, traveling through St. Petersburg and then the three Baltic nations, independent states for just a decade. St. Petersburg—Putin's hometown—seemed to be covered in a layer of dust. The Hermitage held masterpieces on a par with those of any museum in the world, but it lacked what you'd take for granted in the West: fresh paint on the walls, central air conditioning, a pristine gift shop. The boulevards were grand, but trash piled up on the sidewalks. In parks, menacing-looking men drank out of tall cans. Even the beer had an edge to it, a higher alcohol content that could more quickly make you forget whatever it was you didn't want to remember. On the train ride out of the country, I fell asleep and my camera was stolen out of my backpack. By contrast, the Baltic capitals were largely refurbished, on their way to becoming newly embraced members of the Western clubs—the European Union, NATO. Visiting the Baltics in 2001 was like going to a neighborhood in Brooklyn on the cusp of gentrification.

Kaliningrad, by contrast, felt forgotten by time. The only foreign tourists there other than stray backpackers like me were busloads of Germans, hoping to reconnect with some lost piece of their heritage. They walked in packs, cameras around their necks, the losers of World War II now exponentially wealthier than the Russians who'd conquered them and repopulated their city.

Among the low-rise apartment blocks and storefronts, a tower loomed. The House of Soviets was visible from almost all parts of the city. Construction had begun on the building more than forty years earlier, in 1970, among the ruins of the old Königsberg castle. The House of Soviets would be a living symbol of the fact that Communism triumphed over fascism. But the impulse for triumphalism backfired because the wet soil that the castle ruins sat on was like quicksand beneath the Soviet tower. Once the House of Soviets reached twenty-one stories, the engineers realized that it wasn't going to be safe to complete without risking collapse. Construction was halted in the 1980s, and the giant structure stood empty until I laid eyes on it, an unfinished ruin. It did not take a literary mind to see the unpleasant concrete structure as a metaphor for the Soviet Union itself: an ideal that triumphed in war but proved incapable of meeting the basic needs of human beings or keeping pace with a changing world.

I passed a couple of uneventful days in Kaliningrad. One night, my friend and I went to a bar touted by our guidebook as the kind of place that drew a colorful assortment of gangsters, arms dealers, and artists. Unfortunately, that's exactly who seemed to be there, and we finished our beers while reading danger in every glance thrown our way. As Americans cocooned by our Cold War victory and prosperity, we weren't ready to confront the rough edges of the residue of the empire we had defeated. But still there was a feeling of invincibility that came with the passport tucked into the cloth wallet affixed to my belt, stamped UNITED STATES OF AMERICA. This was the last trip I took outside the United States before 9/11, which changed everything about international travel, legitimized Putin's instinct for brutality, and set in motion the chain of events that would somehow propel me—just seven years later—into the White House.

LOOKING BACK, I see that trip to Kaliningrad as one last journey through the post–Cold War world that America bestrode like a colossus—the total domination of global politics, economics, and institutions, the sense that there was an inevitability to world events, the mindset that the rest of the world was a series of places on a map to be visited and measured against the clearly superior way of life that we'd fine-tuned. Even the calamities visited upon that world—a genocide in Rwanda or a war in the Balkans—were something that America could surely learn from and prevent from happening again, aided by think tank papers and Hollywood movies, like a well-intentioned sovereign striving to do better for his subjects. The idea that this kind of world order was even then contributing to a sense of rage and longing for more ancient identities that would lead to the destruction of the World Trade Center was something that my twenty-three-year-old liberal imagination was incapable of even contemplating. So was the idea that Russia would also eventually strike at the heart of American democracy, motivated by a similar cocktail of humiliation, rage, and longing for past greatness that would bookend my experience in the White House.

That was also the time before smartphones and GPS systems, when you planned itineraries days in advance, worked off guidebooks and folded maps, and made your most interesting discoveries by accident. We ended our time in Kaliningrad by boarding an overnight bus that would take us to Warsaw. As we climbed on, I noticed that nearly all of the other passengers were older women carrying giant black plastic shopping bags. The shopping bags were full of bottles of vodka and cartons of cigarettes, and my more worldly—and Russian-speaking—companion deduced from eavesdropping and clipped conversation that these women made a living buying these goods at Kaliningrad prices, then selling them for a profit on the Polish side of the border.

There was tension in the quiet of the bus as we drove to a checkpoint at the border, where we were told to get off with our things. As we stepped off, the older women started running as fast as they could, clutching their bags tightly. They were pursued by the few border guards present, and I saw that this drama was a simple numbers game—there were far more women than guards, so even though the guards could easily tackle a few to the ground, most of the women escaped into the darkness, to reap the few dollars to be made on a black market that had emerged over the previous decade.

Russian women, running into a country that Russians only recently ruled, to participate in the crudest form of capitalism. People's wives and mothers and sisters. From the country that produced Dostoyevsky, won World War II, and sent the first satellite into space. Standing there, even in my youth and naïveté, I experienced a brief wave of what it must have felt like to be a Russian in that time, a feeling not dissimilar to what one must have felt growing up in the shadow of the House of Soviets: a sense of bottomless humiliation and unutterable rage.

8

The Song Is the Same

SIXTEEN YEARS LATER, in 2017, I traveled to Baden-Baden, a spa town nestled in the Black Forest near Germany's border with France. I was traveling with Obama, who was receiving something called the German Media Award, a sign of the country's enduring affection for him. Before coming to Baden-Baden, we'd visited Angela Merkel in Berlin, and she'd told us about her first meeting with Trump. She'd shown him a map of the former Soviet Union to get across what Putin was up to in Ukraine, an issue that we used to labor over with her, deep in the details of sanctions policy and military maneuvers in a country that used to be a battleground between Nazis and Communists. Trump had dismissed her, saying that the only Ukrainians he knew were corrupt.

On a mild May day, I walked cobblestoned pathways along Baden-Baden's central canal, passed meticulously groomed red clay tennis courts with bright white umpires' chairs, and wandered sprawling formal gardens. Statues of royals long forgotten peered over the hedges. It was four months after Donald Trump's inauguration and I was just beginning to recover some sense of equilibrium—sleeping more, working less, reading books again, spending leisurely mornings with my daughters with no fear of being late for anything. Still, I lived in a state of permanent unease.

I was a thirty-nine-year-old with as little idea what I was going to do with the rest of my life as I'd had as a twenty-three-year-old in Kaliningrad. History was no longer something that took place in rooms where I sat. The near-constant surge of adrenaline that sustained me through those years had been replaced by sometimes debilitating anxiety. Every morning, I woke in fear that some initiative that I'd poured myself into was going to be undone in a litany of lies. Insignificant as I was, I retained just enough notoriety to be the subject of conspiracy theories on the right, which I knew led inexorably to investigations. Journalists were constantly calling, emailing, even showing up unannounced at my door to ask me about Russia's intervention in the 2016 election. Everyone seemed to assume that I knew more than I could say, but anything that I *could* tell people on the subject of Russia was obvious. This was always the tragicomic absurdity of the Russia investigation: everyone searching for some additional clue in a conspiracy that was hiding in plain sight, the evidence everywhere from your own social media accounts to the statements made by the president of the United States. To accept that reality would be to acknowledge that what Russia had done was not a mystery to be unraveled—it was all right there in the open. Russia has simply exploited America's weakness in the same way that America once exploited the Soviet Union's. In this case, a Facebook culture that monetized division and disinformation, media that gleefully reported on stolen emails and gossip as news, a Republican Party that had more in common with Vladimir Putin's worldview than Barack Obama's. These facts were self-evident in other countries but contested in our own.

Baden-Baden had the feel of a place built for exile, a spa town known for its baths since Roman times. I was retracing the steps of men and women who for centuries had sought refuge from illness, madness, and the vagaries of politics. Dostoyevsky himself had extracted a novel, *The Gambler,* from his losses in Baden-Baden's casinos. The French had made the town their headquarters for postwar occupation of part of Germany. Winding staircases took me up in the direction of a church from some previous age, with a view of rolling hills that hadn't changed for centuries no matter what war or upheaval was happening in the wider world. Chattering families passed by, blissfully unconcerned with politics. Germany, the nation that America defeated twice to make the world safe for democracy, was now better than America at democracy.

My only appointment in Baden-Baden was with a woman named Zhanna Nemtsova, who had driven two hundred miles from her home in Bonn to meet me for a drink in a sleepy hotel bar that opened onto a courtyard. Zhanna was a youthful thirty-three, with stylishly parted brown hair that occasionally fell over her eyes, a woman forced by events to be fluent in multiple languages. She had come to tell me her own more bracing story of exile: her decision to leave Russia so that she could pursue the truth about the 2014 assassination of her father, Boris Nemtsov, who had been gunned down in the shadow of the Kremlin. As with Russia's intervention in our election, the dots weren't all connected, but the truth seemed obvious: The man responsible was Putin.

Zhanna wanted Obama's help. In that way, she was like nearly everyone I'd met since Trump's inauguration who wanted Obama to *do something* when all he wanted was a break. But he was stripped of any formal power, and was respecting the long-standing norm of former presidents lying low for a while after their term in office. Zhanna spoke about her efforts to enlist European governments and the U.S. Congress in support of a real investigation. The rest of her family remained in Russia; she'd chosen Germany because it was the first place where she found work as a journalist. Zhanna had a habit of laughing when she reached a particularly difficult turn in her story, as if to suggest that recognizing the dark humor of it all is the only way through. It's a habit I've noticed in myself, a nervous chuckle, but from her it seemed like a deeper, Russian habit—the accumulated tragicomic coping with centuries of absurdity.

That night, I skipped the gala dinner and walked the empty streets again, thinking about Zhanna—the extremity of her trauma and exile relative to mine. I took out my phone and pulled up the statement that I had helped write in Barack Obama's name from my basement White House office a few hours after her father was murdered. "The United States condemns the brutal murder of Boris Nemtsov, and we call upon the Russian government to conduct a prompt, impartial, and transparent investigation into the circumstances of his murder." Surely I'd known that such an investigation was unlikely, if not impossible. "Nemtsov was a tireless advocate for his country, seeking for his fellow Russian citizens the rights to which all people are entitled." Unsaid because it was implicit was the reality that that is what got him killed. "I admired Nemtsov's courageous dedication to the struggle against corruption in Russia and appreciated his willingness to share his candid view with me when we met in Moscow in 2009." How long ago that meeting now seemed, Obama sitting with a group of democracy advocates in a Moscow that I could no longer visit because I was sanctioned by the Russian government. "We offer our sincere condolences to Boris Efimovich's family, and to the Russian people, who have lost one of the most dedicated and eloquent defenders of their rights." *How peculiar,* I thought, to be out of power and meet people like Zhanna who had lived the events that I worked on from the safe confines of the White House. The purpose of statements like this, I knew, was less their immediate impact than their repetition—the idea that if the world's most powerful government sounds the same notes again and again, year after year, the continuous melody would let people struggling for their rights feel less alone, so that the arc of history might bend in a different direction. Wasn't that, in a way, how the Cold War had reached its peaceful end?

Now that melody was silenced, replaced with the cacophony of disinformation, a chorus of bots relentlessly hitting discordant notes on behalf of men like Orban, Putin, and Trump. And underneath that noise, there are the individual stories of human beings like Zhanna.

ZHANNA WAS BORN in 1984, two years before an explosion at a nuclear reactor in Chernobyl released enormous amounts of radiation that ultimately killed thousands of people. The Soviet government's initial refusal to tell the truth about the accident contributed to a collapse of confidence among the people. Back then, Zhanna's father, Boris Nemtsov, was a young physicist living in Nizhny Novgorod, east of Moscow along the Volga. In 1987, he joined a local effort to oppose the construction of a new nuclear plant in the area. The fear of Chernobyl was fresh, and his background as a scientist impelled him to get involved in politics.

Nemtsov saw how the government's tone deafness to Chernobyl was connected to its fundamentally corrupt nature. He traveled to Moscow to interview Andrei Sakharov, the Nobel Peace Prize–winning scientist who helped develop the Soviet Union's nuclear weapons and then became a dissident. "This interview was published in one of the major regional newspapers," Zhanna told me. "They did not talk only about the construction of the nuclear plant in Gorky, they talked also about human rights. But the censorship was still in place back in the late 1980s." She laughed before adding, "And that's why when the interview was published, they took away all the questions and answers related to human rights."

Zhanna has grim memories of the end of the Soviet Union. The city where they lived was largely closed to outsiders because it contained military plants and factories considered critical to national security. There were food shortages and long lines for staple goods. Zhanna's mother used to travel to Moscow to buy sausages. Matters got worse after the Soviet Union's collapse as inflation spiraled, the state went bankrupt, and people lost their savings and pensions.

In 1990, Nemtsov was the only non-Communist elected to the Supreme Soviet, the legislative body of the Russian Republic. He was just thirty. There had been a televised debate among eight candidates. Each had only a few minutes to speak, and the other candidates were full of promises they couldn't keep. "And then was my father's turn," Zhanna recalled, "and he said—'I do not want to make any promises. What I promise is that I won't lie and I won't take bribes.'"

Around this time, Nemtsov met Boris Yeltsin, the Russian leader who stood up to the August 1991 coup that sought to reverse the democratic opening taking place in the Soviet Union. One of my own first political memories is of watching Yeltsin standing on top of a tank, taking a stand for democracy, reinforcing my sense that the world was full of good guys who would inexorably vanquish the bad guys on behalf of freedom. But Yeltsin, though a democrat, proved to be an undisciplined alcoholic and deeply flawed president of the newly sovereign Russian Federation. After Nemtsov supported Yeltsin's stand against the coup, he was appointed governor of Nizhny Novgorod in November 1991. "I was strongly against his political activity," Zhanna told me. "He couldn't spend a lot of time with me. I was interviewed when I was seven years old by one of the most prominent journalists in our city, and she asked me a question: 'What should the governor of Nizhny Novgorod do?' And I replied, 'He should resign!' "

Nemtsov privatized industry, advocated for his constituents, and engaged in freewheeling—sometimes televised—debates with the newly independent media. Zhanna rode bikes, played tennis, and occasionally traveled with her increasingly famous father throughout the region. He won the first popular vote held to elect a governor of Nizhny Novgorod in 1995. She learned English. Westerners like Margaret Thatcher came to meet her young father. Yeltsin famously suggested that Nemtsov would be his successor as president. There is a video of him saying this in 1994 during an impromptu interview on a tennis court in Nemtsov's hometown. "He's ready for the presidency," Yeltsin declares to a crowd, before proceeding to clumsily hit tennis balls with his anointed protégé. There is something intoxicating about this video—the bearish, white-haired Russian president laboring to get a single ball back over the net, the smiling Nemtsov moving purposefully with curly black hair and a sly smile, the crowd cheering: a Russian democracy indulging in the openness and good humor of it all.

Other videos of Nemtsov from this time are striking because of the joy he took in politics, and because they depict scenes that would never be broadcast to a mass audience in Russia today. On camera, he berates men richer and more powerful than he, demanding gasoline for his people or refusing to offer his endorsement of various political agendas. He opposed Russia's brutal war in the breakaway Muslim-majority province of Chechnya, splitting from Yeltsin and confronting him with a literal truckload of signatures on a petition that demanded an immediate stop to the war. "In a nutshell, you can explain his legacy," Zhanna told me with pride. "If I had a choice between the Russian presidency and democracy and reforms, I would prefer democracy and reforms."

In 1997, Yeltsin asked Nemtsov to become deputy prime minister. Yeltsin had barely won a second term and wanted to give his government a more youthful look. The move was political suicide for Nemtsov, who would be leaving a post as a popular governor outside the swamp of Moscow politics. He knew this, saying at the time that "in Moscow, I'll be like a kamikaze." Once there, he took on the emerging class of Russian oligarchs (Nemtsov helped coin the term) who had become fabulously wealthy taking control of state-owned entities that were sold off after the fall of the Soviet Union, men who knew how to navigate around, or through, the aging Yeltsin and the general absence of clear laws governing Russia's new capitalism amid the broader canvas of American-led globalization. Indeed, in contrast to the carefully planned reconstruction of postwar Europe lubricated by American assistance, the American advisers who descended on post-Soviet Russia urged privatization and the embrace of neoliberal principles. Ironically, many of the Russians who profited from this dynamic were former Communists rebranded as capitalists—meet the new bosses, same as the old bosses.

Nemtsov tried to replicate the success he'd had as a governor through doggedness and a willingness to pick fights with powerful interests over principle. "He applied the same tactics," Zhanna recalled, "but it was a completely different situation because he didn't have enough power to fight with oligarchs, who had hold on real power, had incredible influence with Boris Yeltsin." Most consequential among these fights was the privatization of the telecommunications utility Svyazinvest. Two of Russia's most prominent oligarchs, Boris Berezovsky and Vladimir Gusinsky, expected to gain control, having backed Yeltsin's reelection and strong-armed their way to win previous auctions of state-owned entities. Nemtsov balked. "He decided to abandon these practices and have a competitive privatization and to introduce transparent rules," Zhanna said. A different bid won. One of its backers was George Soros. Nemtsov had provoked two of the most powerful men in Russia.

"It's not easy to find the right words," Zhanna said, recalling what happened next. She chuckled, the sign of something dark to come. The two oligarchs owned major television channels and used them to attack Nemtsov. "In a very short period of time," Zhanna recalled, "they completely ruined his reputation. His rate of approval fell from sixty percent to two percent." They ran sensationalist reports of Nemtsov consorting with prostitutes. They mocked the fact that he had greeted the president of Azerbaijan at the airport wearing casual white pants. They cast the blame for the problems of 1990s Russia on him. They gleefully reported the fall of his approval ratings, creating a self-fulfilling prophecy. "So that was just dehumanizing, yes? Dehumanization," Zhanna enunciated to me slowly. "They just wanted to create an image of a very easygoing and not serious person who doesn't deserve to be a member of the government. A man who is not reliable. They ruined his political future forever. Forever." It was hard not to think of Fox News in the United States with their relentless campaigns against Hillary Clinton and Barack Obama over private email servers and golf games, amplified online by Russian bots.

"It was the first time when propaganda worked out very well," Zhanna said. Of course I thought this was an overstatement; propaganda has been around as long as politics. But perhaps it *was* the start of something: the brute force of a new kind of Russian disinformation campaign, intent on destroying anyone who posed a danger to the new, corrupt order of things.

THE 1990S WERE a chaotic time for Russians. The oppressive veil of Soviet totalitarianism was lifted. But the transition to what would come next was turbulent. The privatization of the state's assets—the nation's industry and natural resources—resembled a rigged fire sale. Oil prices, a main source of revenue, collapsed to $12 a barrel. The 1998 Asian financial crisis led to a devaluation of currency that further wiped out people's savings. Meanwhile, all these oligarchs had become billionaires while Russia fell further behind the West—evident in everything from the loss of influence over former Soviet satellites to those women in Kaliningrad making for the border carrying shopping bags full of vodka and cigarettes. Freedom had won, and *this* was the result? The disillusionment that kicked in a decade later in Hungary descended on Russia at the turn of the century.

Nemtsov became a fall guy. His reputation was in tatters, and his patron—Yeltsin—could not, or would not, defend him. He quit the government in 1999 and chose to run in the parliamentary elections as leader of a new liberal party, the Union of Right Forces. Zhanna has fond memories of this time. A teenager by then, she accompanied her father as he launched a campaign across Russia, appealing to educated middle-class liberals with a style that had American echoes. They played soccer during the day, and at night they organized rock concerts to draw crowds. She'd watch her father campaign and then they'd have dinner with Russian rock stars. "It was very inspiring," Zhanna told me. She ticked off from memory the cities they visited, place names on the vast Russian map invisible to Americans like me. There was something free about that campaign, one more chance to be young in Yeltsin's Russia.

Nemtsov's party won 5 million votes and took on a consequential role in a parliament that still had an independent voice. He also initially backed the ascent of the relatively unknown former KGB operative Vladimir Putin to the presidency, which became an inevitability once it was supported by Yeltsin. Looking back, Zhanna speaks of Putin's rise as if it was the end of something for her, the end of those carefree times. "On the day of Putin's victory, I turned sixteen. The twenty-sixth of March, 2000," she said. "I was very young, and I couldn't understand why Putin became president of Russia." Part of the complicated reality of the time is that along with the intelligence services, the same oligarchs who had taken down her father also backed Putin. Once he was anointed as Yeltsin's successor, so did most Russians. His grim, workmanlike demeanor seemed an antidote to the freewheeling Yeltsin years; perhaps a gray KGB man could restore order without upending the newly established post-Soviet elite. Zhanna never felt that way: "I didn't have any positive feelings toward Putin back then. I have never had any positive feelings for Putin."

As Putin's tenure began, life got better for the Russian people. The price of oil skyrocketed, replenishing state coffers and stabilizing the economy. "They see that they get their pension every month," Zhanna said of ordinary Russians, "they see that their wages are going up, they see that their standards of living are on an upward trend, they can buy cars and live a normal life. But they don't understand why. They think that the only reason is that Yeltsin was an untalented ruler, was a drunkard, and now Putin is a normal guy working days and nights."

Putin set to work consolidating power fueled by corruption and cronies, the playbook that Orban would replicate on a smaller scale a decade later. One of his first steps was taking control of Russian television. Like Orban, Putin worked through proxies. Gazprom, the Russian national oil company, bought a leading channel and turned it into a government mouthpiece. Berezovsky and Gusinsky—Nemtsov's old antagonists—were driven out of the country. Russia's reputedly richest man, Mikhail Khodorkovsky, was imprisoned. His oil company, Yukos, was handed over to Igor Sechin, one of Putin's closest friends. The new class of Russian oligarchs would be Putin associates. Many—like him—were veterans of the intelligence services, deeply versed in how to simultaneously utilize power and manage dark money. Nemtsov was out of step with these times. By the next parliamentary election, the rock concert ethos failed. Nemtsov damaged his standing by appearing in a bizarre campaign ad on board a private jet. An effort to indicate that his party was a cosmopolitan force that could deliver prosperity only reinforced his association with the corrupt, freewheeling nineties, liberalism as a soulless, self-interested project. Zhanna laughed at the memory: "They thought they were campaigning in Monaco." Nemtsov's party won only about half as many votes as in the previous election. Putin's party, United Russia, received 37.6 percent of the vote but enjoyed nearly total control over politics. Meanwhile, Putin was wrapping his political project in a Russian nationalist bow. After a series of bombings whose origins have always been mysterious (and rumored to be tied to the Russian security services), he escalated the war in Chechnya, vowing to prevent any further loss of Russian territory. The tactics suggested a determination to put an end to the revolutions that had brought down the Soviet Union and were now seeping into Russian territory.

The Soviet days were increasingly seen as something to recall with nostalgia, not shame. Indeed, Zhanna recalled, one of Putin's first steps as president foreshadowed what was to come: "He changed the Russian national anthem back to the Soviet one." Again, she laughed at the memory and its deeper meaning. "It was one of his first decisions. Now we have the Soviet national anthem. The words are different, but the song is the same."

9

Putin and Obama: Two Worldviews

IN THE SUMMER of 2004, I was working for Lee Hamilton, a former congressman who ran the Wilson Center, a Washington think tank that doubled as our nation's official memorial to President Woodrow Wilson. Hamilton co-chaired the 9/11 Commission, which finished its work that July. The event rolling out the more-than-four-hundred-page 9/11 Commission Report was held in a grand building with Doric columns out front and gilded interiors. In a cavernous room filled with national media representatives, Hamilton and his co-chair, Tom Kean, read an opening statement that I'd drafted. I sat in the audience feeling a wave of adrenaline mixed with nerves. *Something that I wrote was being read on national television.* Afterward, I walked out into the heavy, blinding heat—the Washington Monument and National Mall to my right, the White House just a couple of blocks behind me. What could I do in politics to top this?

Something gnawed at me, though. I'd moved down to Washington just over two years earlier to be a part of the nation's response to the 9/11 attacks. The Wilson Center was in the Ronald Reagan Building. Every day I'd go to work, walking past the slab of the Berlin Wall displayed prominently at the building's entrance like the ancient spoils of some imperial victory. Then I'd walk past Wilson's stirring words carved into a stone wall: WE WILL FIGHT FOR THE THINGS WHICH WE HAVE ALWAYS CARRIED NEAREST OUR HEARTS. FOR DEMOCRACY. It was hard not to feel a sense of America's arc of triumph in reverse on that short walk: from our birth as a superpower in World War I to the fall of the Berlin Wall (of course, Wilson's and Reagan's considerable flaws were left unaccounted in these settings). George W. Bush had presented the Iraq War as the extension of that story: a security imperative for our nation as well as a moral response to an oppressed people calling out for our help. This fight, he said, like the others, was for democracy.

By the summer of 2004, it was clear that none of those things were true. There was no threat from weapons of mass destruction. There was no need to invade a country that had no al-Qaeda presence and nothing to do with the 9/11 attacks. Iraqis didn't want us to occupy their country to set up a democracy. Moreover, America had proven woefully incompetent as an occupier because of our hubris, brutality, ignorance of local culture, and incapacity to think more than a few months ahead. The images of dehumanizing torture at Iraq's Abu Ghraib prison mirrored reports of CIA waterboarding at a network of secret prisons around the world, a violent disregard for human rights or fidelity to the rule of law. All of this confirmed Putin's darkest and most cynical judgments about the United States and what he felt he was justified in doing as Russia's leader.

Just three years after 9/11, fighting terrorism itself felt less like a national purpose and more like a justification for a certain kind of rule from Washington: corporatist, securitized, at times extrajudicial, and hyperfocused on the Middle East. As the rationales for war melted away, the language about democracy was deployed more aggressively by Bush and his circle, a post facto justification for something that had no justification. Democracy itself was discredited.

My work for Hamilton on the 9/11 Commission had reinforced these feelings. He'd assigned me the task of reading all of bin Laden's fatwas against America and examining the lives of the hijackers, some of whom I'd watched from the Brooklyn waterfront at the moment of their death. They were bad men who did evil things, but we were only elevating them—and diminishing our values—when we suggested that they represented a threat to the survival of liberal democracy. It was obvious that invading and occupying Iraq and torturing Muslims was going to stir up more hatred and resentment of the United States among Muslims around the world while offering a sense of impunity to autocratic leaders who American officials occasionally lectured about human rights and the rule of law.

Suffice it to say that by July 2004, I'd begun to question the entire story that my own nation told about itself. It was a beautiful story, of course, that spoke to the highest aspirations of human beings for freedom, dignity, and equality—and that fact only made its corruption for immoral ends all the more demoralizing. If I, a relatively secure and privileged person, felt that way, how must others around the world feel?

The 9/11 Commission Report vaulted to the top of the bestseller list, but there was a cynicism to the whole thing that I couldn't shake. The Commission's work was earnestly celebrated by editorial writers and pundits, many of whom welcomed above all the fact that five Democrats and five Republicans had agreed on its findings, as if that fact were more important than the report's contents. The deep, layered, and complex story that it told was cut into morsels that could be digested by the American political and media organism of the twenty-first century. Republicans seized on the idea that the report showed that 9/11 had not been "preventable" while focusing on the counterterrorism failures of the Clinton years (the fact that these areas of emphasis were in contradiction did not matter to them). Democrats seized on the imperative to implement the recommendations of the 9/11 Commission with a missionary zeal. The details of how these sprawling recommendations would remake the nation's intelligence, counterterrorism, and homeland security apparatus were beside the point: Democrats were seen as "weak," and embracing the 9/11 Commission Report gave them a chance to look "strong." The story that the report told was less relevant than its interpretation by a body politic that was still convinced of the rightness of the nation's staggering overreaction to the terrorist attacks through the war in Iraq and the expanding securitization of American life. I'd come to Washington to connect my own life to my nation's response to 9/11, but what was my nation becoming?

JUST A FEW days after the release of the report, the Democratic National Convention was held in Boston. Forty-two-year-old Barack Obama had just won his Senate primary in Illinois and was slated to be the keynote speaker. In his remarks, he said,

> I stand here knowing that my story is part of the larger American story, that I owe a debt to all of those who came before me, and that, in no other country on earth is my story even possible.

This was the story that I wanted to believe. Where else would a Kenyan foreign student marry a young white woman and have a kid named Barack who would end up on the biggest stage in national politics? There *was* something different about the American story, but it wasn't the arc of military and geopolitical triumph from Wilson to Reagan; it was the struggle to better ourselves, to right the historical wrongs of people like Wilson, who'd embraced segregation, or Reagan, who represented the conservative counterrevolution to the civil rights movement.

Obama went on,

> That is the true genius of America—a faith in simple dreams, an insistence on small miracles. That we can tuck in our children at night and know that they are fed and clothed and safe from harm. That we can say what we think, write what we think, without hearing a sudden knock on the door. That we can have an idea and start our own business without paying a bribe. That we can participate in the political process without fear of retribution, and that our votes will be counted, at least most of the time.

To me, these sounded like the words of someone who wasn't far removed from places where there could be a sudden knock on the door, places where you couldn't start a business without paying a bribe; someone who knew those kinds of things didn't just happen in Russia, they could happen in America, too. Instead of grandiose platitudes, this description of freedom felt grounded in reality and the need to guard against complacency. Even the line at the end, *"at least most of the time,"* showed a politician bringing you in on the joke, the knowledge that part of the whole enterprise isn't on the level and we know that.

> If there is a child on the south side of Chicago who can't read, that matters to me, even if it's not my child. If there's a senior citizen somewhere who can't pay for their prescription drugs and has to choose between medicine and the rent, that makes my life poorer, even if it's not my grandparent. If there's an Arab American family being rounded up without benefit of an attorney or due process, that threatens my civil liberties.

Here was an America of underdogs living on the other end of power, rather than the possession of a privileged few seeking aggrandizement through foreign adventures. The inclusion of the one sentence about Arab Americans contained, in its own way, a rebuke of America's post-9/11 excesses. The obvious—even banal—rightness of these images made our failure to live up to that truth both inexcusable and correctable, the proper work of politics.

> We worship an awesome God in the blue states, and we don't like federal agents poking around in our libraries in the red states. We coach Little League in the blue states and yes, we've got some gay friends in the red states. There are patriots who opposed the war in Iraq and there are patriots who supported the war in Iraq.

After I'd spent two years reviewing the pieces of America's response to 9/11—including the faulty efforts to transform distant countries—this was a plea to pay attention to what kind of country *we* were supposed to be in the first place. It was a politics that inverted the jingoism of the post-9/11 Bush years, the patriotism of flag lapel pins, Freedom Fries, and flyovers at football games. Those words spoke to the reality of a country that contains multitudes of identities because individuals themselves contain multitudes. That was America to me: a place where you could be yourself in full because we respected one another's equal worth. The opposite of Us versus Them; just Us. I printed the speech out and put it in a small folder that I kept in a drawer at my office, to be taken out from time to time for inspiration, distraction, or just a reminder.

A FEW WEEKS after the Democratic Convention, a group of heavily armed Chechen militants took more than a thousand people hostage, including nearly eight hundred children, at a school in the Russian town of Beslan. The perpetrators demanded an end to Russia's war in Chechnya. Two days later, Russian security forces stormed the school in a chaotic operation that led to the death of nearly two hundred children.

To the American observer, it was one more horrific terrorist attack in our shared post-9/11 reality. But in truth it was much more than that. It came at a time when Putin had tightened his fist around the gears of the Russian state and hardened his view of global affairs because of the war in Iraq, which confirmed his belief that America's post–Cold War project was an expansionist effort to depose whatever government opposed our hegemony—including Russia's. Just because that view may have been overstated and subsequently used to justify all manner of Putin's crimes and aggressions doesn't mean it didn't contain a germ of truth, or that it wasn't genuinely believed by Putin himself—a man whose life had been spent in the darker shadows of political power.

Sitting in my windowless office at the Wilson Center, I read the speech that Putin had delivered two days after the catastrophe of Beslan. Then I printed it out and read it again and again. I put it in the same folder as Obama's convention speech, where it stayed for the next several years until I packed up my things and went to work for the Obama campaign. Every now and then, I would read it in the silence of my office. There was something chilling and resonant about that speech. The language was simple and direct. It signaled a clear direction. It showed a leader fully revealing himself and his agenda to his people and the world.

Putin began with the expected reference to the terrorist attack, the loss of children, the condolences for the families. Then he told a story:

> There have been many tragic pages and difficult trials in the history of Russia. Today, we are living in conditions formed after the disintegration of a huge, great country, the country which unfortunately turned out to be nonviable in the conditions of a rapidly changing world. Today, however, despite all difficulties, we managed to preserve the nucleus of that giant, the Soviet Union. We called the new country the Russian Federation.

Putin wasn't telling people what one might expect at the conclusion of such a horrifying tragedy, children gunned down in the crossfire of a military assault on suicidal terrorists. Instead, he was telling them what he believed they needed to know about who they are, what they've been through, and what kind of world it is—whether you're a Kaliningrad woman selling vodka and cigarettes on the black market, an outraged resident of Beslan, or just some guy who lost his pension around the collapse of the Soviet Union. The tragedy is not Beslan. The tragedy is what happened to Russia. The tragedy is the loss of the Soviet Union.

> We all expected changes, changes for the better, but found ourselves absolutely unprepared for much that changed in our lives. The question is why. We live in conditions of a transitional economy and a political system that do not correspond to the development of society. We live in conditions of aggravated internal conflicts and ethnic conflicts that before were harshly suppressed by the governing ideology. We stopped paying due attention to issues of defense and security. We allowed corruption to affect the judiciary and law enforcement systems. In addition to that, our country, which once had one of the mightiest systems of protecting its borders, suddenly found itself unprotected from West or East.

From the fall of the Soviet Union to Beslan, Putin was suggesting, a great nation had been brought to its knees. Russia had abandoned Communism and dictatorship, and the "transitional economy" and political system that followed had failed. The Soviet Union used to suppress the kinds of internal and ethnic conflicts that now came to haunt places like Beslan. The Soviet Union used to be respected and secure in its borders, but now America was illegally invading Iraq while America's NATO Trojan horse was swallowing up former Soviet republics (just that summer, the three Baltic nations had joined NATO). Of course the Soviet Union was flawed—that was why people expected changes, "changes for the better." But that is not what had happened. Beyond the brief reference to corruption, Putin did not have to say anything more about what actually happened in the 1990s. Those were things that Russians felt in their bones.

To Putin, these were the real perpetrators of Beslan: the people, nations, and forces that robbed Russia of its strength and dignity, that left it so naked and vulnerable that people were taking children hostage while America was knocking over Russian allies from Belgrade to Baghdad. Nor was Putin shy about blaming Russians themselves, himself included: "*We* found ourselves absolutely unprepared."

Then his argument reached its perfectly distilled crescendo, a simple assertion of worldview. The most powerful thing that a leader can do is tell people a hard truth with the conviction that they already believe it to be true. Phrased wrong, it can insult, leaving people with a sense that the leader is shifting the blame onto them. But when it is done right, it can open a new space for the leader. It does not necessarily matter whether the hard truth is entirely true. Putin had his story of Russia after the fall of the Soviet Union, but someone like Nemtsov could have told a different one—about poor choices, a lack of sound governance, the failure to embrace necessary reforms, the corruption of the gray men from the intelligence and security services. History looks very different depending upon which window you open to look at it.

What matters in politics is whether the person speaking can convince you that he believes what he is saying—whether he conveys a convincing explanation for what has happened and a sense of what *needs* to happen. In just a few sentences, Putin did this—offering a thesis statement for his political project and all that he has done since:

> We have to admit that we failed to recognize the complexity and danger of the processes going on in our own country and the world as a whole. At any rate, we failed to react to them adequately. We demonstrated weakness, and the weak are beaten.

We demonstrated weakness, and the weak are beaten.

"In these conditions," Putin continued, "we simply cannot, we should not, live as carelessly as before." Russia was moving into a new epoch, beyond the chaos of the post–Cold War years, one that required "a complex of measures aimed at strengthening the unity of our country." Those measures would include an end to the direct election of governors, so they could be handpicked by the Kremlin; new rules for parliamentary elections that favored his party, United Russia; new laws that cracked down on foreign-funded NGOs. What mattered was that Russia had to come together as an Us with Putin at the helm, to take on Them—terrorists, yes, but also the American-led post–Cold War forces that had humiliated Russia.

The counterrevolution had begun.

IT'S A PECULIAR coincidence of history that these two speeches were delivered within a few weeks of each other. Think about how many words are said every single day—the endless arguments, snippets of conversation, and seemingly important public assertions that disappear as soon as the sound fades. How rare it is for sentences strung together to signal some new direction that can be recognized from the future. In a way, these two speeches anticipated the extent to which the West was approaching a collapse of the post–Cold War consensus—a process that had been accelerated by 9/11 and Iraq and that would reach its breaking point with the 2008 financial crisis. Both Obama and Putin were trying to tap into people's desire for a new story that offered belonging, purpose, and a sense of possibility. Both Obama and Putin were speaking from a perspective informed by the failure of the Iraq War. Both Obama and Putin described what made their nations exceptional. But their answers, their stories, and their politics led in opposite directions that continue to shape our political debates almost two decades later.

Putin would stop paying attention to words and rules that were inconvenient. Acting with the brute force and disregard for international opinion that characterized America's invasion of Iraq, Russia would invade Georgia in 2008 and Ukraine in 2014. It would also weaponize those aspects of the American order that suited its purposes—oil wealth, the corruption afforded by capitalism, the limitless propaganda function of the Internet and social media.

Years later, just before I left Washington, I had coffee with a journalist who had spent a lot of time looking at Russia's use of disinformation. I described how it had taken years for me to understand the psychological toll that came from a daily bombardment of messages on social media that dehumanized and threatened me. How it was impossible to know what was someone's real voice and what was automated, what was American and what was Russian.

"That's part of the point, right?" he said. "To demoralize the opponent."

As obvious as that was, it had never occurred to me in quite that way before—that my mental state was one tiny front in a war that Putin had been waging since Beslan, that he had projected back onto America what he found ugly about us and in turn shaped us into something that bore a closer resemblance to his view of the world, a place in which truth and individual human beings are incidental to the raw will to power.

10

The System Is Rigged

WHEN I FIRST connected with Alexey Navalny, over FaceTime, he asked with dark humor and a trace of condescension if I was writing a book about "how to do color revolutions better." He was using the term for the popular uprisings for democracy that had been stymied by Russia in places like Ukraine and Georgia, the term deriving from these movements' symbolic use of a particular color or flower. I sensed that he was simultaneously mocking Putin, who claims to see color revolutions being plotted everywhere; American supporters of democracy, whose enthusiasm for color revolutions and financing of civil society organizations can play into Putin's conspiracy theories; and the global media, which reduce complex movements to cartoonish shorthand. He seemed annoyed at the whole edifice. I liked him immediately.

When I explained that I was more interested in understanding his brand of opposition politics through the prism of Russia's story since the Cold War, I may have risen a little in his esteem. He mentioned, as if to strike up a sense of solidarity, that he'd noticed that I had been spied on by Black Cube. He had been too, he said. He'd learned that a Russian billionaire had ordered the operation so that he could give Putin the results as a birthday present. The problem was that the Russian security services already knew everything there was to know about Navalny—a man who has been imprisoned over a dozen times and is constantly followed and harassed. Besides, he was an open book, more than happy for people to know his story.

Navalny remembered becoming politically conscious as the privatization schemes of the 1990s were unfolding and the nation's wealth was being transferred to that handful of oligarchs. The America that likes to think of itself as a source of inspiration to democratic opposition figures did not make a good first impression. Instead, Navalny saw the rotating cast of American technocrats, Ivy League academics like Jeffrey Sachs and Larry Summers, and political consultants who advised Yeltsin and his top deputy, Anatoly Chubais, as—essentially—unwitting co-conspirators in screwing the Russian people. "The privatization was a fraud," Navalny said. "These people who came from the U.S. who were advisers for Yeltsin and for the Russian government—maybe they were personally not a fraud but they worked for crooks and thieves."

Most of the American accounts of that time that I'd read described Yeltsin as a flawed but well-meaning man working with the support of Americans eager to spread democracy and free markets. Navalny said the result tells a different story. "The result was a lot of billionaires. And we have nothing. We still have nothing." Yeltsin's victory in the 1996 election had been viewed as a triumph in America, a narrow defeat of the Communists, a victory for our man in Moscow who even employed American political consultants to help run his campaign. To Navalny, it was a calamity—a validation of corruption, a victory that assured that liberals would be blamed for the unraveling that continued, a dynamic that led to Putin.

Navalny got a law degree and went into politics. In the early 2000s, he went to work for Yabloko, the biggest of Russia's liberal parties. As chief of staff for the Moscow branch of the party, he saw the futility of traditional politics as Putin was steadily taking control of the media—first television, then the newspapers—until self-censorship took hold among Russian journalists. "Without any [explicit] instructions, they understand that you cannot write about these guys," he said, meaning Yabloko and the other liberal parties. Navalny would try to generate media attention for Yabloko's events and agenda, but it all felt like a waste of time. "You're spending much more effort to beg journalists to write something than on the events themselves."

Around 2005, as Putin's transformation of Russia was accelerating after the Beslan disaster, Navalny's attention was increasingly on corruption. Like Sandor Lederer in Budapest, he noticed the schemes that were remaking Moscow. He started talking to people across the city, getting out into neighborhoods where people were being muscled out of their homes to make way for development. "They capture the yard in front of your house, and they're trying to build a skyscraper," Navalny recalled. "They don't have any documentation, they're paying bribes to everyone in the mayor's office."

Navalny began what would become his life's work—connecting dots for people, making them realize that their personal circumstances were directly related to a corrupt political system. He recalled how these conversations with aggrieved residents would go. "Why are they taking land by your house? Because of money. Why are they paying bribes? Because of money." He established the Muscovite Protection Committee, which he described as 99 percent committed to fighting corruption. Navalny would demand documents legitimizing the property seizures and the developers would refuse to provide them. They'd threaten Navalny and then he'd sue them, only to find out that they were paying off the judge reviewing the suit. The people he was up against did not want any publicity, but even when he succeeded in generating it, they operated with impunity. "Back then," Navalny recalled, "people from this construction business are just thugs, mafia bosses, sometimes literally mafia bosses. It's very easy for them to hire a couple of people with baseball bats and just beat you somewhere."

Putin had created the impression that he had reined in the excesses of the nineties when the press was freer, the schemes were plain to see, and the pie was smaller because oil prices were low. But as Russia got richer, the corruption was only expanding, shaping the entire system in which Russians lived. Many of the same people who once ran the Soviet Union were now getting rich in Putin's Russia, joined by the cohort of Putin's own friends and associates who could run networks of graft and criminality drawing on their experience in the shadowy world of intelligence. The words had changed, but the song was still the same. "Corruption is the essence of such a regime," Navalny told me. "Lies and corruption. They're lying all the time to have more money. Of course there is a lot of design with the ideology," he said, referring to Russian nationalism and longing for greatness lost. "But they just want to be very rich men. They just want to have their palaces and their very luxurious lifestyles."

Navalny's own evolving political views in the 2000s were hard to pin down. He made common cause with far-right figures and skinheads who protested Putin in marches, drawing criticism that dogs him to this day. He had a falling-out with the leadership of Yabloko, which wasn't surprising, since he'd demanded that they all resign over disagreements about the party's strategy. By his own admission, he didn't fit easily into the structure of a political party with its coalitions and consensus building. But more fundamentally, all of that political work—and even the traditional left/right debates—seemed pointless when the whole system was rigged.

By 2007, as Putin was preparing to hand off the presidency to his handpicked successor, Dmitry Medvedev, Navalny was at something of a crossroads. At that point, he was just a guy with a blog, but he couldn't shake politics. He wasn't animated by any particular set of policies; what sustained him was anger. He was, he told me, determined to "preserve and keep my level of rage to stay in politics."

What sustained the rage? I asked him.

"It was lying," he said. "The Soviet Union was an empire based on a lie. And Putin's Russia is a country based on a lie." He had seen it firsthand, confronting those corruption schemes in Moscow courts and finding that the legal apparatus that was supposed to enforce fairness was on the take. "You are facing these people in the courts and they are lying to you."

* * *

Navalny's second act in public life, the one that launched him to prominence, was as an online anticorruption crusader. He started a blog and set out to use whatever means were available to him to expose the corruption and lies of the Putin government. He realized that his training as a lawyer and some brief experience in finance could give him a foothold to challenge the system. He bought just a few shares of stock in some of the largest Russian oil and gas companies, which gave him standing to look at their books and challenge them in the courts. He noticed that these companies were paying far more than necessary to middlemen to sell the oil, people also connected to Putin—as much as $30 billion in total. "They were skimming money from every barrel sold," he told me. So he sued them. "My demand was very simple: Please explain why you are using this company to sell your oil. You could sell it directly. So why are you giving money to the closest Putin friends?"

Ironically, Putin's control over the media only heightened Navalny's profile online. By 2008, he realized that the censorship and intimidation of traditional media were driving more and more Russians to his form of Internet activism and investigative journalism. "There was no information at all, so people came to my blog to read something, and it became a sort of theater, a sort of show for people." Navalny was good at theater. In April 2008, he went to the annual shareholders meeting from the mysterious Russian oil giant Surgutneftegas. The meeting was held in the city of Surgut, Siberia, in a cavernous old Soviet Palace of Culture. "You can see all these tough Russian guys," Navalny said, recalling the scene. He got up to ask a question and grilled the CEO, Vladimir Bogdanov, about who the real owners of the company were. Bogdanov admitted that he didn't know.

Another part of the show was the lawsuits against the oligarchs. Navalny offered to help people write complaints. Thousands of people wrote to him, and he established himself as a thorn in the side of Russia's new power structure. That's when he saw the political potential of what he was doing, a grassroots anticorruption movement. The next step was direct fundraising for his efforts, and by 2009 he was raising money for what would become an anticorruption foundation that now has several dozen offices across the country. But he never deviated from his core mission. Every day for years, he wrote an article for his blog detailing his anticorruption efforts, the running script of a hit show. He chafed at the common charge that this made him a single-issue politician, without a program other than anticorruption. "If you're fighting the regime, you're fighting corruption."

Even though he was acting as an investigative journalist and media personality, he always thought of himself as a politician—albeit not a traditional one. "This anticorruption activity was sort of a camouflage for politics," he said. "Because when you're suing Putin's friend for corruption, for stealing oil, of course it's politics." Still, he resisted joining any of the opposition political parties. To him, they had submitted to playing by the rules of a game that was rigged. "I'm a politician," he said, "but I don't have any political party. I realized that it's much better to be out of the game, to create your own game."

As Navalny became more prominent, he confronted an apathy among Russians that was perhaps more widespread than their support for Putin. As the corruption of Russia's economy was impossible to ignore, one of Putin's goals was to discourage people from thinking that participation in politics was worth the effort. To accomplish that goal, he didn't need to convince people that he wasn't corrupt, he simply needed to convince people that *everyone* was corrupt, and the media gave him a huge platform to do that. "They're promoting the idea that you can buy anyone, everyone is corrupt, and the opposition—you can buy them like everyone else," Navalny said. In the same way that Nemtsov was cast as a force behind the corruption of the 1990s, Putin-friendly media cast Navalny himself as no different from Nemtsov and the reviled Anatoly Chubais, author of the privatization schemes. To be a democrat was to be aligned with the corruption of those days and the political agenda of the Americans.

Putin made a version of the same argument about other countries. He cast every other government—every other political model—as hopelessly corrupt as well. If that's the game, Russians might as well have a strong, competent leader who shares their grievances and sense of national greatness. "It's just a business," Navalny said, characterizing Putin's argument. "All over the world, it's the same rules. That's exactly what Putin is saying." The democracies, like America, were just as bad as anyone else. "It's absolutely the same, they're just hiding it better. Everyone is corrupt. Everyone is cynical. There are no rules. There is no democracy. Every election is bought." Referring to Putin, Orban, and the corrupt strongmen who run most of the other Soviet republics, Navalny summed up their somewhat contradictory political message. "Two points of their agenda: First, the West is bad, they don't have any morality; second, it's actually the same, the system is the same, everyone is the same."

On the one hand, it's easy to dismiss Putin's argument. In most of the world's democracies, the basic freedoms that Obama referred to in his 2004 speech are real—the idea that you can say what you want without getting a knock on the door, that you can start a business without paying a bribe. But America has also offered ample evidence to support Putin's message, even before we elected our own corrupt autocrat to the highest office in the land. I asked Navalny whether the 2008 financial crisis reinforced Putin's message that there was no difference between Russian corruption and the corruption of the West. "Absolutely," he replied. "The whole 'too big to fail' conception is a nice way to explain that there is no justice and there is the same corruption everywhere, including the U.S.A."

Think about it from a Russian perspective. You see your own billionaires and know they get rich because of their ties to Putin. Public resources like oil and gas handed off to a well-connected few. Criminal wealth laundered into real estate interests, shell companies, and dummy corporations. Then you look at America and what do you see? You see American banks that took reckless risks getting bailed out and you see billionaires profiting at every turn. The owners of oil and gas interests pouring money into politics. The wealthy able to avoid taxation by spreading their money around, moving it offshore, and creating their own shell companies. If you look carefully enough, despite the American rhetoric about democracy, the same wealthy Russians who everyone knows to be corrupt circulate in the same global elite. "All these bastards, all these bad guys in the very black hats," Navalny said of the oligarchs he's tracked, "they're absolutely fine with going to the U.S. and have meetings with the establishment, with the politicians, they are working it in Davos."

All over the world, it's the same rules.

IN 2013, NAVALNY made his first foray into electoral politics, running for mayor of Moscow. After Putin announced his plan to return to the presidency in 2011, Navalny had begun acting more like a politician, speaking at a series of mass protests in Moscow that helped springboard his candidacy. His goal was to force the Kremlin-backed candidate into a runoff by denying him 50 percent of the vote. Despite having no access to traditional media and being harassed and constrained in his campaigning, Navalny cracked 30 percent and insists that his opponent fraudulently eked his way above 50 percent. It must have been clear to Putin then that Navalny wasn't just an irritant, he was a political threat.

Perhaps not coincidentally, the years after Putin announced his return to the presidency are also the years when Navalny started to be arrested. Sometimes it was just a short-term detention or house arrest to break up a protest. But it would evolve into trumped-up charges on fraud and embezzlement. Being in prison allowed him to get to know a different cross-section of Russians—not just the Muscovite middle class, but also those on the margins of society, insight that he said made him a better politician. But he's straightforward about the fear that goes with prison. "I'm a normal guy," he told me. "Of course I have a sense of danger. Of course it's uncomfortable when they're arresting you. Of course it's uncomfortable when you're in this cell and the metal door closes behind you. And you realize they can do anything." One of the things they did during one of his early stints in prison was poison him. The authorities claimed it was an allergic reaction, though Navalny has never had any other allergic reactions and poison has been a common political weapon in Putin's Russia. "They make this so obvious and so open," he said. "It is a message. It's a strange message, how they poison people inside Russia. They try to show that they can poison you, and maybe they can control you."

Through the years of persecution, anger remained the sustaining force for Navalny. Some of that anger was directed not at the government, but at those who believe that Navalny is not actually an oppositionist. It's a subject that he came back to again and again. It all started, he said, when he confronted Bogdanov in Siberia and was allowed to ask his questions unmolested. From that point on, conspiracy theories started to spread that he was acting as an agent of Putin himself. "People were so shocked that they allowed me to go to the stage and say something about this company, and criticize them to their face—they refused to believe I am doing it on my own. They think maybe I am FSB."

These conspiracy theories ignored the sacrifices that Navalny made, the fact that his own brother was imprisoned for four years on trumped-up charges—some of that time in solitary confinement. So he found himself squeezed between doubters in parts of the opposition and a government that would clearly benefit from spreading conspiracy theories that Navalny is a double agent. Listening to him express incredulity at all this, it was hard for me not to think of the rampant conspiracy theories that have infected American politics, often amplified by Russian disinformation. Of course those with power would want to make people think that their opponents are all part of the same game. He laughed at the absurdity of the conspiracy theory, entering a conversation that he's clearly had many times in his head. " 'Why do they not kill you? Could you explain why they haven't killed you?'" he mimicked his critics. "And I have to explain, 'Sorry, guys, for not being killed.'"

Despite his persecution at the hands of Putin, and the maddening conspiracy theories that he's actually an agent of the Kremlin, Navalny spoke with a focused calm that channeled his outrage. He made his choice two decades ago, to live this kind of life, when he faced judges running interference for corrupt real estate schemes. "If I need inspiration," he joked, "I would go to a Russian court, because what a Russian judge would do would give me inspiration."

There was one more source of anger as well: anger at himself. When Navalny was growing up, the Russian parliament had challenged Yeltsin's policies of liberalization in the early 1990s, right after the dissolution of the Soviet Union. A tense standoff ensued. The parliament attempted to impeach Yeltsin, and Yeltsin attempted to dissolve the parliament. Things came to a head that October when Yeltsin responded to demonstrations with military force. More than a hundred people were killed and hundreds more wounded in street battles that went on for nearly two weeks. This bloody circuit breaker allowed Yeltsin to consolidate his power and move forward with his reforms. "When I'm in prison, I think maybe it's payment for my support for these tanks that are shooting at the parliament," Navalny told me. "They came from the town that I grew up in. I was very supportive, *they should crush them all.* When I'm sitting in jail, I'm thinking all the time: Maybe it's my personal payment for when I'm supporting them so much."

It's not hard to see why Navalny poses a bigger threat to Putin than someone like Nemtsov, who carried with him an abiding faith in liberalism, who couldn't shake his association with the freewheeling days of the nineties. Navalny held tight to the more acute grievances of his time—the boy humiliated by those rations from the West German army and the collapse of the Soviet Union; the man who saw successive corrupt administrations use the powers of government to steal from the people. He was not unlike many of those Russians who had originally turned to Putin after the nineties, and he was willing to be angry with himself for his own moment of trusting Russian authorities. He was relentlessly focused on the one vulnerability at the heart of Putinism: that for all the rhetoric about Russia, it's all just one big corrupt cabal. If Putin deflected those charges by pointing at the corruption of America, Navalny didn't bear any of the hallmarks of being in league with the Americans either. He hadn't featured in the color revolutions.

Navalny is charming and gregarious over FaceTime, even as his grievances are not far beneath the surface. I recognized in him something that I'd felt myself, something that built during my years in politics and the years since: visceral, dumbfounded anger at the circumstances around me—the lies, hypocrisy, and absurdity of it all; incredulity that basic beliefs like the need for a government that isn't corrupted by moneyed interests should be so widely and fiercely contested; the sense of powerlessness in the face of conspiracy theories in which you're cast as someone you're not; the feeling that a global enterprise has been built to sustain the power and wealth of a very particular group of people. Even his anger at himself for supporting Yeltsin recalled my anger at myself for believing the lies told in the run-up to the Iraq War right after I'd moved to Washington. Of course, the circumstances around him, and the price that he has paid, are far greater than anything I have experienced. But it was familiar all the same—a guy who didn't expect to be doing what he was doing, who was motivated by anger and yet still energized by the whole experience, incapable of doing anything else.

11

The Crimean War

KIEV-RUS WAS A federation of ethnic Slavs founded by a Viking prince in the late ninth century. The kingdom spanned the territory from the Ukrainian capital of Kiev to the Russian capital of Moscow and embraced the orthodox Christianity that predominates in Russia to this day. In the thirteenth century, it was overrun by Mongol invaders and divided into separate nations. The fates of Russia and Ukraine have been intermingled ever since through periods of union, war, and separation—an ethnic, religious, and psychic bond that continues to shape the idea of Europe, the identity of Slavs, and the politics of both countries. There was never any question that Putin's counterrevolution would come to this place that, in his view, belonged to Russia; otherwise, European democracy risked coming to Moscow through Kiev.

In 2004, the Orange Revolution prevented a corrupt Ukrainian government loyal to the Kremlin from stealing an election. I remember a presentation at the Wilson Center from a former U.S. ambassador just back from Kiev. Far from your typical think tank presentation, his overflowed with enthusiasm as he narrated a slide show that captured—from the American perspective—this noble and slightly exotic revolution on Russia's doorstep. On a large screen, he showed pictures of the crowds along with protest leaders: Yulia Tymoshenko, a striking blonde with her hair braided like a Ukrainian Valkyrie, who has remained a political fixture drifting toward the nationalist right; Viktor Yushchenko, who would soon be poisoned and then serve a single term as president before being replaced by a corrupt government loyal to the Kremlin; Boris Nemtsov, who had turned up in Kiev, speaking to larger crowds than he could in Russia, and went on to serve as an adviser to Yushchenko. But in that moment fifteen years after the fall of the Berlin Wall, the whole presentation on the Orange Revolution was premised on the continuum of freedom's inevitable spread.

The enthusiasm I experienced during that presentation was rooted in an American certainty about progress, a faith in happy democratic endings. At the time, the Bush administration heralded the Orange Revolution as validation that its missionary zeal to spread democracy was bearing fruit. But the deck was stacked against the Ukrainians. While American attention would inevitably ebb and move on to other things (including the ongoing wars in Iraq and Afghanistan), Putin had many cards to play in a country that shared a twelve-hundred-mile border with Russia. The flow of oil and gas into Ukraine was controlled by Russia, which gave it enormous leverage. Russia also had deep reach into the wealthy class of oligarchs in Ukraine, the criminal underworld, and the security services—plenty of levers to pull for a government that demonstrated the lengths that it was willing to go when it was almost certainly responsible for poisoning Yushchenko.

Still, the Bush administration pressed ahead with an effort to pull Ukraine toward the West. By 2008, Ukraine and another former Soviet republic—Georgia—were invited to pursue action plans to join NATO, the first step toward membership in the military alliance. It was a move that touched Putin's most sensitive nerve, the encroachment of NATO into the former Soviet republics along Russia's borders. It was also hard to believe that Americans would be willing to go to war with Russia over these two former Soviet republics. Within a matter of months, in August 2008, Russia invaded Georgia and ended up occupying two of its provinces. Putin had been on his back foot when the Baltic countries joined NATO in 2004; by 2008, conditions were different.

We were in the last weeks of the Obama campaign when the Georgia invasion took place. For a few days, John McCain sought to make Russia's aggression a central issue, but there was little appetite among the American public for his hawkish approach, especially with the Iraq War grinding through its sixth year. I remember a few frantic days of calibrating our line of support for Georgia with support for diplomacy, wondering how it was that America put itself out on a limb offering membership in a mutual defense alliance to a country half a world away that most Americans had never heard of. Then, just a few weeks later, Lehman Brothers collapsed, and the attention of the American electorate—and the entire world—shifted to the financial crisis.

By this point, Putin was safely ensconced in his behind-the-scenes role as prime minister, with Dmitry Medvedev as the front-man president. But the financial crisis was not without risk for Putin's broader enterprise. He could no longer rely on high oil prices that had buttressed his legitimacy, keeping the people and his corrupt networks fully satiated. "If you look at the graph of oil prices," Zhanna told me, "they skyrocketed from 1999 until 2008, and then they tumbled. I think you remember that," she said, laughing. "During the inauguration of President Obama." With more precarious finances and economic circumstances at home, Putin knew he could brook little dissent and would have to dial up the nationalism that was his other source of legitimacy.

ON NEW YEAR'S EVE 2010, Zhanna accompanied her father to a modest demonstration in support of Article 31 of the Russian constitution, which protects the right to peaceful demonstrations. By this point, she'd abandoned a career in politics. After the Orange Revolution, her emboldened father had urged her to run for Moscow's city council. Her competitor from Putin's party never campaigned, but he had a massive administrative advantage: On the day of the election, busloads of soldiers were taken to the polls to vote for him. Needless to say, she lost. She went to work for a time at an asset management firm, plugging into the burgeoning young Muscovite middle class.

Nemtsov stood on a small platform and addressed the crowd, insisting on the rights guaranteed by Russia's post-Soviet constitution. Afterward, he did a television interview during which he introduced Zhanna as his eldest daughter; the video shows her smiling proudly. Shortly after the interview was over, with the cameras still rolling, they were swarmed by special police units dressed all in black, who pulled Nemtsov away and put him on a police bus. Nemtsov, the once heir apparent to Yeltsin, was driven to a Moscow prison and thrown into a windowless cell with some other men. They shared a single toilet with no privacy and slept on a concrete floor. After fifteen days, he was taken before a judge. "I came to court and he asked for a chair and the judged refused to give him a chair," Zhanna recalled. "So he stood for the whole process and it lasted for six, seven hours. I realized that the situation was getting tougher and tougher." Nemtsov's period of detention would be short-lived, but the effort at intimidation and threat of ambiguous consequences were now constant.

In 2011, huge demonstrations broke out in Moscow after widespread claims of fraud in the parliamentary elections that returned Putin's party to power with a diminished majority. The opposition was motivated in part by Putin's announcement that he would run for another term as president in 2012. The turnout showed that beneath the layer of repression that cocooned public life, there were real pockets of opposition in the country—people who opposed Putin's return to power, shared Navalny's rage at corruption, and were generally dissatisfied with the direction of things. This, Zhanna recalled, energized her father, who ran in a regional election in 2013 and won a seat on a local council, returning to public office for the first time in over a decade. Echoing Navalny's tactics, he began to release reports about Putin with titles like "Ten Years of Putin Outcomes," "Putin's Corruption," and "The Olympic Games in the

Subtropics"—which detailed how the 2014 Sochi Olympics resulted in tens of billions of dollars in corrupt rewards for Putin cronies.

For Putin, the 2011 opposition to his return to power provided added motivation and incentive to dial up the nationalism. Splashy events like the Sochi Olympics were central to this strategy. So was a more assertive foreign policy that took an even sharper approach against the United States and the West. Edward Snowden was given sanctuary in Moscow. Russian support for Bashar al-Assad's murderous campaign against his own people steadily increased. Then, in 2014, there was a repeat of the Orange Revolution in Ukraine as people occupied Kiev's central square—the Maidan—for months, protesting a corrupt government loyal to the Kremlin. Despite a deal supported by Europe, the United States, and Russia that called for new elections, the corrupt pro-Kremlin president, Viktor Yanukovych, fled the country, taking refuge inside Russia.

Protests against his man in Ukraine were an embarrassment to Putin in addition to being a potential threat—successful anticorruption protests next door hit close to home. Within days, he dispatched Russian special forces into the Ukrainian province of Crimea and claimed it for Russia. Then he invaded and occupied two provinces of Eastern Ukraine. Putin had ignored the rules of the post–World War II order through his nineteenth-century-style annexation of a neighbor's territory, though he would consistently try to deflect accountability by pointing to America's invasion of Iraq and our meddling in the affairs of other countries. The machinery he'd built up for more than a decade—corrupt influence, irregular security forces, information warfare—was literally made for war in Ukraine. Despite the hit to Russia's economy from U.S. sanctions, taking a piece of Ukraine was sure to elevate his political standing at home.

By this point, Zhanna was working as a journalist focused on the financial markets at RBC, a Russian business news channel. "Crimea led to so-called patriotic euphoria in Russia," she recalled. "Putin's rate of approval skyrocketed. It was incredible. It was literally eighty-five percent. And of course those people who were critical, those rare voices, were under extreme pressure. So Putin refocused voters' attention from financial crisis, from electoral fraud, from other things, to this thing." Zhanna thought it might finally be time for her and her father to emigrate from Russia, but Nemtsov was adamant on staying.

The fighting in Eastern Ukraine soon became a brutal war that would take tens of thousands of lives. Putin denied that Russia was behind the violence, even as people like me in the U.S. government were putting out aerial imagery that showed huge supply lines of Russian military vehicles flowing across the border. To Zhanna, the cocktail of lies and nationalist fervor was just evidence of how everything, for Putin, is about nothing more than power. "Nobody can explain what Putin means in ideological terms, in serious terms. Of course it means corruption and dictatorship, but what the ideology is nobody knows. So they proclaim some traditional set of values, this idea of imperial glories. Something like that. It's a mix of religion and patriotism but actually they just use those as a tool." She laughed again. "He had this slogan during one of his campaigns, 'Putin's Plan Is the Victory of Russia.'" Her laughter trailed off. "It's very awkward."

IN JUNE 2014, I traveled with Obama to Normandy to commemorate the seventieth anniversary of D-Day. We arrived at the end of a long trip that had been devoted to shoring up European support for sanctions on Russia over its annexation of Crimea and invasion of Eastern Ukraine. The effort had largely been a success, even as cracks emerged in the united Western front. Several European countries held out, worried about losing Russian business; others, like Hungary, showed little concern for what Putin had done. But Obama had strong-armed the key players, aided by Germany's Angela Merkel, and the event in Normandy would both underscore the historic bond of America's alliance with Europe and create an awkward diplomatic encounter with Putin.

If there is a moment in my imagination that marks the emergence of the American superpower, it was June 6, 1944. You don't become the most powerful nation on earth just because you happen to live an ocean away from the other empires or have access to seemingly limitless natural resources. Primacy has to be earned at some point by a collection of human beings who do something hard. It was a moment without ambiguity—one side good, the other evil; the difficulty of charging onshore in a hail of gunfire is easy to understand. But to Russians, our devotion to commemorating D-Day obscured their own, much larger sacrifice. While we were planning an amphibious invasion, they were losing many millions of people holding out against the Nazis in places like Stalingrad, and then fighting mile by bloody mile to retake the heart of the Third Reich. The war touched every Russian in a way that it simply didn't touch Americans, reinforcing the long-standing sentiment that they always experienced the harder, more brutish aspects of the world.

In our own retelling of the D-Day story, Americans defined ourselves. Obama used to talk to me about the old war movies set during or after the battle, how there was usually some unit at the center of the story that shorthanded the diversity of America—the wisecracking Jew from Brooklyn, the Southern-accented sharpshooter, the Irish guy from Chicago, the jock from somewhere out west, all coming together to do this great and necessary thing. There wasn't usually a Black guy, unless the cast was sprawling enough to have room for cooks and valets. Still, he saw something aspirational in this positive mythologizing of diversity—a national identity forged out of differences.

For a person of my generation, Ronald Reagan crystallized the D-Day myth on the fortieth anniversary of the Normandy landings. Standing with his back to cliffs scaled by American troops, he told the story of one unit of Rangers—how they'd fought, and struggled, and helped one another get over the top. Then he addressed those same Rangers, now gone gray, assembled before him: "These are the boys of Pointe du Hoc. These are the men who took the cliffs. These are the champions who helped free a continent. These are the heroes who helped end a war."

My whole life, I had a hard time reading those words without getting chills. Simple and direct, even as I knew that the Reagan-era mythologizing of America's greatness ignored all the rougher edges. When I came into the White House as a speechwriter, I resolved to echo Reagan's tones in my first war speech. It came in Obama's second month in office, as he announced a timeline to draw down U.S. troops from Iraq. There would be none of the triumph of D-Day, no victory to mark. But there was still the same courage to honor. So I ended the speech with a tribute to two young Marines who had died in Iraq's Anbar Province: "In an age when suicide is a weapon, they were suddenly faced with an oncoming truck filled with explosives. These two Marines stood their ground. These two Marines opened fire. These two Marines stopped that truck." The heroism lay not in the liberation of a continent but in saving the lives of their fellow Americans. "Their names are written on bridges and town squares," I wrote. "They are etched into stones at Arlington and in quiet places of rest across our land. They are spoken in schools and on city blocks. They live on in the memories of those who wear your uniform, in the hearts of those they loved, and in the freedom of the nation they served."

These are words I wanted to believe about post-9/11 America and its wars, but whereas D-Day had been unambiguous, everything about our time seemed to be the opposite. Instead of scaling cliffs to liberate allies, we'd asked our troops to fight off suicide truck bombs in a country that didn't want us there. While we used to unite around a president commemorating our history overseas, Obama's every utterance and gesture was scoured by Republicans looking to cast him as less than American. The Soviet enemy used to compel us to carve out a space where we set aside our differences, but my time in the White House was marked by unprecedented vitriol directed against the president I served. A Black man had been put in charge of the unit, and that didn't sit well with a lot of Americans. Putin, by contrast, was firmly in command of a brand of nationalism that was becoming increasingly attractive not just to Russians, but to factions of the Republican Party in the United States.

WE SPENT THE night before the Normandy commemoration in Paris. I was done with my work for the trip, since the D-Day events were purely ceremonial, so a group of us went out on the town. Over the course of the night, more of my French came back with each drink, and I proudly directed a series of taxi drives to after-hours spots for a dwindling number of us. Finally, fortified by absinthe and wine, a small group euphorically trekked to Notre Dame at sunrise. It had been a tough year, what with Ukraine, the rise of ISIS, a creeping Ebola outbreak, and ceaseless Republican investigations back home. With just over two years left in the eight years allotted to us, the night felt like a respite, a chance to blow off steam in the city that America had liberated seventy years earlier.

By the time we got to Normandy the next morning, my euphoria had turned into a hangover that carried the weight of the last several years. Like Reagan, Obama stood near the Channel and spoke. "If prayer were made of sound," he said, "the skies over England that night would have deafened the world. Captains paced their decks. Pilots tapped their gauges. Commanders pored over maps." The story was the same, but I figured it would not be received that way back home from an opposition that preferred to insist that Obama apologized for America abroad.

After Obama's speech, he joined the other world leaders at a grand lunch in a sprawling château. As I nibbled on pastries and nursed a glass of red wine in a staff area adjacent to the château, Pete Souza—Obama's photographer—came running in my direction. "Come on," he shouted, gesturing wildly. "He's meeting with Putin." A surge of adrenaline roused me. Obama hadn't been face-to-face with Putin since the annexation of Crimea. Whatever they discussed was likely to be summarized inaccurately by the Russians and of immense interest to the media. I jogged a few paces behind Pete into the château, ignoring the prohibition on staff—a typically American assertion of superpower status that becomes second nature when you serve in government. I dodged world leaders like a kick returner as I made for Obama and Putin in the center of the room.

It wasn't hard to find them. In a surreal scene, many of the dozens of leaders present were standing and holding smartphones up in the air, taking pictures of the interaction like paparazzi outside an awards ceremony. As I took my position just behind Obama, I was relieved to see that Susan Rice, the National Security Advisor, was already present. Obama leaned down over the much shorter Putin, urging him to pursue a plan for peace negotiations with the leaders of Ukraine, France, and Germany—an arrangement that would become known as the Normandy Group. Putin agreed, but he obfuscated about what he was doing in Eastern Ukraine. He also, strangely, told his aide how attractive Susan was and blew her a kiss.

When the meeting was over, the adrenaline drained out of me. I went in search of a restroom, somewhere I could splash some cold water on my face and consider how to read the meeting out to the press. Finding one, I tried to open the door. In that awkward moment when you don't know whether a door is stuck or locked, I pushed against it a few times, jiggling the knob, before taking a step back, resolved to the fact that someone was in there. Just then, the door opened and out walked the queen of England. She was unaccompanied, given that the area was supposed to be reserved for leaders only. She stood ramrod straight, looked me up and down with a glance that would have once sent someone to the gallows, and walked away.

Solemnly, we then all filed out to a series of bleachers that had been erected on a beach that the Allies had stormed seventy years earlier, the English Channel in the near distance. Whether out of some French sense of diplomacy or simple mischief, the American delegation was seated directly in front of the Russians. As I took my seat, I noticed that the omnipresent Russian foreign minister, Sergei Lavrov, was seated directly behind me alongside a row of sullen-looking men. Lavrov was a survivor, having served in the position for over a decade—defined by loyalty to Putin, a capacity to strike up friendships with adversaries, and a casual willingness to lie.

A jumbotron in front of us showed the different world leaders taking their places. The camera settled on Putin and the crowd booed loudly; then it shifted to Obama and a cheer rang out. I think of that moment as one last expression of the world's preference for a particular brand of politics before it was eclipsed by the darker forces that found expression in Brexit and Donald Trump. Perhaps sensing the drama of the moment, the French jumbotron operator switched the image to a split screen of Obama and Putin—a diplomatic audio-visual play that forced the crowd to cheer for both of them, two embodiments of very different views of how politics should function in the world.

To mark the occasion, the French had choreographed a series of interpretive dances acting out the key events of World War II. The dances took place on a huge map of Europe that had been placed atop the sand where men once charged into bullets. I didn't fully grasp the concept until a group of dancers dressed in black uniforms meant to be the Gestapo took captive a group of dancers dressed in overalls meant to be Jews. The only way to know exactly which part of World War II was being reenacted was to watch the jumbotron, which showed footage of events ranging from the Holocaust to the surrender of German troops. After some time watching this, I gave up and just stared vacantly at the dancers; Lavrov, I noticed, was doing the same. Reviving my recent embarrassment, one video reel showed a young Queen Elizabeth serving as a wartime driver and mechanic, symbol of the unified efforts of an entire generation.

Obama was sitting next to the queen, and there was something hopeful at the thought of this pairing of the West's fortitude in the face of fascism and its capacity to change—a reminder that despite all the mistakes and hypocrisy and corruption, we were still the good guys. Whatever world order could generate that pairing had something to offer the world that *was* worth fighting for—the evolution from empires to liberated colonies, the fortitude of the wartime generation bridging the meritocratic elevation of someone born with brown skin and no wealth or station to the highest office in the world, a rebuke to dictators who still see maps as something to be redrawn at the muzzle of a gun. But I also knew, even then, that the picture obscured the virus that was spreading within the West. Even as the two of them occupied those chairs, there was a creeping sense that the whole enterprise risked being eaten away from within and without.

When the ceremony was over, I met up with Obama. "You know," he said, "there's something cheesy about the cultural programs at these European events sometimes." He recalled a different event at which the Dutch had opened a summit devoted to preventing nuclear terrorism with a performance that included dancing robots.

"I didn't think I'd ever see the Holocaust reenacted by dancers," I said.

Obama told me that he'd found himself wondering what the queen thought, having lived through the Blitz. "Can you imagine what Putin thought, sitting there?" Obama said.

"He probably thought, 'Russia did a lot more to win the war,'" I answered.

"No," Obama said. "He probably thought, *Man, the West has gotten soft.*"

IN FEBRUARY 2015, the "Normandy Group" established during that meeting between Putin and Obama reached an agreement in the Belarusian city of Minsk to resolve the war in Eastern Ukraine—a formula by which autonomy would be granted to the affected regions and the Russian-backed separatists would disarm. The fighting slowed but did not stop.

Around this time, Zhanna moderated a television program because a colleague was on vacation. She invited three guests onto the show—the chair of the Russian Duma's committee on defense, a separatist from Eastern Ukraine, and an organizer of a Russian march against the war—and they had a real debate. "Oh, it was fantastic," she recalled. "Some people on social media wrote, 'What has just happened on RBC? It has never happened before. It was a real program. They put forward real facts.'" Afterward, the Duma member called Zhanna's boss to complain. "You know," one of Zhanna's superiors told her, "we value you not as a political commentator, but as a financial markets commentator."

Zhanna also reported on the diplomatic efforts of Western leaders. "Barack Obama and Merkel and Hollande, they put a lot of effort into launching the effort for cease-fire in Eastern Ukraine," she remembered reporting. One of her superiors called her once again to complain. "And he asked me one question: *What about Putin! Do you realize how much effort Putin has put into trying to ensure peace in Eastern Ukraine?*" Her father advised her to ignore the pressure, saying that she shouldn't censor herself. At the time, he was preparing a report on the scale of Russia's involvement in Ukraine, which was being concealed from the Russian people. He was also helping to organize a protest march against the war.

On February 27, 2015, Nemtsov was finishing preparations for the march. He went to dinner with his Ukrainian girlfriend, Anna Duritskaya. Around 11:30, they were walking home across the Bolshoy Moskvoretsky Bridge, just a stone's throw from the Kremlin, the place where Nemtsov could once have credibly imagined himself serving as Russia's president. A man approached them from behind and fired several bullets into Nemtsov, hitting him in the head, heart, and stomach. No shots were fired at Duritskaya.

One wonders whether Nemtsov even had a split second for a final thought to pass through his head, to wonder at how his own life had taken him so far from those early, optimistic days when he was a young man finding his voice at a moment of new beginnings for Russia. One more casualty of Putin's war: *We demonstrated weakness, and the weak are beaten.*

12

Democratic Nationalism

ALEXEY NAVALNY HAS been a difficult adversary for Putin in part because he's not the kind of Russian oppositionist who tells Americans what they want to hear. This became obvious as soon as I broached the subject of Ukraine, the country that—in some way—had precipitated everything from Russia's offensive against American democracy to Trump's first impeachment. "You cannot just give Crimea back," he told me.

Navalny reminded me that his father was Ukrainian and his mother Russian, so he grew up spending time in both countries. He described childhood visits to his Ukrainian family after the collapse of the Soviet Union, when these visits were now to an independent country. "All through the nineties, we have a family argument—every dinner, every family gathering—we have this discussion: What is better, to preserve the Soviet Union, or to be divided?"

From the Ukrainian perspective, the answer was clear. "We were feeding you," he recalled his Ukrainian family telling him, since Ukraine was the breadbasket of the Soviet Union. "Now we're independent and we're going to live much, much better. And this was kind of a central idea." Central to the forces that drove Ukrainians into the streets in the Orange Revolution in 2005 and onto the Maidan in 2014. Central to Ukraine's desire to draw closer to Europe, to join the European Union and NATO. To be more prosperous, and free of Russian domination—that was the Ukrainian desire.

From the Russian perspective, he said, the answer was also clear.

"My mother, who is Russian, and I would say, 'Give us Crimea and get the hell out of here,'" he recalled. Crimea is separated from mainland Ukraine and Russia, a peninsula that sticks out into the Black Sea. Its population is majority ethnic Russian, but the territory was shifted to Ukraine in the middle of the twentieth century, part of the opaque Kremlin maneuvering of people and places designed to shore up their empire. "It was something deep inside every Russian—this understanding that the people in Crimea are Russian people. And without any real reason, they were given to Ukraine by Khrushchev."

Despite his desire to keep Crimea, Navalny volunteered that he admired part of Obama's efforts to punish Putin for his annexation of the region. It wasn't *what* Obama was doing that he agreed with, it was how he carried himself on the world stage. With so much corruption circling around Ukraine, a place that has attracted all manner of Russian and American grifters and influence peddlers over the years, Obama seemed to just be a guy doing his job. "Obama, when he started attacking Putin after Crimea and Ukraine, was an example for me," he said. "Look, this is just an honest guy who was elected despite the fact that he was not rich, he was not connected, he was based in morality."

Navalny clearly saw himself as someone who could become the president of his country while remaining honest. And this, in his view, meant not succumbing to the American position on Crimea. "If I'm president," he said, "I want to have something fair. A real, fair referendum under independent observers." This he contrasted with the rushed Potemkin referendum on Crimea's future that took place under the watch of Russian occupiers in 2014. "Everyone will understand the results of this referendum," Navalny told me, anticipating—of course—that the result would be the same: Crimea would remain a part of Russia.

Instead of criticizing the outcome of Putin's annexation of Crimea, Navalny focused on his motivation: Putin's fixation on the United States and an encroaching West, the constant warnings that

Crimea would become a base for NATO ships or nuclear weapons. "He's playing with something real," he said of Putin's Ukraine policy and broader political project—that sense of making amends for the humiliations of the past. "But he's twisting it, he's perverting it, he's using the huge apparatus of propaganda and media to connect it to anti-American and anti-Western propaganda."

To Navalny, approaching the issue of Crimea as a kind of geopolitical chess move diminished the very legitimacy that should buttress the union of Crimea with Russia, the fact that it was—to him—the right thing on the merits. It also bespoke a dangerous and self-destructive habit of Russian leaders to seek legitimacy at home through the pursuit of conquest or power abroad. "These delusions about empire," he said, "this is the most dangerous stuff for Russia. Because it is why we were poor all the time. We were poor back in the Russian empire with the czars because they spent everything on empire. The same in the Soviet Union. Back in the USSR, we paid for Cuba, we paid for half of Africa, we paid for half of Asia. So we were poor. People don't have a color TV set in their apartment, they don't have any cars even in the eighties, but we spent billions of dollars around the world."

This imperial pursuit also allowed leaders to obscure their own corruption, distracting people from their own lot in life by offering a connection to some glory-seeking project. *Putin's Plan Is the Victory of Russia*. Obama used to always tell me: In the longer game, a politician's strength can always become his weakness. This could become true for Putin and his total identification with the effort of once again projecting Russian strength abroad. "Can't we spend our energy and the money of our country for ourselves?" Navalny asked incredulously. "Syria," he said, referring to Putin's intervention on behalf of Assad, which has been viewed as a strategic masterstroke by many Western analysts, "it doesn't work at all. They wanted to repeat this trick from Crimea and the Ukraine War. But people are so annoyed. Syria?" he repeated, as if the absurdity was self-evident.

"Why should we fight with these kinds of guys? We're restoring Aleppo. Repair some roads here!"

COVID-19 underscored this danger for Putin. As Navalny and I spoke, Russia's economy was spiraling into a deeper hole, even as Putin was ramming through "constitutional reforms" to allow himself to stay in power well into the 2030s. The pandemic itself was mismanaged, alternatively denied and attacked, responsibility delegated down to lower-level officials who were never empowered to do their jobs. Navalny complained about the shipment of vital medical supplies that Putin had sent to the United States and Western European countries early in the pandemic as evidence of his increasing fixation on his geopolitical standing, a trolling czar. "It's fun to be such a generous and noble person, to give a lot of presents to a lot of people. But if you're the poorest guy in the room, why are you giving stuff away to a rich guy?"

As usual, the thing that grated most on Navalny about Putin's rhetorical broadsides against the West was how they elided the extent to which everything Putin did was in service of power and profit. "What is the best response to Putin?" Navalny asked, clearly prepared to answer his own question. "Look, if the West is so mean and bad and ugly and there are gays everywhere and the gay marriages and morality is dying—which they are talking about all the time—my response is: I'm showing that these guys who are blaming the West have a palace somewhere in France. Showing people they are using their families, and their nostalgia to live in a great country—Make Russia Great Again—they're using it for their own personal good and personal profit." Navalny paused for effect. "We can have a great country, who can be a leader of Europe, and one of the best countries in the world, without that stuff."

This was a potent message. These were the words of someone who wanted Russia to stand on its own two feet but wanted the benefits to flow to ordinary Russians. He wasn't asking that the blunt force of American foreign policy come to his aid, he was more focused on the example that America set. For years, he told me, he had made an argument for what he calls democratic nationalism, the idea that the advanced democracies are richer because they have less corruption. Then the argument was disproven. "All those years I was promoting that honesty is the best policy. Here's why Trump is a tragedy for us. All my literature is based on the idea that free elections are a system where a better guy becomes higher and a worse guy becomes lower. And now, what is the example? At the high point of this democracy there is someone corrupted." That, more than anything else, is the return that Putin got on his investment in Trump. "It's now very easy for Putin and for independent observers—just a guy who is reading the newspaper—to explain the idea that the Western world doesn't have any purpose, they don't have any idea what they're doing, and they're very much hypocrites and cynical."

Navalny still believed that Putin's house of cards was going to collapse at some point, the same way the czars did, the same way that the Soviets did, perhaps the same way that the United States did under Trump. Putinism may have started from something pure, something visceral, that humiliation I saw on a night bus from Kaliningrad; but it had been corrupted, twisted, and rendered devoid of meaning—particularly as Putinism spread beyond Russia's borders. Perhaps Putin was marching himself over the precipice, to be followed by acolytes like Orban who were similarly out of ideas, out of justifications for their corrupt enterprises. "When he's talking about national humiliation," Navalny said of Putin, "he's blaming some other people—outsiders, America, Europe, the West. It's an interesting phenomenon of Soros. Why Soros? Nowadays no one knows who Soros is. I look at the far-right American and European propaganda, and Orban is talking about Soros all the time."

It was a feeling I'd often had, a sense of tragicomic incredulity, looking at American right-wing media and conspiracy theories. With everything that's gone wrong in the world, why are we entering our fourth decade talking about this one man, George Soros?

Because he offers a target that strikes the darkest chords of historical memory and nationalist, reactionary politics: an immigrant, a financier, a globalist, a Jew.

NAVALNY MADE NO secret of his ambition. "I can beat them," he said of Putin and his cabal, as a matter of fact. "I understand that our movement, if we're registered as a party, in the first election we would be in second place. And in the second election, we would beat them."

To him, all of the sacrifices he has made would be worth little if they added up only to a lonely and futile pursuit of justice. This is where he contrasted himself with the Soviet-era dissidents, most of whom made their choice to oppose the regime without much hope that they would bring about actual political change. Navalny drew this contrast in ways that could sound similar to Putin, emphasizing that he was from the military towns outside Moscow rather than from the city's cosmopolitan elite. The Soviet-era dissidents, he said, were people doing something right without broad support, just some flashes of recognition from a handful of friends and foreign journalists. "I have no idea how they did it," he told me. "I am asking myself all the time." Instead, he goes out of his way to convey a different impression. "I'm trying to preserve an organization with offices—to look like a real organization with people who are sitting at their desks with their laptops, their MacBooks, not dissidents who are working underground."

Even at forty-three, I've lived enough lifetimes in politics to see warning signs in every movement or personality that comes along. No one person has all the answers, particularly those who act as if they do. There are plenty of Russian liberals I know who see Navalny as a kind of Putin Lite, a nationalist with a personality-driven approach to politics. As a liberal wary of nationalism, I caught myself at times trying too hard to project what I liked about Navalny onto him while eliding the rougher edges that he made no effort to conceal. The comfortable assertion of a nationalism that, with an issue like Crimea, drifted into blood-and-soil territory. The leadership of an organization that appeared to be fueled by something of a cult of personality embedded in anticorruption. But I've also lived enough lifetimes in politics to know that those things made him a more effective politician and viable leader of Russia, and to know that thinking Americans have any capacity to pick our ideal Russian leader (or American one, for that matter) is a foolish impulse destined to lead to dashed expectations.

We have to live in the world as it is. So why did I find Navalny so appealing?

First, he at least put forward a nationalism that isn't corrupt, that tries to offer Russians a sense of dignity and national identity that isn't determined by a cabal of rich oligarchs skimming off the top. This is where an anticorruption agenda leads inexorably to a set of affirmative principles, with available models that suggest corruption need not be an inevitability, some unshakable bug in the Russian character. "I have a very clear understanding of what kind of country we should build," Navalny told me, with that occasionally jarring certainty. "I have a positive agenda. I do believe in market economy. I do believe in free media. I do believe in free elections. I do believe that Russia is not worse than Finland, we can live as a nice rich country."

Second, it was impossible not to admire the risks that Navalny was taking, which suggested that the pursuit of power alone could not have been the wellspring of his actions. He knew better than anyone the likelihood that the organization he had built would be smashed. At his forty headquarters across Russia, he told me there had been three hundred searches. Raids. People arrested. MacBooks confiscated. But he'd clearly priced that in, along with his own arrests, detentions, death threats, the shadow of physical harm. He trusted—maybe too much—in his own fame in ways that also suggested a generosity toward those who lacked it. "Honestly," he told me, "I became sort of a famous guy. I'm in less danger than some regional activists."

But there was another reason that I was drawn to him: that sense of righteous anger. We were speaking on FaceTime, each in some form of COVID quarantine. I had decamped for a few days to my mother-in-law's at the end of a tidy cul-de-sac in Huntington Beach, California. The houses were ringed with walls that concealed small swimming pools; the real estate appreciated steadily given the proximity to the ocean; my children slept soundlessly in the adjacent room. During the days, quarantine was slightly easier here because they could ride their scooters on the empty suburban streets. This was about as far from Moscow as one could get.

Navalny wore a white undershirt, just another guy in his forties with kids contending with the daily inconveniences of a pandemic in a world governed by people ill prepared to deal with it. And the more we talked, the more I felt an unlikely sort of kinship with this son of the military towns. Part of it was the fact that we found ourselves on the wrong end of the same political trend in the world, even though the dangers he faced were exponentially greater. Part of it was the fact that we shared the same cynicism about what had gone wrong over the last thirty years, even as we'd taken very different paths to get there. But there was something more essential, a motivation that I recognized, something that was hard for me to put into words but was present in nearly everything that Navalny said. "There are different types of people," Navalny told me. "Some people under the pressure, they are scared, and some people, they are more enraged."

If I am honest with myself, my own motivations draw on rage, even as I know that rage can at times distort your thinking and lead you down blind alleys, even as I worked for a politician who was better at hope than anyone else these last thirty years. It was rage over 9/11 that propelled me down to Washington. It was rage over the Iraq War that propelled me into politics. The longer I served in government, the more it was rage—over hypocrisy, over obstructionism, over meanness, over the endless gamesmanship, over unacknowledged racism—that kept me going day after day when all my other sources of motivation had dissipated or run up against the limits of an uncooperative world. It was rage over the daily realities of Trump's America that had eaten away at me for the last several years—there it was, a little dose of rage like a fix each morning with the news; the larger indignities of seeing things I'd worked on dismantled; above all, rage over the toxic cloud of mediocrity and mendacity that encroached like an invisible force.

From the moment I left the White House, I was often told by others with ambitions for future government service that I should be less angry, more circumspect in my comments. To assume a public role as an angry person was, in American politics, to define yourself as a less serious person, an identity that has become more dangerous for a Democrat to assume than a Republican: a partisan. To attack prominent people, even Republicans who had more than earned the attacks, was to deal yourself out of future positions that require the confirmation votes of Senate Republicans or the acceptance of a Washington society that wants people to pretend to like each other, even—perhaps especially—when they don't. But I kept returning to rage, for reasons that I didn't really consider. Talking to Navalny, I felt comfortable that the reason I did so was to replenish my own motivation, the impetus and organizing principle for everything I was doing—including writing this book.

Perhaps, in the end, it *is* futile. You look at the obvious corruption that shapes things around you—from who gets wealthy, to how the wealthy maintain power, to how the powerful design systems to enrich themselves and maintain power, to the ravaging impact that that power can have on individual lives. The more you look, the more you see how the last thirty years of American hegemony has designed, wittingly or unwittingly, a system that others could easily manipulate—from big banks that are bailed out, to Putin and his cronies moving vast sums of oil money around an infrastructure of shell companies, real estate interests, and opaque corporations facilitated by a poorly regulated global economy, to the service industry that profits by running interference for the wealthy and powerful, be it disinformation campaigns, private espionage, or the occasional act of violence. Seeing all that, you can either decide, rationally, to dive into the system—as I had done in 2008—and accept its structural flaws while trying to make some discernible impact on it; or you can step outside it and give voice to your rage at the injustice of it all.

Having been spat out by the very system I had served, I had come to believe—rightly or wrongly—that it was, in some intangible way, irredeemable without a more profound overhaul. That the corruption of a man like Putin was inseparable from the broader corruption upon which the world ran. Navalny understood this. He sensed it intellectually. He felt it intuitively. Rage, after all, is an essential starting point for any revolution, even as success depends upon much more. Navalny was focused on the first step, and that was enough for me, even though my own lived experience suggested that success was far from likely.

ON AUGUST 20, 2020, Alexey Navalny was poisoned and nearly killed.

Coincidentally, that was the night that Obama was addressing the Democratic National Convention. The stakes were both lower and higher than those of his last four convention speeches: lower in that he was no longer the front man, higher because everything he had done or stood for was on the ballot. Over the past four years, I'd often experienced Obama's sense of rage over the direction of things. In private, he could be withering about Trump, though in public he was circumspect—continuing to model appropriate behavior, couching his warnings in recommendations for what needed to be done. But in his withdrawal from the arena, I recognized a different form of rage—the disappointment of someone watching a serious enterprise like the presidency be debased, the sense of betrayal that must come from watching an entire nation do something as unfathomably stupid as electing Donald Trump.

And that night he gave people a glimpse of the anger he felt. "They're hoping to make it as hard as possible for you to vote, and to convince you that your vote doesn't matter," he said, emotion creeping into his voice. "That's how a democracy withers, until it's no democracy at all. We can't let that happen. Do not let them take away your power. Don't let them take away your democracy." For a moment, his delivery was poised upon the precipice of tears of frustration. *Were we really going to give up the whole enterprise for this, for Donald J. Trump?*

A couple of hours later, scanning the reactions to his speech on Twitter, I noticed an item about Navalny. The initial reports suggested that his tea had been poisoned at an airport before he boarded a flight to Siberia. I saw the comment from his spokesman: He had taken ill on a plane and was in intensive care. I saw the alarming reports: He was in a coma. I saw the brazen hand of the Russian government: videos that somehow quickly made it online of Navalny drinking tea in an airport. Videos that could come only from surveillance controlled by the Russian government. Like Boris Nemtsov's death or the foreign intervention in the 2016 American presidential election, the details of the story were murky and would change over time, but the gist of it was again clear: Putin was behind this. Watching this, thinking of all the various reasons that Putin may have had for doing it—the messages he intended to send to Navalny, other oppositionists, or the wider world—I knew that his motivations boiled down to one thing: *He did it because he could.*

For the rest of the night, I felt the stakes of politics in the world all around me like a heaviness in the air. I already knew there were people prepared to go to extraordinary lengths to perpetuate the corrupted state of things. This was yet another escalation of that dynamic. And while I knew my own government was not responsible, I also knew that it was led by somebody who would stay silent about it. And he did.

For a frequent traveler, there is nothing more mundane than getting a coffee or a tea in the minutes before entering the airport and boarding a plane. The action itself is so routine that I struggled that night to recall a distinct memory of any one of the hundreds of times that I had done this. I wondered how it had been for Navalny. What convergence of thirst, boredom, or fatigue had led him to decide that he'd grab a tea before his flight? Did it cross his mind, when eating and drinking in public spaces, that he was facing the same level of danger as when he heard the cell door clang shut behind him? When he began to feel the first stirrings of illness on board the plane, did he know immediately what it was?

Of one thing I felt certain: When he fell to the ground in pain, fading toward unconsciousness, that well of motivation was replenished, the undistilled rage that can arise only from pure injustice. The moments when the choices before people are cast in the most black-and-white version possible. Do we want to live in a world where innocent people are poisoned with impunity in airports? What kind of people would do that, and what dynamics enable them to get away with it? Sometimes people like Navalny are able to actually win power, to see things change. But perhaps even more powerfully in their darkest moments, they show us the true nature of those they oppose.

13

A War Without Violence

THE UNITED STATES and Russia have been intertwined for a century, each shaping its own story in opposition to the other: the Communist Revolution that frightened capitalist America to its core; wartime allies who then sorted the world into blocs made into competing exemplars for our respective ideologies and agendas; Cold War superpowers competing through proxy wars, neocolonial outposts, and the looming specter of nuclear war. After the Cold War, Russia (partly by American design) became more like America as it opened things up. But then, over the last decade, America (partly by Russian design) became more like Russia, as nationalism and conspiracy theorizing shaped our politics. Ironically, this Russian effort was made much easier by American-made social media and online culture.

As I was leaving the White House, the reality of the scale of Russia's ambitions settled around me like Orban's comment about the fog settling on the landscape. With just two weeks left before Trump's inauguration, I sat in the Oval Office as the leaders of the U.S. intelligence community methodically walked us through Russia's sprawling and successful effort to shape the outcome of America's election. There was no doubt about these findings—the hacking and release of emails; the creation and dissemination of huge volumes of fake news; the smoke screen around how much of this effort was welcomed by or coordinated with the campaign of the incoming president of the United States of America. I remember Joe Biden looking incredulous as decades of assumptions about the guardrails around American politics were shown to have been upended. *Is this guy some kind of Russian asset?* he asked. The question hung unanswered in the air. Obama was more sanguine, even unsurprised, at how easy it had been for Putin—perhaps because, unlike Biden or me, he was a Black man who lacked illusions about the inevitable rightness of America. All Russia had done, he'd tell me again and again, was take advantage of the dark openings in American politics and culture, particularly online, where a vast industry of right-wing conspiracy theories had created a market for disinformation. We were an easy mark.

Perhaps nothing in my lifetime symbolizes the triumph and spread of American-led globalization more than the Internet and social media: American creations that somehow mirrored America's raucous commitment to free speech, unregulated capitalism, and unadulterated entrepreneurship: our unique capacity to connect the world. These forces had been unleashed on Russia in the 1990s, only to be repurposed and fired back into America with a far more destructive result than any Soviet weapon ever achieved. *We demonstrated weakness, and the weak are beaten.*

IN 2017, I was forced for the first time to consider what it meant to be an American while living in a country that no longer made sense to me. As a child, I could take comfort in my Americanness by measuring it against the Soviet enemy. Even in the depths of the Iraq War, it seemed that my country had made a terrible mistake—not that it was, in some essential way, a different place than I believed it to be. I now had to measure what I had *thought* it had meant to be American against an enemy within, an enemy that had been elevated to the highest office in the world. If I thought America represented diversity, Trump represented white supremacy. If I thought America was about hope for the future, Trump offered a crude longing for an ill-defined past. The worldview embedded in Putin's Beslan speech was now mirrored by the White House, which was dedicated to attacking the worldview embedded in Obama's 2004 convention speech. In my own less risky way, I had become like the Russians I'd met over the years—a citizen struggling to hold on to my own identity as my country comes to stand for something else.

I found my mind drawn back to a moment in early 2016 when I met with a group of Russian writers in a small room in the West Wing. It was one of those meetings that broke up the monotony of my days, that peculiar opportunity you have, when serving at high levels of government, to choose to meet with a group of interesting people. In this case, it was a handful of writers sponsored by PEN, the organization that supports journalists and authors facing oppression around the world. I remember the familiar feeling of meeting with a group of people whom I could not possibly seem to help. Throughout the meeting, I was distracted by the fact that one of the women looked uncannily like my mother, which led my mind to wander and wonder just how far east my family's journey had begun before the pogroms drove them across Poland and then to America. I asked the writers if they had any concerns about being affiliated with an American organization like PEN, or about meeting with people like me. No, they answered. It was their choice. What they wanted was not so much help as the simple opportunity to share their experience and perspective, which is, after all, a starting point for writing itself.

One of the writers in that 2016 meeting was Maria Stepanova. Maria had come of age in the nineties and established herself as one of Russia's leading poets in addition to being a novelist, a journalist, and the publisher of a crowdfunded website on news and culture—like Szabolcs Panyi in Hungary, a voice adapting to the spaces closing for discourse in her country. In the spring of 2020, I noticed an interview in which Maria spoke about the dark humor of being Russian, the realization that everyone had two identities: the one put forward in public and political spaces, and the private life lived behind closed doors. I thought she could help me make sense of the ways in which politics and identity in our two countries had blended in such a disorienting way.

I asked Maria how she felt things had changed since the 1990s, that time of humiliation and hopefulness. "The nineties were about the future," she said. "Now everything is about the past. But not the actual, historical past." Instead, she said, leaders like Putin, Orban, and Trump invented a past to suit their needs. "There is an enchantment and obsession with the past, but it is a fictional reality that doesn't have anything real." For Russia, she said, this transformation was completed with the 2014 annexation of Crimea and the return of the Russian empire, though it had been in motion for many years, the end results of years of smaller changes.

In Maria's telling, Putin's first two terms as president, from 1999 to 2008, seem almost quaint when compared to his current stint. There were, of course, a rising standard of living and newly created wealth in oil-rich Russia. But there was also, she said, a degree of political freedom. You could be outspoken. Putin's creeping authoritarianism was still rooted in an orientation toward Europe and the United States, that age-old balancing act between East and West. "It was all about following the Western way," she said, "the Western mode, we want to belong to this family of nations." Russia may have become authoritarian again, but it was still pointed in the direction of nations that embodied a set of liberal values.

Maria remembered feeling this way as recently as Dmitry Medvedev's inauguration in May 2008. On that day, she went out with a few colleagues from the website that she was editing. They were drinking coffee in a Moscow café, looking out at a pleasant courtyard. "We were talking about the end of history," she said, that post–Cold War sense that the big questions had been resolved. Medvedev may have been Putin's lackey, but he was a Western character who wanted to be in decent standing in the Western clubs. During Medvedev's time in office, Obama had pursued a "reset" in relations with Russia, which led to cooperation on everything from nuclear arms control to trade. But there was also a vacuum. After the collapse of the Soviet Union, Maria said, "Russia had become a country that has forgotten what it means to have a history, a country that has fallen out of history." It had become, even more than Hungary, a country with a history filled with ghosts—the enormous suffering of the Soviet years, along with the sense of loss that accompanied the collapse of the Soviet Union. And it was ripe for something to fill that vacuum.

When Putin retook the presidency in 2012, Maria sensed a shift in him. From my perspective, this reflected the political calculation of a man who could no longer count on high oil prices to lubricate his corruption and consolidation of power, a man in need of legitimacy who turned to a convenient nationalism. But to Maria, Putin's shift also reflected a man who felt politically and personally wounded at home when his return to office was met by huge demonstrations led by the likes of Alexey Navalny. "These were beneficiaries of his reign," Maria said, referring to the middle-class Muscovites who took to the streets. "People that he was identifying himself with in a way." Perhaps Putin was like Russia—a man who felt himself falling out of history. Perhaps the cold, corrupt logic of power was not his sole source of motivation—to a man like Putin, falling out of history can engender its own rage.

After his reelection, Putin gave a speech to an enormous crowd in Moscow in which he quoted the great Russian poet Mikhail Lermontov. In one of Lermontov's most famous poems, he wrote about the Napoleonic Wars, the first of two crises when Russians put aside their differences to repel an enemy at the gates. "We shall die before Moscow, as died our brothers. To die we swore, and our oath of fealty kept on the field of Borodino." When Putin read these lines, Maria recalled, he had tears in his eyes. Perhaps to Putin the collapse of the Soviet Union and the ensuing tide of globalization represented another advance on Moscow, embodied in those 2011 protests led by Western-oriented Muscovites.

In Ukraine, Putin rejoined history—the history that has dominated most of humanity's time on the planet, when nations fought wars over territory and reconquered places that had been taken away. The same understanding of history that illuminated Orban's rhetoric about avenging lost lands, albeit without the military power. Blood and soil. Of course, Putin framed that conquest as necessary to stop another enemy at the gates of Moscow. Like everyone else I talked to, Maria noticed the omnipresence of a virulent patriotism inseparable from the person of Putin. But she also noticed a broader effort to reshape the consciousness of the nation. "I noticed the difference in the amount of violence around you," she said, "on television, social networks, etcetera. It is violence you feel in the air. But the level of actual violence was quite low."

Compared to the battles of Russia's past, the actual fighting in Eastern Ukraine was a small endeavor affecting mainly the people there and the few thousand Russians sent furtively across Ukraine's borders. But there was something brutal and infectious about the propaganda that went along with it. I noticed it at the time. In memes that anticipated American conspiracy theories like QAnon, Russia's enemies were cast as pedophiles, sexual deviants, and diabolical criminals. This ability to manipulate and mobilize the national psyche while keeping the stakes relatively low represented a breakthrough for Putin, making easy use of America's unregulated and sensationalizing social media networks. "People are happy to be violent in the social networks," Maria said. "In that space, there has been rhetorical violence in Russia for the last ten years, through the discourse of hate on social networks."

I thought of my own daily experience of social media, the emotions that could be stirred by a single tweet, the reduction of discourse to a set of characters that could trigger someone in response, the endless online battle that can have no winner but that seems to carry with it the highest possible stakes. This is our most prevalent experience of how politics meets culture today: the ceaseless immersion in social media and how they shape our perception of ourselves, our countries, and the world at large. Ironically, a space with no borders in which we try to assert what our nations mean. Neither Putin nor Orban nor Trump created this reality; it was simply available to them. "They didn't invent it," she said, "but they are riding this wave, which travels a short distance. They are unable to build things, so they destroy things." This includes the very concept of objective reality and expertise upon which national decisions are supposed to be based.

Given that the majority of culture has migrated online, someone like Putin doesn't have to suppress ideas so much as he needs only to overwhelm them with—to use the American jargon—"content." To do this, Putin can count on trolls of the Russian state and what Maria called "voluntary supporters"—the countless online profiles who can also be counted upon to fuel messages of hate and nationalism. "They are just aiding a feeling of instability. People are living in bubbles and they are filtering the information that comes in. And they are experiencing the whole world of contradictory images that are in constant struggle with each other. That leaves you dizzy, unable to form a political vision or cultural identity while endlessly distracted." Listening to Maria, I found it impossible to distinguish between Russia and America. "You don't feel any sort of ground under your feet. The world is becoming terrifyingly flexible."

Just as Sandor Lederer spoke of the unresolved history of Nazism and Communism in post–Cold War Hungary, Maria observed the discourse was now "tracking something in the unconscious from the dystopia of the twentieth century." For Russia, that included everything from Stalin's purges to their war in Afghanistan to the collapse of the Soviet Union. Even the violence of Chechnya, the terrorism of the early 2000s, the murdered children of Beslan, still lingered. Whether it was out of conviction, for political convenience, or—more likely—some mix of both, Putin knew how to make Russians feel that they were reentering history. The assassination of Boris Nemtsov and poisoning of Alexey Navalny can be seen as an extension of that trauma, actions that keep history alive.

* * *

ON AMERICA'S ELECTION DAY in 2016, Maria was in New York with friends and went out to a bar where people were buying one another drinks in anticipation of Hillary Clinton's victory. By the end of the night, everything had changed. "I didn't recognize this country I love," Maria said. "When it comes to Russia, one is cautious enough to predict the worst." America was supposed to be different.

This isn't a feeling that has gone away simply because Trump has been voted out. Time and again, I encountered the stark reassessment of people abroad: It wasn't just the fact that Donald Trump was president that caused a reassessment of America around the world; it was the fact that American voters elected him in the first place and therefore could do something that reckless again. Maria said the experience of the last few years had flipped the dynamic that I'd first encountered when I met her in 2016. When traveling abroad, she said, people often asked her: *What can we do to help you?* I myself had been one of those people. "I found this endearing and encouraging," she said. "There is nothing one can do to help Russia, but when one can think the situation can be helped, it gives you a certain kind of optimism." Maria knew that things had changed when she faced an audience shortly after the 2016 election and an American asked her if she had any advice that could help Americans.

I told Maria that I was asking her the same question. I had my own views about social media, about the need for regulation to slow the spread of disinformation and make companies liable for hateful content on their platforms. But how could we overcome the more fundamental crisis of identity that made all of this hate so alluring in the first place, the seeming breakdown of order that had been steadily progressing over the last thirty years?

Maria volunteered that if she had the opportunity to vote for Navalny for mayor of Moscow again, she would do so. But while his single-minded focus on corruption represented a needed change, she did not think it was sufficient. Instead, she said, a more radical shift had to take place. To her, this was the other side of the coin from

Navalny's interest in upending a corrupt cabal: the simple notion that politics and government had to be rooted in truth. "People are yearning for a sense of truth, for a certain sense of reality that is always being distorted. People are asking for something that is based on an ethical frame."

The danger of the other path is catastrophe. The history that Putin had reentered is the older kind, which inevitably leads nations down rivers to the heart of darkness, borne on the currents that gave rise to fascism and Communism, Hitler and Stalin, two men who had caused the death of tens of millions of Russians. When history appeared to come to an end at the conclusion of the Cold War, the specter of another world war was lifted, and with it some of the sense of drama that Putin had tapped into. And while wars fought online were not often tied to actual violence, a dizzying array of narratives online recirculated those old twentieth-century forces in new packaging—in particular, a creeping and sometimes casual fascism that suited Putin and had reshaped the American right wing.

As a Russian, Maria knew how this kind of history can hurt people in ways that Americans, too often, do not. Every Russian had been touched by World War II. Every Russian family had suffered in some way through the Soviet times. This was the main thing she had to tell us Americans, I realized—this warning. She feels the return of history. "I am afraid of some catastrophe that is going to happen," she said, referring to her mindset these last few years. "I feel it in my bones. I am sharing this with my compatriots: There is going to be a new war, World War III, or the gulags, or the trials." What she hadn't anticipated, she said, was a pandemic.

Talking to her at the height of lockdown, with the death toll in the United States soaring toward two hundred thousand and my own life upended along with everyone else's, I understood what she was saying: that we could all be reentering history through some other door, one that might ultimately lead somewhere better than war. We are all confronted with this virus. We even used the language of war in describing our efforts to defeat it. But there was something different about this moment when what was most obviously required was expertise and common effort. "It is a war without an enemy," she said, "without the language of hate or the necessity to fight."

Perhaps, she suggested, this could reawaken respect for truth and expertise. Perhaps it could highlight the danger of people living inside their own distorted narratives. Perhaps it could finally drive home the lesson that we are living in a world in which danger—a pandemic now, climate change later—reveals the absurdity of hardening borders and clinging to revanchist nationalism. Maria knew as well as anyone that the opposite could also happen. The disorder unleashed by the pandemic will surely take years to unfold, just as it took a decade for the consequences of the financial crisis to become apparent. But to Maria, at least, there was the potential for an inflection point that could steer things in a different direction, the hidden hand of history. "It gives me hope," she said, "because it is something new, something global."

VLADIMIR PUTIN HAS done his part to avenge the humiliations that came with the end of the Cold War. Historians will debate how much America might have instigated some of this retribution, or might have done things differently to forestall it. How complicit were we in the chaotic privatization and transition to capitalism in the 1990s, which created a new class of oligarchs while enraging the Russian public? Were we too triumphalist in our foreign policy, lording it over the defeated Russians through the expansion of NATO, the push to include former Soviet republics like Georgia and Ukraine, which Putin subsequently invaded? Were we too casually belligerent in our hegemony, meddling in the affairs of other countries and trying to engineer their politics, until there was—inevitably—a backlash in which an adversary did the same to us? Was Obama too timid in the face of Putin's increasing belligerence in Ukraine and Syria, incapable of finding a formula to push back against an adversary who'd gone on offense?

These debates are important, but they make up only part of the picture. The more I considered the ways in which the stories of America and Russia have been intertwined, the more I realized that our bigger failures lay in choices made by Americans without Russia in mind. After the end of the Cold War, we often failed to elevate America's purpose in the world above the methodical expansion of global markets, allowing America to become tethered to the dislocations and inequality produced by late-stage capitalism. Our embrace of a global War on Terror created a basis for leaders like Putin to securitize their own grip on power, while the invasion of Iraq introduced a destabilizing new normal to global politics: Laws and norms were for the weak, and the strong could do anything they wanted, even invade and occupy a foreign country on a false pretense. We embraced new technologies and promoted their spread without thinking through how they could be used to undermine democracy and the objective reality required for an informed citizenry to make decisions. With the cloud of nuclear apocalypse lifted, our own political culture descended into triviality and racialized grievance, opening the door to both Donald Trump and the online Russian cavalry that came to his assistance. We became a nation at war with an invisible enemy, only it wasn't a pandemic or climate change—it was a war with ourselves, a war that took us out of history and rendered us a diminished giant, humiliated by our embrace of incompetent authoritarianism.

But what has Putin really accomplished? Beyond enriching himself and his associates, and claiming some small pieces of the former Soviet Union for Russia, he has proved to be far more adept at destroying than at building. Russia has been economically and socially weakened, enthralled with an ideal of its own past and incapable of offering the world a model for the future beyond a cautionary tale about the vagaries of corruption and vindictive nationalism. This great nation that gave the world Dostoyevsky and Tolstoy, that once saved Europe from fascism and sent the first satellite into space, now exports a toxic stew of conspiracy theories and disinformation that will make as little sense to people in the future as it does to anyone living in reality today. Even in the games of geopolitical chess that Putin relishes and sometimes excels at with his instinct to attack, he has allowed himself to become a junior partner to a Chinese Communist Party that appears much more confident in the model that it is building. At home, the bullets and poison dispensed on his behalf only illuminate the fears of a ruler who lacks confidence in the sustainability of his own project. Whether he is defeated by a Navalny or clings to power for as long as he wants, Putin, at some point, will be gone; that much is certain. What will be his legacy?

IN MY FINAL trip before the first COVID lockdown, I met with Congressman Adam Schiff, chairman of the House Intelligence Committee, in Washington. He'd recently completed the noble and ultimately incomplete ordeal of the impeachment of President Donald J. Trump, which also amounted to an autopsy of what Russia had done to America and what we had done to ourselves. I'd come to know Adam well when I was in government and he was a less prominent congressman. He was thoughtful, earnest, and soft-spoken—the rare congressman who would spend an hour with you just because he was curious about something, not because he wanted anything. The normally reserved man I'd come to know had become almost unrecognizably passionate—even desperate at times—a person articulating what it's like to feel the ground evaporating beneath your feet, trying to recapture a sense of objective reality through the assertion of fact after fact after fact. I wanted to know what he'd taken away from it all.

When we met in his office, he was trailed by a plainclothes security detail—a precaution, I was told, because of the volume of death threats he received from the hate-filled corners of our online culture, one more front in a ceaseless war. We trundled down to the basement of a House office building and got coffee from Dunkin' Donuts. Schiff politely asked a woman if we could sit at the other end of her table. She nodded, annoyed, over something that she was reading.

I asked Adam what he thought he'd learned about Russia. He said that Putin seemed to have little ideology beyond a fierce Russian nationalism, a will to power and profit, and a desire to harm the United States. "Putin has a perception that the best way to aggrandize Russia," he said, "is pulling down the United States." But as much as we could critique Putin's intentions, the results were impossible to ignore. Adam seemed intent on not losing his shock at the course that events had taken, though he had also come to understand how much Americans had also made Putin's task easier. He seemed to have integrated the incredulity that I'd seen on Biden's face in the Oval Office with Obama's colder realization that we'd turned ourselves into an easy mark. Both, after all, were correct responses. "Can you imagine," Adam asked, as if still trying to wrap his mind around Putin's success, "in his wildest dreams, that the president of the United States would parrot his talking points? It was the intelligence coup of the century."

With the passage of time, it was less important to deconstruct the tactics of this intelligence coup—the misadventures of Russian intelligence agents and Trump associates, the hacking of emails whose contents seemed sensational at the time and feel meaningless today, the disinformation that could feel like a drop in the ocean of our own toxic national discourse. "We were," Adam said, "ripe for exploitation." He checked his watch. Soon he would have to attend a memorial event for Elijah Cummings, the Black congressman from Baltimore who had recently passed away after being accused by Trump of representing a rat-infested district, the kind of thinly veiled racism easily exploited by Putin and his army of trolls.

"Putin wants to weaken Western societies," Adam said. "He knows the fault lines well. He knows how to manipulate them on social media. It's cheap and deniable." The violence, as Maria had said, without the actual violence. The worry, Adam said, is that Russia is exporting these methodologies, causing them to mushroom across the United States and around the world—the counterrevolution gone viral. Still, Russia itself was not likely to be the beneficiary, for the same reasons that Navalny had seized upon—the corruption that is only about the perpetuation of wealth and power for a particular group of people in a particular time. "Putin runs the government like a Ponzi scheme. And eventually, Ponzi schemes implode."

The more ominous danger, Adam said, came from China. "Putin's Russia is the threat of a wounded animal. China is the threat of a growing, strengthening, burgeoning power." It was a power that had the capacity to do more than tear things down—the stopgap nationalism of a Putin or Orban. Russia could destroy; China could *build*. So perhaps, after Putin tore down pieces of the post–Cold War Western world, it was China that would replace the old order, with consequences for our politics, culture, and identity for a century to come—in large part because of technology.

If Russia represented the vengeance extracted from fights rooted in the past, China represented the future coming into view. "The Chinese have been more risk averse to date," Adam said. "But they have massive troves of data that can be used to build a surveillance world that Orwell doesn't do justice to."

Part III

THE CHINESE DREAM

Passivity is fatal to us.
Our goal is to make the enemy passive.

—MAO ZEDONG

14

Meet the New Boss

I HAD JUST drifted to sleep in my Shanghai hotel room when the landline woke me up with a persistent ring. I mumbled hello and a polite voice said, "Mr. Rhodes, the vice foreign minister is here to see you," as if it were the most normal thing in the world.

It took me a moment to get my bearings. I was no longer a government official. The clock by the bed told me it was around ten. It was late 2017 and I was traveling with Barack Obama, now a former president of the United States. I got up, put on some clothes, and arranged a couple of chairs at the foot of the bed. When I answered the knock on the door, I was surprised to find two men standing there. One was the vice foreign minister with responsibility for North America, a younger guy whom I recognized from times when we'd both been in enormous bilateral meetings with rows of silent staff flanking our bosses. He spoke in meticulous English with the faint trace of a British accent—vestiges of the nineteenth-century British Empire that became America's twentieth-century hegemony, the expectation that Americans could communicate in our own language even in uncomfortable circumstances. The other man didn't say a word.

We took our seats and the vice foreign minister plowed into a presentation. President Xi and the Chinese people, he said, appreciated the "positive, cooperative and comprehensive relationship" that President Obama had forged in office. There were many achievements to be proud of, he asserted. I almost enjoyed the familiarity of the exchange, still wondering why we were there.

"I understand you are going on to India next," he said.

"Yes," I replied. "To Delhi," as if that offered some necessary clarity.

I noticed the other man begin to watch intently. "We understand," the vice foreign minister continued, "that President Obama is considering a meeting with the leader of the Tibetan separatist movement." He was referring, in the way that Chinese officials do, to the Dalai Lama. And with that, he got to the point: It would be a "personal insult" to Chinese people and Xi Jinping, he said, if the meeting took place so soon after Obama had been welcomed in China.

Speaking in the diplomatic code that had become second nature in government, I said that we very much appreciated their feelings on the matter, and President Obama would make his own decisions about whom to meet. It was the typical way of saying that we'd meet with the Dalai Lama without coming out and saying it. In this way, in a kind of metaphor for how U.S.-China relations have been managed over the decades, we could say offensive things to each other without being offensive. At the end of the exchange, everyone seemed satisfied, and I was left alone.

Closing the door, I thought: *We had not announced a meeting with the Dalai Lama*. I had only recently been put in email contact with the Dalai Lama's representatives after they learned of Obama's trip to India, where the Dalai Lama has lived in exile for well over a half century. Despite the recency of my government service and my famous boss in a nearby suite, my guests had no problem letting me know they were monitoring my communications.

With my hope of any jet-lagged sleep ruined, I walked outside to get some air. The hotel was right next to the Bund, the riverfront area that offers a breathtaking view of Shanghai's multicolored skyline. Shades of pink, purple, yellow, and blue beamed off a set of futuristic towers and glistened in the darkened water below. Pockets of tourists all stood with their backs to this image of postmodernity, taking selfies, their phones grasped in sticks held aloft in the night air. Here was the blend of politics, culture, and economics that America had created—skyscrapers, technology, and social media that allowed someone to create an idealized version of their own existence, transformed into a demonstration of Chinese ascendance: from the British to the American to the twenty-first century's empire. To someone from the Chinese countryside or a similarly developing nation, the scene must have seemed an awesome and improbable achievement: the construction of this almost entirely new city on top of its old colonial center, indicating that the West's supremacy need not be exclusive or indefinite.

The wealth on display was tied to indisputable progress that had lifted hundreds of millions of people out of poverty—economic growth that put food in stomachs and roofs over heads. An achievement of American-led globalization and the Chinese Communist Party, which had made the decision to plug into it. But there was something soulless about the scene and what it represented. To me, an American, it seemed to strip the century-long achievement of the American superpower of meaning: American wealth begetting wealth in other places, exporting inequality; the individual reduced to pursuing an image to post on social media that millions of other people have already posted; those same technologies offering a totalitarian government or faceless corporation access to limitless troves of data that indicate our political preferences, commercial interests, and personal desires. Like a scientist in some laboratory, the Chinese Communist Party had taken American globalization and separated out any pretense of individual liberty—preserving the supply chains and movement of people and capital, but carefully removing the freedoms. In their place was the promise of wealth, security, and pride in national greatness—or at least the *feeling* of empowerment that might come with proximity to wealth, security, and national greatness. I hit the button on my iPhone screen that froze an image of the Bund and uploaded it to Instagram.

I was an American in a world that America had made in its own image, a world that now felt oddly foreign in its familiarity. I was an individual who felt unmoored amid the forces shaping the world, my own identity as incidental as a flicker of light in the panorama that reflected off the water. I was a political exile of sorts, cast among the figures of the past who objected to the general direction of events, clinging to pride in the fact that I'd soon meet with a Tibetan Buddhist who was almost sure to die in a foreign land.

I turned to walk the few paces back to the hotel, taking momentary solace in the "likes" that began to register on the screen of my phone, like an addict being given tiny doses of an opioid by some giant unseen beast.

DURING THAT TRIP to Shanghai, Obama had spoken to an organization named the Global Alliance of Small and Medium Sized Enterprises (SMEs). It's one of those rites of passage for a postpresidency—you can't really make a normal living, so you fly around the world speaking to groups like this. The name itself suggested a borderless and opaque form of capitalism. The event had been curiously chaotic by the standards of these normally staid affairs. After giving the first of two speeches, Obama stood in a photo line in front of a neutral backdrop and had his picture taken with dozens of the people who had sponsored the event. Apparently, some of the Chinese had been scalping their tickets for this photo line. There was just one problem with this practice: To get past security, your name had to match the name on the ticket, so people started to be turned away. This led to shouts and shoving, and ultimately a fight broke out. So there we were, in a windowless room, wondering just how out of hand things could get. "Well," Obama said, "that's never happened before."

I had skipped the first speech. "You have to see this," he told me, with amusement, taking a sip from his tea. "No one listened to a word I had to say." This was an attribute of Obama's that I'd found appealing from the beginning of his first run for the presidency: a capacity to step outside himself and observe the absurdity of his circumstances.

I followed him into the ballroom where he was going to make his second speech. Bright yellow lights beamed from the ceiling, lending the nondescript curtained room a slightly futuristic vibe. As soon as Obama began talking, nearly the entire audience stood, turned their backs to him, and started taking selfies. There was an undercurrent of noise as people elbowed each other to try and get Obama, speaking at the podium, into the frame. Presumably, these people had paid to hear a former U.S. president, but their foremost intention had been to get that selfie. Obama dutifully plowed through a short set of remarks about globalization that nobody seemed to be listening to, an apt metaphor for the geopolitical moment.

"If you ever write a novel about what it's like to be a former president," I told him as he walked offstage, "this has to be the opening scene."

He laughed and, as he often does, connected this seemingly obscure event to a larger truth. To Americans in 2017, he said, the Chinese seem as Americans must have seemed to Europeans a hundred years ago: the ill-mannered yet emerging new rich. Within that analogy was a harder-edged reality: that the crass Americans had displaced the more refined Europeans in much the same way that the Chinese were now poised to do to us.

The previous night, we'd dined with Xi Jinping at an old imperial palace in Beijing. Lanterns lit winding pathways amid manicured gardens. At a large round table, Xi hosted us for a multicourse meal punctuated with occasional shots of Chinese liquor. Xi was, as usual, calm and assured. He'd recently presided over a Chinese Politburo meeting where he'd taken yet another step toward consolidating his power. The conversation moved easily over a mix of geopolitical issues, Chinese economic plans, and reminiscence. Both leaders took care to only walk up to the edge of addressing the Trump in the room. When the dinner was over, as I watched Obama introduce each of his staffers to Xi, it occurred to me that I was looking at the most powerful man in the world who was not—for the first time in a long time—an American president. And Xi had none of the sense of defensiveness and grievance that characterized interactions with Putin. This was a guy who was totally comfortable sitting at the top of the pyramid, methodically asserting his power over more than a billion people, refining a totalitarian system, waiting out, strong-arming, or steamrolling the next obstacle in front of him.

CHINA IS DIFFERENT from nations like Hungary and Russia because it never made any pretense of embracing liberal democracy at the end of the Cold War. And unlike Hungary or Russia, China has the size, wealth, and self-confidence to eclipse the light of liberal democracy that has been something of a North Star since the end of World War II.

For most of the last few hundred years, the center of geopolitical gravity was in Europe: home to the Enlightenment, the emergence of nation-states, the rise of empires, the catastrophe of world wars, the Cold War competition between the American and Russian superpowers. China was on the periphery of this world: a great civilization turned into a divided and partially colonized country, a Japanese-conquered member of the World War II allies, an impoverished Communist regime that helped determine the outcome of the Cold War by shifting its weight slightly away from the Soviet Union and toward the United States. In the span of just thirty years, the center of gravity has shifted. Today, Viktor Orban's Hungary represents the emerging brand of nationalist authoritarianism that has infected the West in the wake of globalization's failures. Vladimir Putin's Russia represents the disruption of the post–World War II global order of international laws, norms, and institutions through a return to an old and aggressive definition of national security and sovereignty. Xi Jinping's China represents the emerging model of capitalism blended with techno-totalitarianism that could be our future, as it is taking hold on nearly every continent. Far from the periphery, Beijing could become the new center of global events.

The United States made this possible. Since the end of the Cold War, we have developed a symbiotic relationship with the Chinese.

Our businesses eagerly decamped to China to make cheap goods that they could then sell back to Americans hungry for ever-improving standards of living; it's almost impossible to imagine an American household that doesn't have something in it that was made in China, even as much of the wealth created through this process was accumulated by the very few Americans who sat at the top of our own economic pyramid, the people who ran companies, traded stocks, held portfolios, and repeatedly had their taxes cut.

As the Chinese became richer, they became not just a factory but a market for American businesses—a vast frontier of emerging wealth to buy cars, computers, software, semiconductors, soybeans, sneakers, Starbucks coffee, Hollywood movies, NBA basketball, and more than a trillion dollars' worth of U.S. debt. It was no secret that as this process unfolded, the Chinese were also stealing American technologies and intellectual property—using them first to catch up with us and then to pull ahead of us in the new frontiers of Artificial Intelligence that will increasingly shape life on earth.

At every turn, the profit motive and economic interdependence between our countries ensured that concerns over democratic values would be subordinate to other interests. The U.S. government always had higher priorities. The American moguls who served as thought leaders on China and gatekeepers to the Chinese market—men like Henry Kissinger, Hank Paulson, Steve Schwartzman, and Mike Bloomberg—really had only one idea to offer: Do what the Chinese want, and you can make money there. U.S. businesses acquiesced to the self-censorship that comes with operating in China. U.S. venture capital helped build a Chinese tech sector that was perfecting methods of surveillance. U.S. popular culture gradually expunged the democratic themes that would make a movie, show, or game less welcome in the Chinese market. The United States and China had made a series of historic decisions over the last half century to draw closer together, but the values America purports to stand for in the world were never a part of those decisions.

It's therefore no surprise that China has become more like America in apolitical spheres—the way they've plugged into the grid of the global economy, the pollution they spew into the atmosphere, the pop culture they consume, the technology-driven nature of life in the twenty-first century. Think of American capitalism and culture devoid of liberal values and democratic politics, and you'll get something approximating the Chinese Communist Party.

But in recent years, the balance has also shifted. It is now America that is becoming more like China—a place of growing economic inequality, grievance-based nationalism, vast data collection, and creeping authoritarianism. The shifting position of our two nations has been on stark display through the ordeal of COVID-19, which spread from the Chinese city of Wuhan in part because the first instinct of a controlling Chinese government was to suppress the news about its lethality and risk of contagion. When COVID did inevitably spread, China was able to move its massive ship of state quickly to lock down whole cities and control the virus, while an America governed by a disinterested authoritarian regime proved incapable of any collective action. While China made a show of its rising influence within institutions like the World Health Organization, the United States made a show of withdrawing from the WHO and performed so incompetently that Americans were barred from entry by many countries around the world. American politics became characterized by a paranoid and sometimes bipartisan demagoguery about a "rising China" that feels one step behind the times: China isn't rising, it has risen.

In 1990, the U.S. economy dwarfed China's and our political model was rapidly ascendant all across the world. How did things change so dramatically?

15

The Outlier

I FIRST MET Bao Pu in a coffee shop in Hong Kong after months of protests had dominated the life of the city. In his early fifties, he was youthful in appearance and in the certainty of his statements, though his views were tinged with fatalism. He had the conflicted air of a man who doesn't trust people easily but has a lot to say. You don't understand China by looking at the present, he would continually insist through our conversations; you have to understand the history. "The most significant question," he told me, "is what can explain China as an outlier compared to the rest of the world after the Cold War." Over the course of our time together, he tried to answer that question.

In 1989, Bao Pu was a senior at university. He remembered the 1980s as a time of relative openness, at least for young people coming of age in China's major cities. "Reading translated works was fashionable, but only among certain people, better-educated people." China had only recently lived through the Cultural Revolution, Mao Zedong's fanatical effort to eliminate counterrevolutionary elements, which had purged intellectuals and killed millions of people over the course of a decade ending around Mao's death in 1976. "After the Cultural Revolution, the mood was for change," Bao told me. "And so ideas were contested within the party apparatus, as well as within the society at large among the educated urban elites. There were debates back and forth that reflected the eighties, the competition of two ideas focusing basically on one issue. The issue was whether the Communist Party could actually use capitalist means to develop its economy, because Mao's economic model had failed."

There was little need for debate about the failure of Mao's economic model. A 1950s effort to modernize China's economy—the so-called Great Leap Forward intended to grow China's economy to the size of Great Britain's—had instead initiated the Great Famine that killed tens of millions of Chinese by the early 1960s. That horror had been followed by the Cultural Revolution. After Mao's death in 1976, China's new leader—Deng Xiaoping—opened up China's economy to capitalism, shaping the world in which Bao Pu would come of age.

Through the 1980s, as China began to plug into the grid of global capitalism, the nascent debates described by Bao Pu addressed China's political model—a different version of debates happening across the Communist bloc. In Hungary, popular frustration with Soviet-backed Communism was making sweeping change inevitable. In Russia, Mikhail Gorbachev was testing whether economic and political reform could be controlled, even as Soviet elites were beginning to prepare for a post-Soviet future. In China, there wasn't a similar tipping point that had ripened in the society. But there was a sense that the leadership would soon face a choice about whether China's economic opening should be accompanied by political reforms: freedom of speech, freedom of the press, efforts to combat corruption, and ultimately a multiparty system rooted in democratic accountability.

In April 1989, Chinese student protests began in Beijing after the heart attack and death of Hu Yaobang, a reformist who had recently been ousted from his position as general secretary of the Communist Party. The largely student-driven movement drew crowds that swelled to a million people around Tiananmen Square. Bao Pu was one of them. "Nineteen eighty-nine was an accident," he told me, with little bravado, "because the timing was triggered by someone's unexpected death. So it's not like society actually reached this boiling point and then the last straw happened." Instead, it represented the moment when the elite debate that had been taking place moved into the streets of the capital city. "It spilled over from the Party's internal dispute to the society."

Gorbachev was scheduled to visit Beijing that May. With the spotlight on that visit, Deng's hands were tied. He had worked to repair relations between the Soviet and Chinese Communist Parties, which had suffered over the last three decades. That initiative was set to culminate in the visit of the reformist Gorbachev, and Deng didn't want to distract from that achievement. "In Deng Xiaoping's mind," Bao told me, "*Mao parted with the Soviet Communists. I'm the one who brought the two big Communist parties together. This is my historical accomplishment.* So because of that timing constraint, Deng Xiaoping had to wait until May 18, after Gorbachev left Beijing, to deal with the student protests. That allowed for a whole month of occupying Tiananmen, giving the illusion that the Communist Party had no power to contain the protests." Bao paused slightly. "But they had all the power."

In this telling, Tiananmen is both a product of history and an accident of history. It was a product because younger people, like some of the elite cadre of the Chinese Communist Party and students across the Communist bloc, were questioning the failure of the Communist model throughout the 1980s. It was an accident because the protests started after the untimely death of a reformer and endured for weeks because of the impending visit of the reformist leader of the Soviet Union.

At the time, Bao Pu's father was a close aide to Zhao Ziyang, the general secretary of the Communist Party. The two of them wanted to have a dialogue with the students, to recognize the legitimacy of their concerns, to accept that China should move in a reformist direction. Deng Xiaoping had different ideas. "Basically, Deng believed that politically they could not open up," Bao said. Deng himself had experience with this kind of debate. Decades earlier, Nikita Khrushchev had written a secret report criticizing Stalin and his more repressive tactics, setting in motion the Soviet Union's distancing itself from Stalinism and ultimately embracing détente with the United

States. The man who delivered Khrushchev's secret report to Mao was Deng. Mao saw the report as a profound threat to his own absolute power and legacy; that analysis, in turn, helped precipitate the very breach between the Soviet and Chinese Communist Parties that Deng was mending in 1989. "Deng learned from Mao," Bao told me. "How Mao assessed the secret report that criticized Stalin and then the Hungarian and Polish uprisings. This experience made Deng inclined to use the army to crack down on mass movements. He was ready to use hard power. He did use it."

Within a couple of weeks of Gorbachev's departure, a quarter of a million troops were brought into Beijing to crack down on the students. Tanks rolled into Tiananmen Square. Live fire was used against the students. Thousands were killed. Bao Pu watched as protesters were shot down around him. His father was imprisoned and then placed under surveillance in Beijing. It was a pivotal moment in Bao Pu's life. He ultimately came to the United States, became a U.S. citizen, and then settled in Hong Kong in the early 2000s, where he started an independent publishing company with his wife. He carved out a niche publishing histories that challenged the Chinese Communist Party's version of events—secret papers about the Tiananmen crackdown, memoirs by reformist members of the Party, books that probed lurid and corrupt corners of the Party. I remember, growing up at the time of Tiananmen and the years after, seeing Deng Xiaoping as a small, friendly-looking old man who opened up China's economy to Coca-Cola and factories that made cheap American products. In reality, he'd spent decades as one of Mao's enforcers, presiding over the killing and starvation of hundreds of thousands of people long before 1989.

History was on the move at the outset of the 1990s. Gorbachev was opening up the Soviet political system. Eastern European countries like Hungary democratized. Soviet republics like Ukraine declared independence. America distanced itself from autocratic right-wing allies who had formed a bulwark against Communism around the world. Democracy bloomed in Latin America and in parts of Africa and Southeast Asia. Nelson Mandela walked out of prison. The Dalai Lama was awarded the Nobel Peace Prize. China opened up its economy, but not its political system. "The Communist Party," Bao Pu said, "they see the outcome of the Cold War. And so now they unanimously conclude that if we don't actually strengthen Party control, we're finished—just like the Soviet Communists."

I EXPECTED BAO PU to be a recognizable advocate, the oppositionist who speaks the language of Western democracy. But despite his antipathy for the Communist Party, he also rejected the frame of the twentieth-century debates—West versus East, capitalism versus Communism, democracy versus the dictators—as a Western construct. Like Navalny, he has been shaped by his own country and experience. "The Communist Party," he argued, "is built on the Western model that claims an ideology to create a social program. And when it doesn't work, they lie." In this telling, the Chinese Communist Party is rooted in the Western idea of Marxism imposed on an ancient civilization. As the nineties dawned and the Soviet Union died, Bao said, the Party recognized it needed to change course. "After 1992, they found that the rest of the world was operating under a market economy; so now, if we control money we control everything. It was just a practical choice." And so they went shopping for another Western idea available to the Party: capitalism, in place of Marxism, as a form of social and political control.

That's the choice the Chinese Communist Party made. By opening up, they could accumulate the money that was power in the post–Cold War world. But they needed other forms of legitimacy; they needed a story to tell about who they were and why they were in charge. So they leaned harder on nationalism, a mix of history and culture, Chinese grievances and supremacy. "The Cold War was all about the ideological struggle," Bao Pu said. "But that has gone out of fashion. The twenty-first century is about *identity.* Identity is something that you cannot put into a framework. But that's where the emotion is." And that identity, of course, is defined by both who you are and who you are against. "The driving force," Bao Pu told me, "is the rise of a Chinese identity versus the West, versus Japan. So this is the major issue—the modern Chinese identity is the key to understanding every present-day China issue on the world stage."

Bao Pu went through his own list: China's humiliations at the hands of Western powers in the nineteenth century; China's subjugation by Japan during World War II; the American abandonment of the Chinese Republic to Mao's advancing armies in the war's aftermath. To Bao, these veins of humiliation, betrayal, and fear of chaos run deep through the Chinese body politic, and the Party has proved capable of tapping them. Throughout the 1990s and 2000s, the Party dialed up anti-Western and anti-Japanese themes in official media, stirring up lingering resentments over Western colonization and Japanese atrocities. They scrubbed the school curriculum of the Western materials that Bao Pu recalled from the 1980s. They buried the historical memory of Mao's catastrophic mistakes and rehabilitated Confucius, the preeminent ancient Chinese philosopher whose thought had been sidelined under Mao, as a justification for a society focused on collective effort over individual rights. "Confucius was rejected in the twentieth century," Bao told me. "They trashed Confucius to the point of no return. But the ideology turned out to be bankrupt, and they were trapped in their own empty framework." Trapped, that is, by an embrace of Marxism, which could never deliver results in China.

Once they were freed from this framework, the Chinese Communist Party thrived as never before. The economy took off and grew at an unprecedented clip, generating its own brand of legitimacy. "For most people who still remember the poverty of the twentieth century," Bao Pu said, "life is pretty good now. Of course they have to put up with a lot of bullshit in their daily lives when they clash with the authorities. But overall, for most people, living standards have improved dramatically. They have wealth and a certain amount of power. They see that the Chinese government projects a certain kind of image that they already have world influence. It's all trying to feed a sense of pride, and nothing but that. Having wealth and power has always been the goal of China in the modern era."

The rise in Chinese living standards dwarfed the wealth created in Russia by the spike in oil revenues in the 2000s. Hundreds of millions of people were lifted out of poverty, one of the great leaps forward for humanity in recent history. This was made possible by the melding of American capitalism with Chinese governance: the global economy we'd built, the trade arrangements that we welcomed China into, the top-down system that enabled massive changes and compulsory work to satiate the consumer demand in the West. And it was buttressed by the construction of a new Chinese nationalism designed in opposition to the very Western countries that were buying all of those Chinese-made goods.

IT SEEMS OBVIOUS in retrospect that a blend of state-controlled prosperity and nationalist fervor could allow the Chinese Communist Party to navigate the turn of the century. But as an outsider, an American comfortable with my status in the world, I found it easy not to feel threatened by a process that was opaque to me, not to ask too many questions about the assumptions underpinning it. I remember a familiar refrain that Xi Jinping would use in conversations with Obama: that Confucian values spoke to the Chinese people's need to belong to a broader collective, whereas American society was built around the individual. It sounded interesting, and unlike Putin's aggressive brand of Russian nationalism, Xi seemed to truly believe it without wanting to impose it on you. Of course, there was something self-justifying in the story. In the same way that American politicians can find justification for just about anything they want in the writings of our Founding Fathers while ignoring all the disturbing parts, Xi could simultaneously extol Confucian values while embracing Mao, who suppressed Confucian thought.

To Bao Pu, the Party's co-opting of Confucianism is offensive. Chinese culture, he told me, was anchored in a civilization distinct from the short-term interests of the Party. "There's a colossal force still there, because of a tradition that has existed for two thousand years, and it's not been forgotten. The Party just use it as window dressing to give the impression that they represent Chineseness. But the Communist Party, being a Leninist party, has nothing to do with Chinese civilization." Confucius, for instance, featured prominently at the 2008 Olympic Games in Beijing, meant to herald China's emergence on the world stage. This, to Bao Pu, was emblematic of a hijacking of traditional Chinese identity for crude political ends. He cited a soaring statue of Confucius that was erected around the games. "Who built that kind of statue? It was totally fascist in style. It really had nothing to do with Confucianism. Modern Chinese identity is more complex. It arose with the challenge of the West, but it has deeper roots in its culture and is really a colossal force. Unfortunately, the Communist Party is the only one in the position to use that force, and it does so for its own benefit."

I considered America's own debates around our two hundred fifty years of independence. We have existed as a country for a fraction of China's history, with a population that is a fraction of China's. Could, as Bao suggests, a more ancient Chinese identity still be a living force among the people despite Mao's systematic destruction of traditional Chinese society over several decades? One irony of China's ascendance is that achieving Mao's vision of a rising China depended upon the Party's abandoning a number of Mao's convictions—Communism, worldwide revolution, self-sufficiency. But not the most important one: *The Chinese Communist Party must rule and is the sole arbiter of Chinese identity.*

It is an identity that Bao Pu has spent a lot of time thinking about, and his resentment of the Party leadership is rooted partly in the way that he believes it has been repeatedly Westernized. Communism, capitalism, and—finally—totalitarianism. To Bao Pu, China's more enduring culture allows for a greater degree of self-criticism and evolution than the rigid system that has hardened in the twenty-first century, even as he glosses over China's own history of authoritarian control. "The Chinese civilization offers an alternative way of thinking about ideology," he said. "Western culture traditionally tended to distinguish between good and evil in absolute terms, defining a clear line. The Chinese never think that way. Instead, Confucius tradition focuses on personal virtue." This focus would compel leaders to admit error and evolve—the opposite of how the Chinese Communist Party operates. "As a ruler, you are supposed to perfect your virtue. When you fail, you hold yourself accountable. The ideal leader in the Confucius tradition would not try to put total control over a society."

LIKE BAO PU, Ching Cheong was shaped by Tiananmen as a young journalist reporting on the protests. In the ensuing decades, he reported on—and experienced—how the Communist Party strengthened its control over society. A friend took me to see him in Hong Kong, insisting that he could describe this matter of how Chinese nationalism has been part of the Party's effort to assert control. I sat across the table as he sipped tea and nibbled on snacks. Like an oracle, he was accustomed to being listened to.

In his younger days, he had worked for the Communist Party's media on the mainland. When I asked when he left that job, he said "June fourth, 1989"—the peak of the Tiananmen crackdown. His post-Tiananmen career took him to the *Straits Times*, a Singapore-based newspaper. In the 2000s, he was imprisoned for a thousand days by the Chinese for publishing "state secrets"—a severe charge used to intimidate or punish journalists who publish things the government doesn't like. In prison, he was subjected to brutal interrogation and more than one hundred days in solitary confinement with no windows, no light, and no idea what was going to happen to him.

Ching Cheong spoke with certainty about enormous questions and events—perhaps shaped by his experience of oppression. As if relaying a secret source of knowledge, he told me that the dividing line in terms of the introduction of Chinese nationalism and identity politics was a 1993 Party document on China's response to the collapse of the Soviet Union. "In that document," Ching told me, "it said that after the Soviet collapse, Marxism-Leninism no longer has a market in China. So we should return to Chinese nationalism and promote Chinese culture."

Before that, the Chinese Communist Party was wedded to the Soviet ideology of a global Marxist revolution that knew no borders. As Bao Pu had told me, with the collapse of the USSR, that was no longer going to work. "So they turn to traditional culture," Ching Cheong told me. "They turn to nationalism. The propaganda department began to produce documents on promoting patriotism and nationalism." As this nationalism emerged over the last three decades, the memory of Tiananmen was whitewashed from history. The events of those days are not taught in schools. Internet searches related to the protests are restricted. Those who show interest in the topic could end up, as Ching Cheong did, detained with no knowledge of what's going to happen to them.

For the broader population, these more contested aspects of politics can disappear from view. I asked a Chinese acquaintance who was born around the time of the Tiananmen protests what her generation's schooling had been on the subject. "Most people of my generation don't know that it happened," she told me. "Or people who know don't really know what happened—how many people were killed, what it was about."

16

The Chinese Dream

IN 2008, CHINA hosted the Olympic Games in Beijing. As the number 8 is associated with prosperity in Chinese culture, the opening ceremony was on August 8—8/8/2008. It cost over $100 million and involved more than fifteen thousand performers. Over the span of four hours, the sprawling story of Chinese culture was told, from the terra-cotta warriors up to the marvels of postmodern technology. There was nothing subtle about it; the Chinese Communist Party was announcing China's ascent in the community of nations, drawing on the legitimacy of China's great civilization. Weather-altering technology ensured that the polluted skies were clear and it didn't rain. The Olympic torch was lit by a young Chinese gymnast who was made to appear to fly through the air. The spectacle was televised to an audience of billions. One wonders how a young person anywhere in the world could watch it and not think they were looking at the future.

George W. Bush represented the United States in the stadium, a diminished man nearing the end of his tenure. The Iraq War was grinding into its sixth year. While Bush and the Republican Party were celebrating the results of the Surge—a relatively small increase in the number of U.S. forces fighting across a relatively small country in the Middle East—as some defining moment of national greatness, China was doing . . . *this*. The day before the opening ceremony, Russia invaded Georgia. The American-led order was fraying at the seams.

My British friend in Singapore—the one who described the "elongated reason cycle"—recalled to me the moment when he believes the seams finally popped. It was a few weeks after the Beijing Olympics, when Alan Greenspan testified before Congress as the American financial system was melting down. Here was the man who presided over the massive economic growth in the two decades after the end of the Cold War, the maestro who was the invisible hand behind the Federal Reserve for much of that time, the steady, competent force who could be depended upon in financial capitals around the world even when American politics resembled a playground of dysfunction. Even the Chinese implicitly accepted the premise that they had to defer to Americans of Greenspan's stature on the basic operation of the global financial system.

During his testimony, Greenspan was asked, in essence, *How did this happen?* "I have found a flaw," Greenspan responded, referring to his basic worldview. "I don't know how significant or permanent it is. But I have been very distressed by that fact."

"Bam," my friend said, describing the moment. "Shivers-down-the-spine moment. That was the intellectual gunshot that was heard very loudly in Asia." He called it "a hinge of history."

Here was perhaps the most prominent embodiment of the American-led global economy acknowledging that the whole system was flawed. "I made a mistake," Greenspan went on, "in presuming that the self-interests of organizations, specifically banks and others, were such that they were best capable of protecting their own shareholders and their equity in the firms."

The same global audience that marveled at the images of an ascendant superpower during the opening ceremonies in Beijing now felt their livelihoods endangered by that flaw at the heart of the global economy. People who had tacitly accepted the consensus of American-led globalization now saw both its failure and its potential replacement. "The emergence of a Beijing consensus directly challenged the Washington consensus," Ching Cheong told me. "The financial meltdown showed clearly that it is the greed of those capitalists that brought a lot of problems to a lot of people. That was the time that people saw the failure of the American model versus the success of Chinese authoritarianism."

A YEAR LATER, in the fall of 2009, I traveled to China for Barack Obama's first visit to that country. All that year, Obama had gone to international summits trying to rescue the American and global economy, in part by asking the Chinese to stimulate demand to replace American spending that had disappeared—in other words, by having Chinese people buy more stuff and shift toward a more consumer-based economy. Obama had leveraged his political capital and the fear of a global depression to get enough grudging nations to do their share, but no one was going to erase the memory of what America had done: the reckless deregulation of the American economy from the 1980s onward, the yawning chasm of inequality, the unaffordable mortgages urged on homeowners by banks that should have known better.

By the time we got to Shanghai, the worst of the crisis was behind us. To penetrate the veneer of officialdom that clouds any engagement with the Party leadership, we had a youth town hall event scheduled. We anticipated Chinese efforts to control the event, so we made a plan with the U.S. ambassador, Jon Huntsman: If the Chinese students seemed to be asking questions that were either fed to them by the authorities or self-censored to avoid sensitive topics, Huntsman would ask a question that had been submitted to the embassy's website. I drafted remarks for Obama that made the case for democratic values. "These freedoms of expression and worship—of access to information and political participation—we believe are universal rights," he said. "They should be available to all people, including ethnic and religious minorities—whether they are in the United States, China, or any nation." Then the questions came, and they were clearly designed to avoid certain subjects.

"Shanghai will hold the World Exposition next year. Will you bring your family to visit the Expo?"

"In Confucius's books, there is a great saying that harmony is good, but also we uphold differences. . . . What would you do to respect the different cultures and histories of other countries?"

"In your opinion, what's the main reason that you were honored with the Nobel Prize for Peace?"

It was hard to imagine that these were really the most pressing concerns of the young people in the audience. Most Chinese would never hear the words Obama said about democracy, but they would see the pictures of a charismatic American president and smiling Chinese students, heirs of the brave new world. In a way, the same thing has happened to countless American brands whose allure has been repackaged for a Chinese audience, stripped of any trace of democracy. Huntsman jumped in with a question that had been submitted to the embassy: "In a country with three hundred fifty million Internet users and sixty million bloggers, do you know of the firewall? And second, should we be able to use Twitter freely?" Obama responded with a long answer about the importance of a free and open Internet, access to the latest technologies, and freedom of speech and thought in general. The audience sat passively.

The so-called Great Firewall referred to in the question was China's nascent effort to build the first distinct national Internet. At first undesirable foreign websites were banned—Twitter, Facebook, YouTube. Thousands of search terms were off-limits, things that were too dangerous for people to learn about—like the Tiananmen protests. The Internet didn't provide all of human knowledge to all human beings after all; it was selective, like any human endeavor.

The firewall was the Chinese government's response to one of the only remaining vulnerabilities for the Party. In the early 2000s, young Chinese lived within a strange duality: People consumed the latest popular culture from around the world while being taught to distrust the individual liberty that enabled the creativity that produced comic-book worlds, Beyoncé, and the NBA. The younger Chinese I talked to remembered an emerging discourse through the 2000s about political issues, particularly on tens of millions of microblogs, a version of the opening that Bao Pu had experienced in classrooms in the 1980s. There were debates about corruption and mismanagement, particularly at the local level, and growing activism around a more equitable rule of law. By the time we went to Shanghai, the Party had decided that this trend was unacceptable. They also had no interest in listening to Americans lecture them about their internal affairs, particularly as Americans were asking for China's help in getting out of the financial crisis of their own making.

By 2011, it had become fashionable to think that social media was the virus that would prove untreatable by authoritarian regimes. In the Arab Spring, mass mobilization fueled by social media toppled dictators across the Middle East—in Tunisia, Egypt, Libya, and Yemen. But the Communist Party saw that social media wasn't simply a threat. It could be controlled with the right firewall, and it was also a nearly ideal tool for surveillance and disinformation. Within China's Golden Shield program, the Party monitored Internet activity within China and blocked more sensitive keywords from Internet users. Emerging Chinese tech companies were made to understand that their own growth depended upon strict regulation of political content. An untold number of Chinese government cyberpolice agents patrolled social media for subversion, while paid propagandists and—as Maria Stepanova would say—voluntary supporters filled it with messages lauding the Party or denigrating its opponents.

The China that had been emboldened around 2008 was unabashed in cultivating its own version of globalization, one that made use of technological progress and open markets while turning those tools against the freedom of the Chinese people. Then China found the right leader for its moment of ascendance, the man who would take the next step in pursuit of the Chinese Dream.

XI JINPING IS the son of a member of the Chinese Communist Party's founding generation. When he was a teenager, his father was purged in the run-up to the Cultural Revolution. At the age of fifteen, Xi himself was sent to the countryside for a dose of hard labor. Instead of turning him away from the Party, the experience instilled in him a fervent desire to join and rise through the ranks. It foreshadowed a certain aspect of Xi's character, one that recalled a line from V. S. Naipaul that Obama and I recited to each other when faced with the rougher edges of life and power: "The world is what it is; men who are nothing, who allow themselves to be nothing, have no place in it."

Xi muscled his way up to the top of China's leadership pyramid, the heir apparent to Hu Jintao. He was an unusually large personality for a Chinese politician, married to a popular singer. Upon taking power in 2013, Xi introduced the concept of the Chinese Dream, which spoke to a more showy and ambitious style than that of Hu, a mild-mannered man devoid of charisma who never broke from carefully prepared talking points in his meetings with Obama. Xi reportedly introduced the slogan at a private meeting of the Party faithful at a museum exhibit focused on China's historical suffering at the hands of Western powers.

"We must make persistent efforts," Xi said in a speech in March 2013, "press ahead with indomitable will, continue to push forward the great cause of socialism with Chinese characteristics, and strive to achieve the Chinese Dream of great rejuvenation of the Chinese nation." Whereas past Chinese leaders like Deng Xiaoping had talked about the need to "hide your capabilities, bide your time," Xi was casting off that sense of restraint. In an echo of the goals of Mao's Great Leap Forward, the Chinese Dream involved China's achieving "the two 100s"—a "moderately well-off society" by 2020 (the hundredth anniversary of the Party), and a "fully developed nation" by

2049 (the hundredth anniversary of the People's Republic). The Chinese Dream was the subject of a relentless nationalist propaganda campaign that also harked back to the days of Mao—complete with songs and dances. Xi launched a massive anticorruption campaign, which simultaneously acknowledged the public's frustration with rampant corruption and served as a useful tool for Xi to sideline potential opponents. Factory owners could use the initiative to justify endless hours for their workers, who were called upon to produce the goods that would make China a great nation (and factory owners rich). And Xi promoted a cult of personality that emphasized his own charisma instead of just putting himself forward as the leader of the Party—students were forced to study his writings, Party members recited his sayings, and television cast him as the star in China's story of ascent.

I first met Xi in June 2013 at a summit at Sunnylands—a golf resort and retreat in Palm Springs, California, that recalled a faded American glory and had been a favorite of presidents like Nixon and Reagan. I liked Xi from the perspective of a staffer who sits in meetings and doesn't talk. He had a personality, he broke from his talking points, and he brought a bottle of strong Chinese spirits to his dinner with Obama to break the ice. His large frame and protruding waistline drew a contrast with Hu's tendency to recede into his entourage. It suggested a man at ease in his skin and pleased with his power. There was also something ominous, though. Whereas past Chinese leaders spoke about China's "core interests" (a euphemism for interests that would never be compromised and could lead to conflict) with respect to issues like Tibet and Taiwan, Xi's definition was broader and included the entire South China Sea—maritime borders that absurdly snaked around the coastlines of several Southeast Asian nations and encompassed vast natural resources.

Sizing up Xi's ambition, Obama set to work getting him focused on climate change as an issue on which Xi could demonstrate global leadership by dealing with the air pollution that was becoming a more dangerous phenomenon in China. If Xi took aggressive action on climate, Obama reasoned, he could differentiate himself from China's past leaders while unlocking the potential to reach an ambitious global climate change agreement (what became the Paris Agreement). In the first term, we needed China's help to save the global economy; in the second, we needed China's help to save the planet.

To address China's more assertive approach in Asia, Obama accelerated an effort to consolidate a bloc of countries committed to a set of rules and norms for commerce that could be translated into geopolitics through the Trans-Pacific Partnership (TPP), a trade agreement that included traditional U.S. allies as well as nations like Vietnam and Malaysia who were threatened by China's claim to the South China Sea. A Vietnamese official once pointed out the importance of TPP to me as a signal of America's presence in Asia: "We have hated the Chinese for a thousand years, but they are right here," he said, pointing to China's border with Vietnam. "They are going to be here. The question is: Are you?"

Obama had some success in appealing to Xi's ambitions while trying to shape how they evolved. The Chinese government stepped up its efforts on climate, and it was helpful on a handful of other foreign policy issues, from North Korea sanctions to the Iran Nuclear Deal. But Xi's heavy hand also became more apparent. The nationalism within Chinese media increased. In 2013, seven subjects were deemed off-limits for the Chinese classroom: universal values, freedom of the press, independent civil society, civil rights, elite cronyism, judicial independence, and the past mistakes of the Chinese Communist Party. Official surveillance, harassment, and detentions increased—not just for dissidents, but also for lawyers, minority groups, Christians, journalists, and activists of various stripes. Efforts to control the U.S. media in China increased, and the Chinese government revoked visas from reporters working on stories about corruption and repression. The theft of intellectual property from American companies persisted despite our protests.

Time and again, Xi echoed Deng's private conclusion about the collapse of the Soviet Union in his words and deeds: Don't show any weakness, any compromise, or any concession to those who press for change that could affect the Party's control. After Trump's election and swift withdrawal from TPP and any recognizable form of U.S. leadership, Xi's ambitions accelerated. He started talking about the need to build a military that could "fight and win wars." His Made in China 2025 initiative focused on ensuring China's indigenous capacity and technological supremacy as American investment in research and development was falling. Chinese influence in nearly every part of the world increased, along with the heavy-handed tactics of Chinese diplomats. Xi did away with term limits, establishing himself as China's unrivaled leader for as long as he wants.

To my British friend, the meaning of the Chinese Dream is simple, and rooted in that collapse of confidence in the American model in 2008. "I think what it means," he told me, "is 'not the American Dream.'" This view fits neatly into the story that the Chinese Communist Party had been telling its people about the reemergence of China following the humiliations and chaos of the twentieth century, their new identity as citizens of the next superpower. My friend summarized it: "Mao was *Stand up*. Then Deng was *Get rich*. And now Xi is *Become strong*."

TECHNOLOGY IS CENTRAL to the model that Xi and the Party are building, with consequences that could ripple across the entire world. With the development of Artificial Intelligence, the capacity to make use of the vast amount of data available to an authoritarian government is accelerating exponentially. Just as the United States helped create the prosperity that enabled the Party's control, U.S. technology has been copied, repurposed, and enhanced to secure that control—sometimes with investment from U.S. venture capital. Across China, a program known as Police Cloud allows for the collection and integration of previously unimaginable amounts of information: who you're in contact with, what you buy, where you travel, when you shop, whether you pay your parking tickets, and so on. A "social credit" system allows the government to affix a score to someone: How reliable are you? Could you pose a threat of some sort? You live your life with the knowledge that the sum total of your actions could be evaluated by someone, somewhere, with some purpose. This creates incentives and disincentives, given the reach of the Party into people's lives. Disincentives are clear: Say the wrong thing, and you could end up detained. But the incentives may be even more powerful: Want a good job? Want your kids to get into a good school? You may have to consider those aspirations with everything you do.

When I was in government, Human Rights Watch regularly complained to me about the Obama administration's lack of prioritization of human rights. After I left government, I found myself seeking them out. I connected with Maya Wang, who has a Chinese background herself and has focused her research on technology and authoritarianism within China. "The authorities are hoping to use new technologies to build a perfect authoritarian society that is free of dissent, or makes dissent irrelevant," she told me, "with the idea that the surveillance has a repressive side and a service delivery side." Repression if you say or think the wrong thing. Service delivery as technology can anticipate your wants and desires. With more advances in technology, the Party is trying to reach a new reality. She summed up the goal this way: "We are able to predict dissent before it occurs and crack down on it, and completely reengineer people's identity and thoughts."

Just as the Party placed a bet after Tiananmen that they could embrace capitalism but not democracy, they're now placing a bet that responding to people's wants and desires in some areas can erase their wants and desires for other things—like politics. This is done by harnessing technologies that are similar to those that help Amazon predict what I might want to buy while nudging me in certain directions. Maya described this as "creating the kind of new society where the Party serves the people so well that people no longer feel the need for democracy or debate, because we would know you are unhappy about it or we will manipulate it so you won't be unhappy about it." This goes far beyond the mixed authoritarianism of Hungary or the more traditional repression in Russia, where technology can be a tool of surveillance and disinformation but not achieve total social control. "This is a new model of authoritarianism," Maya told me. "Almost all authoritarian leaders eventually face the [people's] desire for freedom. It's a ticking time bomb. The Chinese government is trying to solve that problem and it seems to be working quite well."

Technology is central to the effort to solve that problem. Speaking of the Internet, Xi Jinping once said, "Freedom is what order is meant for, and order is the guarantee of freedom."

Read that several times and make sense of it. Or think about George Orwell's slogan for the Party in *1984: Freedom is slavery.*

The most extreme version of Xi's "new model of authoritarianism" can be seen in China's western Xinjiang Autonomous Region (known as Xinjiang Province), where more than a million ethnic and largely Muslim Uighurs have been detained in camps and the rest live in a kind of open-air surveillance prison. The Communist Party justifies this as a necessary effort to cleanse the region of "Radical Islam" after a spate of terrorist attacks a few years ago. In reality, the Party is trying to reshape Uighur identity—removing devout Islam and certain cultural traditions, while shifting the demographics of the region. Tens of thousands of police have been added. More than a million Han Chinese have moved to Xinjiang in recent years, with an untold number staying as "guests" in Uighur homes.

When you serve in government, you can get numbed to the scale of human suffering in parts of the world. The number of people killed, injured, or detained in a conflict. The quantification of repression in a country. These become numbers in reports, accompanied by the occasional anecdote. You notice, over time, that certain human suffering also becomes more of a focus of media reporting, because of accessible geography or the implication of some easily understood U.S. interest: the danger of terrorism, for instance, or the stability of some U.S.-backed dictator who looks after some important U.S. interest, like oil or refugee flows. Americans can become intimately familiar with the suffering, for instance, of several Americans killed by ISIS, or refugees trying to reach Europe. If the suffering happens somewhere farther afield, perhaps in some African country divorced from any discernible U.S. interest, the images don't reach us. The suffering is more easily forgotten, chalked up to the vagaries of a cruel world.

Over the last few years, the *numbers* out of Xinjiang came into focus, but because the media faces strict restrictions in this remote part of their country, the *picture* does not. There would be no images of crying children, separated families, or dead-eyed prisoners. Perhaps some aerial imagery that shows the development of a camp gives us a glimpse of this systematic effort to grind the identity out of a minority group through the relentless application of control. But this would not be something that we would be forced to reckon with through our own eyes.

This, too, has been a hallmark of the Communist Party's effort to suggest that such things are not the concern of the wider world. We need not even avert our eyes, because there is nothing to see. Why trouble yourself with concern over this place that few people have ever visited, or these people whom you have not met? To do so would only complicate things. Complicate China's own valorous efforts to lift people out of poverty. Complicate the business that American companies want to do in China. The Uighurs are a secondary concern, best left to human rights advocates engaged in a well-meaning but ultimately insignificant business: the complaints of those who don't understand how the world really works. It was reported that Trump himself told Xi that the construction of camps for the Uighurs was a great idea. Why would he care about some insignificant people he had never met, and whose cause might interfere with his more important work of seeking a trade deal that would require China to purchase more American soybeans?

This is the apathy that those with unchecked power seek to engender in others: the idea that it's not even worth caring about something because it's not going to change. That's the strategy the Chinese Communist Party has pursued for decades—for instance, on something like the erasure of the Tibetan people's distinct language, culture, history, and leadership. *It would hurt the feelings of the Chinese people and Xi Jinping if you met with the Dalai Lama.* "It's not worth it," they might as well say. "It's not going to change, and we have more important things to talk about."

But in Maya Wang's telling, informed by countless interviews with Uighurs ("I didn't interview one person who wasn't crying or close to tears"), Xinjiang is really about the future of China. "It's about the whole model of Xinjiang—the ability of authorities to put basically [an area the size of] a third of Western Europe under some kind of lockdown, from prisons to reeducation camps to being detained at home, depending on their level of reliability."

As I talked to Maya, read her detailed reports of what had taken place in Xinjiang, and scoured the other accounts based on Chinese documentation and Uighur testimonials, I found myself forced to look more directly at the human circumstance that was unlike anything experienced before. I found myself imagining what it might *feel* like to be a Uighur, and what their experience might suggest about the future for other Chinese people, and perhaps for ourselves.

There are cameras everywhere; some ostentatiously placed, some invisible. They don't just monitor events; they record your face so as to perfect the facial recognition technologies that make it easier to monitor the population. There are checkpoints everywhere. They don't just stop and question you; they also record images of your face, car, and license plate. You don't know what, exactly, will get you sent to a camp. You can arouse suspicion by being idle or switching jobs. You can be interned for showing religious devotion—attending prayers at the mosque, downloading sermons, covering your hair or growing facial hair, adopting a more pious lifestyle (quitting drinking, for instance). You can be questioned for something that your family members do, including those who live abroad. You have to assume your communications are monitored. You don't know if your phone has been turned into a listening device, your home is surveilled, or your circle of friends is penetrated by informants eager to finger someone as politically questionable, destined for the camps. You can attract attention for knowing too much about what is going on in a place where the authorities only want you to know what they tell you. The curriculum in schools has been changed to sever your children's bonds to what has been a communal identity for generations. You are not permitted to be yourself, to be left alone, and you are presented with no option other than being who the Party wants you to be. Technology renders this destiny, quite literally, inevitable.

One million people in camps. Five years ago, it would have seemed absurd. Today, it barely registers. Why, having succeeded in doing this in Xinjiang, would the Chinese Communist Party not deploy these methods, export these technologies, and create this dystopia elsewhere?

17

Make China Great Again

WE ARE VERY early in the period of time through which the world will adjust to China playing a bigger role in our lives, no matter where we live. Yet while the Communist Party's focus on control at home is clear, what the Chinese Dream means for the rest of us is not. If you look closely, though, a picture is beginning to come into view.

A centerpiece of Xi's global ambitions is the Belt and Road Initiative, a $150 billion per year Chinese-led consortium to build infrastructure involving nearly seventy countries. It started around the time Xi took power, echoing the ancient Silk Road trading route, the age of Marco Polo. Now it has advanced to the point where it is simply one more acronym familiar to government bureaucracies, boardrooms, and readers of *The Economist:* BRI. If you trace the path of BRI, it begins along China's periphery in Southeast Asia. It snakes through Myanmar, where China is building pipelines and a port in the same province where the Burmese military—which shares a real and manufactured dislike of Muslim minorities, and stands to profit off BRI—has ethnically cleansed a million Rohingya Muslims. It curves around the Indian Ocean, including Sri Lanka, where a Chinese port can conveniently double as a potential naval facility. From there, BRI reaches into Africa, the colonial competing ground of the pre–World War I European powers. "If you put the ports and roads side by side with British ports and roads from 1880," my British friend in Singapore told me, "it's the same chart. Geography doesn't change that much. The British didn't mean to become a global hyperpower. They just went out to make some money and then suddenly they had infrastructure, and then suddenly they were a great power." China has also pushed beyond this geography, to places like Hungary, where Viktor Orban signed up for a BRI project—a rail link to Serbia involving a close crony and childhood friend.

In this way, if you look at it through the constancy of powerful people seeking profit, the logic of China's expansion is obvious and no different from that of great powers of the past. The British went abroad for natural resources, built infrastructure to extract and transport those resources, and then began to find new ways to make money by controlling politics in the places where they were dominant. Americans did a version of the same thing in the twentieth century even as we built the kind of international order that could facilitate the rise of a country like China.

It is not military power that is the principal source of China's influence, it is money. Corruption can be a lubricant for the effort to ensure that foreign governments are compliant. Sometimes when we'd be in large bilateral meetings with certain governments, Obama and I would speculate afterward about how many people in the room were being paid in some way by the Chinese government. For smaller, less wealthy countries in particular, this can be completely transactional for China: Pay a bribe to the government, get a foothold of control. One version of this formula is simple: The Chinese use intimidation and bribes to pressure poorer countries to take out huge Chinese loans for infrastructure projects that serve Chinese interests—to extract natural resources, for instance, or to build a road to transport them (often with Chinese labor). Then the countries fall into debt traps where they become beholden to Beijing. Of course, China also prefers to deal with authoritarian governments because it diminishes the danger that democracy will encroach upon China, simplifies the transaction, and makes it less likely that countries will protest when China does things like put a million people in camps.

So while they are extending their influence, the Chinese Communist Party is also exporting authoritarianism—through corruption, geopolitical leverage, and, increasingly, the export of the same technologies that they use to suppress dissent in places like Xinjiang. This creates a particular dilemma for democratic governments: If you seek to isolate authoritarian governments in order to impose some cost for their repression, you only push them further into China's arms. Myanmar, for instance, knows that it will face no sanctions or criticism from China over its treatment of an ethnic Muslim minority group.

The international order of laws, rules, norms, and institutions that America has taken the lead in building since the end of World War II is supposed to at least curb excesses—to serve as a check on flagrant abuses of human rights, to impose penalties for the theft of other nations' territory or the intellectual property of companies, to at least discourage corruption and the bullying of smaller countries by bigger ones. But none of it is self-enforcing. As the United States abandoned any investment in that international order under Trump, China ramped up its efforts to create its own new reality through the sheer force of its size and the dogged nature of its actions. They could also easily argue that their authoritarian model was a better choice than the American one—not just for other governments, but for their people as well. As one prominent African entrepreneur put it to me, summing up how billions of people likely feel around the world: "I mean, one can argue with China and say, well, China is not democratic. But when you look at the results—hundreds of millions of people brought out of poverty in a very short period of time—one must say, well, okay, how do we learn from the way that has happened?"

As I traveled the world throughout the Trump years, these two compatible ideas came up again and again: that Chinese authoritarianism might be more effective than American democracy, and that Trump's abandonment of the international order meant that there was no alternative to increasing Chinese influence. In one Asian country, a foreign leader told me that "the American-led order is gone" and that China represents the future. When I asked him to explain how China exerts influence, he didn't hesitate to provide an example. Referring to a prospective infrastructure project, he said that in the past, the government would have considered bids from Europe, Japan, and China. The decision could have been informed by everything from cost to quality to reputation to considerations of geopolitics. "Now," he said, "we know it has to be the Chinese bid." To cross China is not worth the risk.

Ultimately, this shift in the center of the world's gravity doesn't just shape particular transactions and policies; it begins to shift how we behave, in a version of how a totalitarian government exerts control over the behavior of its citizens. For rich countries, big corporations, and prominent individuals who want access to Chinese markets or investments, there is increasingly an explicit cost in return. Do not meet with people like the Dalai Lama. Do not oppose China's position on matters like the South China Sea. Do not investigate or even inquire about what is happening in Xinjiang. Do not comment on anything that is taking place within China's borders.

IN THE AFTERMATH of Tiananmen, at the height of American leverage over global affairs, George H. W. Bush moved quickly to make amends with the Chinese Communist Party, and Bill Clinton followed suit—welcoming China into the World Trade Organization and the lucrative club of nations that agree upon a set of rules for international trade, even though China routinely broke them. I understand the motivation. From the standpoint of the ordinary American, the Chinese market has been a limitless frontier, a place where cheap goods could be manufactured to lower costs for American consumers, and—as China developed—Chinese consumers could support American jobs by buying more of our stuff. The economy that I've lived in most of my life is shaped by this dynamic. American manufacturing jobs were displaced to China. Cheaper goods facilitated bargain shopping that started at places like Target and Walmart and migrated to Amazon. Electronics emerged from supply chains designed as intricately as your smartphone—ideas from Silicon Valley and chips made in America to be assembled in China and sold back to Americans. Things worked out very well for the people at the top, and everyone else owed the illusion of rising standards of living to a basic bargain—the cost of education and health care and housing kept going up, but at least you could buy cheap household goods, drive a big car, and entertain yourself on a phone that offered the promise—or distraction—of infinite immersion. Meanwhile, the rich people who could own stocks and trade in markets got wealthier and translated that wealth into political, social, and cultural influence.

Obama governed in line with this consensus, even if he was at the progressive end of it. He was consumed by the need to rescue the global economy and find some way to resume economic growth. Those priorities depended upon Chinese spending and stability, a machinery of economic growth that—like America's sprawling banks—had become too big to fail. But over the thirty years since Tiananmen, the balance of influence between America and China has also shifted, almost imperceptibly, like a picture that changes as it comes into sharper focus.

Now, as China surpasses the United States as a source of influence in an increasing number of sectors and regions, it is not surprising to see more aggressive efforts to shape the behaviors of U.S. companies and their employees. In the fall of 2019, I got a call from the Houston Rockets general manager, Daryl Morey, who had gotten himself into hot water for tweeting in support of Hong Kong protests against the heavy hand of China's rule: "Stand for freedom. Support Hong Kong." Twitter is banned in China, so the Chinese government clearly had to choose to make the tweet a story in China and manufacture a sense of nationalist outrage to send a warning shot across the bow of the NBA and any other American company with interests in China. State media was whipped into an anti-NBA frenzy. NBA games were yanked off Chinese television. Lucrative shoe contracts for American athletes were suspended. Billions of dollars were at risk. The Chinese insisted that Morey be fired or disciplined, something that Adam Silver, the NBA commissioner, refused to do.

Morey is a smart and innovative man. He repurposed the data-driven "moneyball" approach that reshaped baseball and used it to assemble successful Rockets teams. But when he called me in the thick of the controversy, he was shocked by his entry into geopolitics. Pacing on a nondescript side street of Los Angeles outside a coffee shop where I was working on this book, I explained to him that the Chinese will always test the limits of how much they can control your actions. That's what they were now doing—testing the NBA. I explained that if there weren't established lines that couldn't be crossed—in this case, China policing the speech of NBA executives, players, and even fans—then they would keep pushing. The Rockets were particularly important to China because Yao Ming, the greatest Chinese basketball player of all time, had been a Rocket and now ran China's basketball association. It was, in miniature, what had happened between our two countries. The Rockets had made Yao a global figure in the same way that America had helped make China an economic juggernaut; now China was using its newfound leverage to control what the Rockets could do and say, in much the same way that they try to leverage America across the board. How many American companies have bent to China's will, restricting the speech of their own employees, making compromise after compromise to avoid offending an authoritarian government? How many powerful Americans had abandoned support for causes like the Dalai Lama's effort to preserve Tibetan identity because they didn't want to get a knock on their hotel room door in the middle of the night, or lose access to the Chinese market? Morey's job had been spared, but he had also deleted the tweet, and the team's star player—James Harden—had apologized.

After the Morey incident, I started to notice things around me that had been a less visible presence before. When my daughter watched a hit Disney movie, for instance, a map of China included its absurd maritime border—a dotted line swallowing up the entire South China Sea. How often does the map of a country indicate its maritime border? The blockbuster movies that sustain Hollywood's bottom line now depend upon Chinese moviegoers even more than American ones. Every film that is released in China is vetted by the Central Propaganda Department. A Chinese company, Wanda, owns the second-largest American movie theater chain. And while it's easy to find major American films that are critical of the American government, try to find a blockbuster movie that takes on the Chinese Communist Party. Instead, American blockbusters are now laced at times with subplots of Chinese ingenuity helping to fend off alien invasions or to rescue Sandra Bullock from space. More subtly, they're devoid of the admittedly simplistic Cold War storylines that I grew up with, when the good guys were fighting for democracy and the bad guys were totalitarian oppressors. It's easier, instead, to have the bad guys be people who don't control a chunk of the global market: Muslim terrorists, for instance, a representation that can justify both America's War on Terror and China's repression in Xinjiang.

In this way, American companies, banks, entertainment conglomerates, sports leagues, and even the U.S. government are operating under the same social credit system that applies to Chinese citizens. The incentives and disincentives are clear. Using the leverage of money within the system of American-designed global capitalism, the Chinese Communist Party is increasingly shaping our choices, and incrementally exerting control over what we say and think.

"NOBODY TOOK THE Chinese nation seriously," Bao Pu said to me. *"It's a poor country. They're never going to get themselves organized."* Unspoken was the implicit bias that likely led many Americans to think a nonwhite nation could never surpass us in influence. "The Internet broke the national border for information, but the Party has created its own border," Bao Pu continued. "Of course the Internet and globalization complicate things. People in the West all of a sudden feel vulnerable, and there are people out there with a willful intention to use that against you." How extraordinary that in my own relatively short life span, the Internet and globalization have become more of a threat to the democracies that set them in motion than to totalitarian regimes like China's.

Bao Pu is unsparing in his assessment of where this is going. "The Communist Party of China is a cancer to humanity," he told me. He saw little hope emanating from China, including its educated ranks. "The Chinese intellectuals are doing nothing but building the Chinese identity, their own project to make China great again." But I sensed a continued internal conflict within Bao Pu. He preferred democracy but was uncomfortable oversimplifying what has happened in an enormous and ancient country like China. He recognized the achievement of the Party but thought they had stumbled into their current position by being in control at the right time. He opposed identity politics but was plainly proud of his Chinese identity. He rejected the grievance-filled nationalism of the Party, but he clearly harbored some of the same grievances. And despite his belief that Tiananmen was an accident of history, doomed to fail, Bao Pu had spent much of his life trying to fight against this whitewashing.

I asked him why the Party had to whitewash Tiananmen from history. "Because they can," he answered, echoing my own sense of why Putin had poisoned Navalny. "It's just because they can. The Tiananmen student protest exemplified nonviolent struggle. But because nonviolence was met with tanks and machine guns, right and wrong was really clear. The Communist Party had no excuse for this massacre, even within their own rhetoric. The history of the Communist Party is littered with inconvenient truths. Cultural Revolution they can't explain. The Great Famine they can't explain. They had to erase them all from history."

In recent years, Bao Pu's publishing business has suffered. He used to sell books largely to mainland Chinese, who would come to Hong Kong and take them back home. Then, in 2014, the Chinese government abducted several Hong Kong booksellers, detained them in China, and—in one case—forced a man to make a videotaped confession of all his trumped-up wrongdoing. Meanwhile, the Chinese government bought out the vast majority of booksellers in Hong Kong, with the result that there is less space for the kind of provocative books that Bao has published. For those who still buy them, there are much more intrusive checks at mainland Chinese ports of entry. For a party that has such control over the information environment inside China, the measures may seem extreme, but that's exactly the point: If even bringing a book inside the country is dangerous, then starting a mass nonviolent movement becomes nearly impossible.

For his part, Bao Pu told me he is shifting from nonfiction to fiction. The battle to shape perceptions of recent history and objective reality has become increasingly impossible to fight. "There are other ways to shape hearts and minds besides using nonfiction," he told me. "I think the people in the twenty-first century receive information from either education or entertainment. Perhaps entertainment would be a better tool."

Bao Pu did volunteer an explanation for the seeming tension within some of his own comments. "Given the totality of that system," he said of China, "people like me spent thirty years to basically reassess what I learned in the first twenty years of my life in China. And I still sometimes come to a realization that I'm programmed to think a certain way. The Communist Party is operating in an Orwellian way. It rewrites history. It monopolizes information, and therefore controls people's minds."

China's Communist Party has spent the thirty years since Tiananmen reprogramming the minds of its people—blending the aspiration for material wealth with a national identity rooted in past grievances and manifest destiny; to trade the Western ideal of Marxism for a version of authoritarian capitalism. This project can be stifling to the individual, which is why Bao Pu resisted it. "I personally make those who change history, who rewrite history, my enemy. Because their willful social engineering is suffocating the creativity of the population."

WHEN YOU WRAP your mind around the scale of the challenge to individual liberty posed by the Chinese Communist Party, it's easy to succumb to a sense of inevitability about the dystopia that lies ahead. But then I remind myself that people were equally certain, back in 1989, that the future would evolve in a particular direction: that America was ascendant and its model of democracy and open markets would inevitably prevail. Who could have foreseen, back then, what events like the Iraq War and the financial crisis and the election of Donald Trump would bring about? In assessing the present, what you cannot account for is the intrusion of hubris and history—the inevitable overreach of a totalitarian government, and the irreducible longing of human beings to live without a boot on their throat. The event that might spark some form of mass mobilization, which in retrospect always seems inevitable.

When I asked Maya Wang about the Party's hijacking of Chinese identity, she pushed back. To Maya, the absence of space for free and open discourse concealed the diversity of the people. "People in China are not one-dimensional," she told me. "The problem is we have no open space," no place to openly debate issues and hold different views. "So there are alternative Chinese identities that are different from the interests of the Party." Like Sandor, she was pointing to those more local, community-based forms of belonging and meaning. Like Navalny, she was holding out a space for a form of nationalism that is not destined to serve a particular national power structure. Like Bao Pu, she believed it was wrong to see being Chinese as something that cannot be distinct from the Party. "People rightly feel defensive about their country. However much nationalism does play a role in politics, people who talk to each other about issues in China, their gears shift." What happens may not take the form of dissent, but it suggests that the Party's rigid framework does not define the people.

She gave me an example. One of her older relatives went back to China. "He knows his friends very well," she told me, "and they were all telling him that the Hong Kong protests are a Hong Kong independence movement," which is very much the Party line—that everyone from peaceful protesters to Daryl Morey are trying to dismember the Chinese nation.

"Who do you hear that from?" her relative asked. "It's not about independence. It's people fighting for their rights." When the group pushed back, he asked them: "Why do you trust the Party when they say this about revolutionaries who were smeared and then rehabilitated after the Cultural Revolution?" All of these people, after all, had lived to see the Party's version of the truth change over time, in the same way that Winston Smith—the protagonist in *1984*—came to distrust everything the Party told him because his own memory recalled a time when history was different.

Maya estimated that the ten people in this group held views that could be matched in the diversity of gatherings of similar size in rooms across China. "There would be two or three people gung-ho for nationalism," she said. "Then you have three or four people who say, 'You are right, we want democracy, but I'm too afraid,' or 'We can't get there,' or 'China would be too chaotic.' And then you'll have two people who are liberal, progressive."

Right now, the prevailing circumstances push those three or four people in the direction of the Party—as they are products of decades of education, propaganda, economic policies, suppression, and surveillance. The question is whether those circumstances can change, and when.

18

One Country, Two Systems

I FELT AN affinity for Hong Kong from my first visit in 2002. With steep mountains ringing a majestic harbor lined with skyscrapers, it had a geography that changed the way I looked at the possibility of a physical space—a futuristic city implanted on an improbable landscape. As a British colonial outpost, Chinese city, and global center of finance, it gave off—street by street—a sense of being a bridge or portal between worlds: East and West, Communism and capitalism, open and closed societies. Here, one could imagine, there had been all manner of intrigue over the decades—opium traders; dissidents escaped from mainland China and the spies looking for them; foreign correspondents and organized crime; Chinese tycoons and Westerners who'd never lived in the West.

During that first visit, I was twenty-five years old and Hong Kong was only five years removed from British rule. From the window of my hotel, I could make out the old English building that housed colonial government offices amid narrow streets marked by traditional Chinese characters. I rode a ferry from central Hong Kong across the harbor to Kowloon, a breeze in my face, looking back at the skyline—the tallest buildings not reaching the height of the houses that dotted the mountaintop behind them. As a New Yorker, I'm vulnerable to falling in love with great cities, and I remember in that moment thinking that the world held an infinite number of discoveries to be made, mysteries to solve. For perhaps the last time in my life, I had no idea what my future held.

I didn't return to Hong Kong until March 2017. It was my first introduction to the kind of speaking that people do when they leave government—in this case, sitting in a conference room in one of those high-rise buildings along the harbor, with video links to offices in other Asian capitals, talking to a slice of a bank's workforce about social media strategy and global trends. I had never before considered the subjects I was talking about from the perspective of making a profit, and I was struck by how obviously that shifted your perspective.

Up above the city, you no longer felt you were in a nation-state; instead, you were in the globalized community of capital markets. Men and women of different nationalities looking for some germ of knowledge that could allow them to make a bet on something—currencies, companies, geopolitical risk—that would pay off. The latest technologies were readily available, the video links more pristine than those that used to connect me with a global community of diplomats and military officers from the White House Situation Room. There was a seemingly limitless supply of bottled water, coffee, and tea. I had the peculiar feeling of being a commodity. In the world of finance, my accumulated knowledge and experience could be plugged into this world of markets, the trillions of transactions that shoot across computer screens every day. The world of politics dealt with the people on the other end of those transactions.

ONE COUNTRY, TWO SYSTEMS. That was the promise made to the people of Hong Kong when they were passed to Chinese sovereignty in 1997. The handover had been negotiated between the British and the Chinese, largely excluding Hong Kongers, and there were a number of contradictions. Hong Kong was a part of China but had not been governed by Beijing for a century. People in mainland China spoke Mandarin, while the people of Hong Kong spoke Cantonese. Hong Kong was a liberal, open society; mainland China was ruled by the Communist Party. "One country, two systems" was meant to reconcile those differences, or at least allow them to coexist. Hong

Kong would become a part of China, but it would be entitled to its own laws, democratic practices, and civil liberties.

This arrangement was to stay in place until 2047, a date that must have seemed impossibly far away when the handover ceremony took place on June 30, 1997. A band played "God Save the Queen" as the Union Jack was lowered one last time just before midnight. After a twelve-second pause, a tiny window of suspended sovereignty, the flag of the People's Republic of China was raised to the tune of "The March of the Volunteers," the Chinese national anthem: *With our flesh and blood, let's build a new Great Wall!* As Prince Charles sailed away aboard the royal yacht, accompanied by the last British governor of Hong Kong, the belief—among many liberals in Hong Kong and the West—was that China would become more like Hong Kong than the other way around. That was wrong. Over the next two decades, China became more nationalist, more authoritarian, and more of a presence in the lives of Hong Kongers.

In 2019, the people rose up, beginning with a series of protests against legislation that would allow mainland fugitives in Hong Kong to be extradited to China. Massive demonstrations filled the city and morphed into a nimble movement of flash protests, sit-ins at the airport and universities, encrypted mobilization, and cultural memes. The stakes were higher than just the politics of Hong Kong. The growing luster of the Chinese Communist Party's model depends upon the proposition that people prefer order and prosperity to the dysfunction and chaos exemplified by American democracy. Give the people economic growth, a nationalist story of ascent to believe in, and the cultural products of a liberal society—American-made superhero movies and opinionless athletes—and they will be happy. So Hong Kong was an uncomfortable twist in the plotline of Chinese ascendancy. There was only one place in the world where people lived under a blend of China's system and the characteristics of an open society. If the Communist Party's model was superior, presumably the people of Hong Kong would want to opt in to it. But throughout 2019, people had been making clear through protests that involved an enormous share of the Hong Kong population that they did not want that.

I traveled to Hong Kong that November to understand why. I considered leaving my electronics at home; *Bring a burner phone and a Chromebook instead,* my friends said. But out of a mixture of laziness (*How does one set up these other electronics?*) and fatalism (*The Chinese are probably already in my stuff*), I made no such adjustments. And so, as I trundled off the seventeen-hour flight into the bright duty-free lights of the airport, my devices caught the available network and presumably fell within the reach of China's monitors, whoever or whatever they are. For all I know, they are reading these lines as I type.

It was nearly midnight by the time I was dropped off in front of my hotel in central Hong Kong—the same one, in fact, that I had stayed at back in 2002. The street was quiet, empty of people or cars. But the question of Hong Kong's identity—and whether it could be separate from China's—was clearly very much in play: the city was uncharacteristically covered in graffiti. On the wall across from the hotel, painted letters were illuminated in the ghostly half-light of the street lamps. *Free Hong Kong. Fuck the popo. If we burn, you burn with us.*

In the morning, I walked to one of Hong Kong's cavernous shopping malls, where I met Wilson Leung, a spokesperson for an organization called the Progressive Lawyers Group—a collective of several hundred Hong Kong lawyers who provide legal analysis and support for the protest movement. It must be noted that my conversations with Wilson took place before a new "national security law" was passed that ambiguously criminalizes conversations with foreigners that could be deemed subversive. More on that later.

We met for breakfast in a buffet room that allowed you to pile Chinese and Western staples together—think dim sum and scrambled eggs—on the same plate. Wilson had been a student at the time of the 1997 handover, a time that he remembers as hopeful. The first decade of Chinese rule was a period of relative calm, without much interference. "We carried on with the annual Tiananmen vigil. You could say mostly what you wanted. There was still active press on both sides." But there were signs of unease in the population, a fear of Chinese authority that was just under the surface. In 2003, when the Hong Kong government tried to pass a national security law that would have encroached on Hong Kong's civil liberties, half a million people demonstrated. Otherwise, demonstrations on behalf of a more democratic system were carried on by a relatively small activist cohort.

As Chinese rule entered its second decade, Beijing's efforts to assert control over Hong Kong began to accelerate in ways that were imperceptible day to day, but transformative over time. "The way that the Chinese government does these things," Wilson explained, "is really through a whole-of-society approach." Businesses that relied on the Chinese market were told their employees should not express political views. Mainland Chinese tycoons with ties to the government began to buy up nearly all the major newspapers and television stations and toe a reliably pro–Communist Party line. Independent media were denied a license to operate. Certain kinds of speech began to disappear—not because any one dictate went out, but simply because they began to be regarded as outside the realm of accepted discourse. Life became less free. Even as these changes were taking place, the relative prosperity and the feeling of openness remained. No Berlin Wall went up; no troops were in the streets. "What's so interesting," Wilson said, "is that life is basically similar, right?"

Wilson told me that the changes in the society accelerated around the time Xi Jinping came to power in 2013. Control from Beijing became tighter. There were more restrictions on what you could say, what kinds of media were available, what kinds of events were permitted. In advance of Hong Kong's 2014 elections, there was a debate about how Hong Kong would select its chief executive—the top official in the government. Many Hong Kongers preferred a free and direct election of the chief executive, in line with the democracy they'd been promised. But Beijing tossed those proposals out. Hong

Kongers would be offered a choice among a very small number of candidates who'd been prescreened by Beijing.

This decision triggered what became known as Occupy Central or the Umbrella Movement. Tens of thousands of Hong Kongers inspired by the Occupy Wall Street movement occupied part of the city's center for several months, another indication that American influence comes not just from what our government is doing but also from our people. The eyes of the world were on Hong Kong's politics. Business was disrupted. Beijing dug in and a tense standoff ensued. The umbrella became a symbol of resistance: In addition to protecting against the rain, it could be a shield against tear gas and pepper spray, or the watchful eye of surveillance.

IN NOVEMBER 2014, at the height of the Umbrella Movement, I traveled to Beijing with President Obama. The focus of the trip was securing an ambitious Chinese pledge to combat climate change: If the United States and China could make a joint announcement about their commitments to slow global warming, the rest of the world could be brought along to achieve what would end up as the Paris Agreement. Hong Kong was in the backdrop, the latest human rights irritant in our relationship with the Chinese government and therefore something Obama would raise in his meeting with Xi. To the American media, there was additional drama revolving around whether Xi Jinping would take questions from the press alongside Obama. In this way, issues related to human rights are reduced to a kind of formulaic play: The U.S. government raises issues privately with little expectation that they will be resolved to our liking; the U.S. media champion issues related to press freedom that are also about whether they get to ask Xi Jinping a question. We Americans get to perform on behalf of human rights, but when we leave, nothing changes.

Obama took a private walk with Xi, the kind of time alone when you can make a hard ask on a sensitive matter. Obama pressed Xi to raise the ambition of China's climate pledge. He succeeded in that effort. It is hard for me not to see the logic of the trade-off in prioritizing climate change over Hong Kong rights in that kind of setting. Without China, it was impossible to achieve a global agreement to fight climate change. Saving the planet seemed like even more of a progressive priority than the Umbrella Movement. Perhaps more acutely, there was little evidence that pressing Xi harder personally on Hong Kong would make any difference; the Chinese routinely reject criticism of what they deem internal matters. There have been trade-offs like this for decades; at every turn, there is some competing priority that makes complete sense in the moment, just as it can seem pointless to press the Chinese Communist Party to move in a direction that they will surely resist. But the problem for people like me is being part of a broader enterprise that has allowed itself, over time, to see human rights as a secondary or even unattainable objective. That's what the U.S. government—as well as American society writ large—has done with China since Tiananmen.

Obama did raise the Hong Kong question in his larger bilateral meeting. Xi was predictably dismissive, blaming the protests on a small group of troublemakers and saying it was an internal matter for China. Obama argued that respecting the right to protest and addressing the concerns of the movement would ultimately bring more stability than repressive measures. But Xi was clearly uninterested in debating these points. Afterward, Xi did agree to take questions at a press conference, which earned us goodwill with our media.

In the press conference, Xi confidently announced, "In my talks with President Obama, I also pointed out that Occupy Central is an illegal movement in Hong Kong. We are firmly supportive of the efforts of the Hong Kong Special Administrative Region Government to handle the situation according to the law so as to maintain social stability in Hong Kong and protect the life and the property of the Hong Kong residents. Hong Kong affairs are exclusively China's internal affairs, and foreign countries should not interfere in those affairs in any form or fashion." This statement was strikingly similar to what Xi said in private. Obama noted that America was not behind the movement in Hong Kong. "The United States," he said, "as a matter of foreign policy but also a matter of our values, is going to consistently speak out on the right of people to express themselves, and encourage the elections that take place in Hong Kong are transparent and fair and reflective of the opinions of people there."

From my seat in one of the front rows, the tableau of the U.S. and Chinese leaders looked like a familiar production, even as this unusual movement had taken hold in Hong Kong that was aimed at capturing their attention and the attention of the world. I watched as Xi was asked a question by the *People's Daily,* a state-run newspaper: "As China further develops, how does China see its own position in international affairs?" As if to emphasize the extent to which the whole thing was a charade, Xi quite obviously read an answer that had been prepared for that particular question in advance, as colorless as a progress report at a Politburo meeting.

At the banquet lunch that followed, the Chinese seated me next to an affable older man who had been Hong Kong's first chief executive after the handover. The Chinese do their homework. Presumably they knew that I would be one of the staffers most likely to press Obama to be outspoken on Hong Kong, and that I would be asked about it by the media myself. The man smilingly explained that the vast majority of people in Hong Kong did not support the Umbrella Movement because of their good feelings for China and their desire to get back to normal. I noted that to Americans, the movement seemed to reflect fairly obvious concerns among the people of Hong Kong, particularly young people. *It will all be over soon,* he told me, smiling.

IT WAS OVER soon. Beijing and the Hong Kong authorities waited out the Umbrella Movement. After seventy-nine days, the protesters had to go back to work and the leaders of the movement were arrested. The election remained within Beijing's control. The message was clear: Time was on the side of the Chinese Communist Party, which could treat a social movement like a minor speed bump in its assertion of control over Hong Kong.

Around the same time, the Hong Kong booksellers were detained and taken to China. "These guys were not prominent activists," Wilson told me. "I don't even know if they can be called dissidents because they're just publishing things, they're not writing." What unsettled people, he said, was how random the detentions were. One bookseller was taken from Hong Kong, another from Thailand, suggesting a lack of safety anywhere, foreshadowing the extradition law. "The most shocking thing is that it was not shocking," he told me. *The most shocking thing is that it was not shocking.* It was a sentence that had become like a reflex to me during the Trump presidency. To Wilson, the lack of popular resistance in Hong Kong was just as disturbing as the actions being taken by Beijing. The pro-democracy movement spoke up, but not the rest of society. "A lot of them," he remembered, "were silent."

This fact is central to understanding the success of China's model of control: Fear silences people as much as any particular governmental dictate. "There's self-censorship," Wilson told me. "In these semiauthoritarian or authoritarian regimes, they're very good at shutting down people from saying anything that might be quote-unquote 'political.' And in that context, 'political' usually means something that's critical of the government. On mainland China, there are very lively debates on many issues. But nothing that would touch the government. You know, as soon as someone tries to say something in the chat room about the government, everyone falls silent because everyone knows that you don't go there."

Self-censorship had become a prominent feature of life in Hong Kong. If you want to get ahead in politics, don't criticize the Chinese government. If you want to get ahead in business, don't criticize the Chinese government. Even without a social credit system in place, the effect is already present. Wilson pointed out a different, more social form of self-censorship. "Authoritarian regimes are very good at equating 'political' with 'bad,'" he said. "So if anyone's a political person, that means they are some kind of devious or bad person. So you always get the message from the pro-Beijing camp: Keep politics off campus. But what they actually mean is 'Don't have students who oppose the government.' They're fine with students who praise Beijing, and praise One Belt, One Road, and so on. But they're not fine with students who support democracy."

This reminded me of Márta Pardavi in Budapest, watching potential donors to her civil society organization opt for the ballet instead; or, in America, the warnings I got at times to tone down my anti-Trump commentary for fear of appearing hysterical, unserious. "I think," Wilson told me, "this feeds into the general atmosphere of society where you think *I better not say anything.* And then there's the element, which might even be common with the U.S., where you just don't want to get into it."

Wilson decided to become political despite the risks. In the wake of the Umbrella Movement, he helped form the Progressive Lawyers Group. Many lawyers in Hong Kong were reluctant to pick fights with China because their firms had business there. As an independent lawyer, Wilson didn't have the same constraint. I wondered, as I talked to him, whether someone was watching, just as I'd wondered whether my communications were being monitored. So I asked about his decision to become political. "You either have to stay silent or have to come out," he told me. Once you have spoken out, he said, "you're kind of too late, you know? So, for example, our group was named in pro-Beijing newspapers as some die-hard opposition group. Once you're on that list, you're stuck."

For a few years after the Umbrella Movement, things settled back into a new kind of status quo. Carrie Lam, a nondescript, prescreened, pro-Beijing politician, was elected chief executive in 2017. Then in early 2019, her government introduced the extradition law—basically, it felt as if anyone could end up like those booksellers. People took to the streets. "It's very easy for people to understand," Wilson told me, "the simple idea that you'll be taken over the border."

This time the protests united the city. This included the more traditional democrats who think of Hong Kong as part of China but want what was promised under "one country, two systems," and what Wilson called "localists," who emphasized the preservation of Hong Kong identity. Beyond that, there was an assortment of students, religious groups, chambers of commerce, businesspeople, and those who had been squeezed by Hong Kong's booming real estate prices. The marches were small at first; most people believed the bill would just be rammed through the Hong Kong legislature. But in June 2019, more than a million people turned out in the streets. "There was a recognition that we have to be united," Wilson said, referring to the scale. "We can't afford division because we're already in a much weaker position. And it's even worse if you argue among yourselves about tactics." He cited one of the movement's slogans: "We each climb the mountain, each in our own way."

The movement learned from the failure of the Umbrella Movement. Because people can't take off work for months at a time, this time the protests would be episodic—a flash mob on a lunch break, a surge of people on a weekend, in shifting locations. Because an identified leadership could be arrested, this time there was no leadership—instead, a kind of direct democracy prevailed; in some cases protesters went into mass groups on encrypted online message boards and voted on a time and place for protest. This is how the movement tried to avoid being crushed by Beijing, like a virus evolving to survive. No disunity. No single venue. No leader. Secure communication.

Over the summer of 2019, the authorities started blocking peaceful mass protests. In this second phase of the protests, the police set up roadblocks and clashed with protesters who turned out. Many people who'd participated in the mass marches started staying home, and the streets were left to what became known as "frontline protesters"—people who chose to climb the mountain through confrontation. As the protests stubbornly continued every day, with crowds that swelled on the weekends, the approach toughened. "They started shutting it down as soon as people appeared in the streets," Wilson told me, "firing tear gas and so on."

WILSON AND I were surrounded by the trappings of a prosperity unknown in most of the world—a shopping mall filled with designer stores, the brand names inseparable from the one percent that had been the subject of the first Occupy protest on Wall Street: Prada, Louis Vuitton, Tiffany. The prosperity itself was suffocating, the promise that you could aspire to buy these things if you just shut up and stayed home. "I think there's little illusion as to how ruthless the government, the CCP, is in keeping control," Wilson said. "People here can see what they do in Xinjiang, what they do in Tibet, where there's a whole system of society set up to monitor, control what you do. And also to erase your separate identity." While this upscale shopping mall could feel a million miles from the unseen lands of western China to an American like me, it didn't to Wilson. "I think that's certainly something that weighs on people's minds here. That some of the things that they do in Xinjiang could come to Hong Kong as well."

I asked Wilson what the people of Hong Kong wanted. He gave a simple answer: "To be left alone." It was a less ambitious definition of freedom: *to be left alone*. One country, two systems. "You're pretty much left to do what you want, say what you want, educate your people in the way you want. You can criticize China in the same way as you can criticize the queen or the prime minister if you're in Scotland." Summing it up, he said, "Your separate system and separate identity are respected." This feeling, he noted, was overwhelming among the youth.

19

"The Narrative of Liberalism and Democracy Collapsed"

NOVEMBER 24, 2019, was election day in Hong Kong. The elections were for District Councils, local bodies whose power was limited and focused on concerns like trash collection and traffic patterns. But the District Councils are the only fully democratically elected political institutions in the city, so their election every four years represents a clear barometer of public opinion. The protest movement hoped they could send a message, even if only symbolic, at the ballot box; the authorities wanted to convey a sense of normality, and hoped to use the election to take some steam out of the protests. Therefore, a truce of sorts had been called. This would be the first weekend in many months without a protest. The remaining flash point was a protracted standoff at the Hong Kong Polytechnic University, which had been cordoned off as police laid siege to a few dozen remaining protesters armed with Molotov cocktails and makeshift bows and arrows. When I first got to Hong Kong, someone pointed out plumes of smoke coming from the university across the river, silent in the distant sky.

Before going to see some polling sites, I met in the lounge of the hotel with an official from the Hong Kong government—a body with significantly more power than the District Council but less than the colossus of the Communist Party to the north. He wished to remain anonymous. Even though it was on a weekend, he was neatly dressed with carefully combed hair—a man who exuded the care and dignity of a technocrat who tried to do the best he could, even if he couldn't control the circumstances that shaped his work. His thoughts were already carefully prepared when I told him that I was trying to understand the ascendant authoritarianism and nationalism in the world, and how they connected to what was happening in Hong Kong.

"The nationalism in the U.S. and Europe is somewhat different," he told me. "Yours started with the financial crisis in 2008. That's when liberalism started to lose its appeal, when people saw this isn't working. The narrative of liberalism and democracy collapsed. This spilled over into China, too. This is when China started to think—*Should we really follow a Western model? Look what's happened.* That's when you start to hear more about a Chinese model. So the nationalism movements in East and West were both a response to the collapse of the Western model."

He had basically summed up in a few sentences what I'd been wrestling with for two years. Yet I had come to realize that this was only the surface level of what was happening. Underneath, there was the question of how people everywhere were adjusting to this shift toward nationalism or resisting it, those questions of identity that were supplanting the ideological debates of the last century. And the tectonic plates of geopolitics seemed to run right under Hong Kong, a city where the last twenty-five years have seen expectations upended, with consequences looming for every Hong Konger.

"My generation is more sympathetic to China," the official told me, explaining his feelings about the 1997 handover. In the early years of Chinese rule, he said, many people like him had made excuses for China's repression on the mainland. *China has been divided and kept down by the West, so it has to be wary. China is very poor, so it has to cut corners on the path to development.* Still, there was also an expectation that Hong Kong would be largely left alone by Beijing. "Hong Kong was valuable to China and it was in their interest to maintain a high degree of autonomy," he explained. Hong Kong, after all, was an international financial capital that could be a gateway for investment into China, a capitalist bridge between a Communist country that was opening up and the world that wanted access to China's market. If the price of having that gateway was an open society in Hong Kong, where Westerners would be comfortable living and the locals governed themselves, China would see that as a price worth paying. For that first decade after the handover, it felt to the official like China and Hong Kong were proceeding comfortably on parallel tracks—one country, two systems. "But after 2008," he said, "we thought we are no longer on the same track."

He briefly sketched how a more prosperous China became more assertive over the last decade. More mainlanders started moving to Hong Kong, speaking Mandarin instead of Cantonese. The government started to try to change the curriculum in Hong Kong schools to mandate propaganda that celebrated the Communist Party. The media was increasingly bought up by those pro-mainland tycoons Wilson talked to me about. Particularly after Xi Jinping came to power, governance became more top-down, and Beijing's "liaison office" in Hong Kong, its official representation in the city, became more aggressive on the issues that it cared about.

This whole time, the official had served in Hong Kong's government. On the surface, he said, some things were the same. When it came to issues like transportation, housing, and other local issues, "most of the time they don't give a shit," he said, referring to Beijing. "It's how to deal with politics—that's when the Chinese government came in." This could be seen, for instance, in the selection of Hong Kong's chief executive, and the way that some members of the legislature were backed by powerful Chinese interests. "Their guys win elections, that's the measure of their performance." If you wanted to get ahead, you had to toe the Beijing line. The liaison office began to perform the role of the "whip" in Hong Kong's legislature, bringing pressure to bear to make sure important votes went Beijing's way. This created the precarious state that the Hong Kong government found itself in by 2019. "Anger has been building for many years," he told me. When the extradition bill was introduced, "it was like a bomb."

I asked him how a bill like this gets proposed by a government that knows it will be unpopular. Ostensibly, the reason had been a murder case: A Hong Kong resident had killed his pregnant girlfriend in Taiwan before returning to Hong Kong, and the authorities wanted to be able to extradite him to Taiwan. Despite the fact that Taiwan is not governed by China, the government argued that the right to extradite someone to Taiwan would enable extradition to mainland China as well. Beyond this individual case, the broader political objective—erasing the lines between China and Hong Kong—was obvious. "It's a feeling of 'kill two birds with one stone,'" the official said. He told me that Beijing didn't order the Hong Kong government to introduce the extradition bill; instead, they had simply made it known that there were a bunch of measures that they expected to see enacted over a period of time—*including* the extradition bill. "You deal with this one murder case, and you check this one item off the list." The timing was up to the Hong Kong government, but the message was clear. "You do what you can to get ahead," he said. And the way to get ahead, to bolster your social credit score, so to speak, was to do what the Chinese Communist Party wanted.

A wan smile crept across the official's face as he recalled with nostalgia Barack Obama's election in 2008 and how he had inspired people across the political spectrum in Hong Kong. I had the familiar feeling of sitting in silence with someone remembering that hopeful moment, even as the die of the financial crisis that the official had spoken about had already been cast. He explained that Obama was the kind of inspirational figure who couldn't exist in Hong Kong. "You have to understand," he told me, "one of the legacies of colonialism is that we do not have good politicians." For that reason, the protest movement didn't have a clear sense of direction. Surprisingly, he said something similar about Beijing. "China may not have an overall plan," he told me. "Their approach is the hard approach and then you have to stick with it."

For the rest of the day, I wandered the city from polling site to polling site. For a place that had been rocked by upheaval, the scenes were quiet and orderly. Huge lines formed. Families stood together. People snapped selfies. Nobody appeared impatient even though some lines went on for hours. One young voter told me he lived in the UK but had flown back home so that he could participate; there were many others like him, he said. I was reluctant to linger too long at any one location, mindful of the propaganda point about foreign interference.

I came to one of the main train stations that connected the city by rail to the airport, where demonstrators had proved earlier that fall that they could grind air traffic to a halt. There'd been an impact on Hong Kong's economy from the protests: fewer mainlanders coming to shop, more international conferences relocated to Singapore, contingency plans for banks to move some of their employees there as well. But in the train station, the shops were immaculately lit and an orderly procession of Hong Kongers passed through infrastructure that would make Americans envious. This was the promise of wealth, order, and connectivity to the world that was supposed to be the allure of being swallowed within China's political boundaries and accepting the story of the Communist Party's steady ascent. Back outside, the high-rise apartment buildings hinted at the limits of that promise. Many young Hong Kongers can't afford the housing prices, which have been driven up by the influx of mainland Chinese tycoons and the continued presence of foreigners. Some work all day and spend their nights cocooned in small rooms along with others. The wealth on display is out of reach; the reward is a small piece of a small room and the ability to feel that you are a part of a greater whole. If the American Dream, in economic terms, is embodied by visionaries who upend a status quo, the Chinese Dream is embodied by those who don't. Perhaps, with the right mix of hard work and fealty to the Party, you could rise like the Chinese nation, could achieve the Chinese Dream.

Earnest campaign workers handed out flyers for their preferred candidates. You could tell the progressives by their youth, people still in their early twenties, as young as I had been on that ferry back in 2002. I took their leaflets and smiled back, thinking that it could be both their first and last experience of a free election.

I MET WITH two young men who were active in the protests. I'll call them Adam and David. They were both in their twenties and not out of place in the somewhat upscale bar where we ordered drinks that sat largely untouched on a white-clothed table.

David, a so-called frontline protester, spoke differently from the others I'd met in Hong Kong. His own identity seemed immersed in the movement in a way that even Wilson Leung's wasn't. For the last six months, he'd gone out once or twice each week. He was at the airport when protesters clashed with the authorities. He wore black masks. He'd taken part in strikes. He'd joined human chains against police in the streets. He'd been teargassed. He spoke with a dispassionate tone. This was a matter of logistics and tactics; the necessity of participation was obvious. The movement would likely fail, but that didn't matter; the protests were as much an end as a means.

At the beginning, David and Adam said, it could take three to four days to set up a protest. Now it was much faster. There are different online forums for different protests. Someone proposes a location, and whatever gets the most "likes" becomes the protest site. A phone was handed to me; in just one Telegram group, I saw, there were 288,419 people. New comments flashed in Chinese characters, a living organism that never stopped growing online. Sometimes, the decision making was driven by events: People see protesters getting beaten up by police and people organize another protest, and so it goes. Adam told a story about how a young protester was shot recently and within hours there was a flash mob. The details of the event were discussed and agreed to online with urgent efficiency. *We're going to have a candlelight vigil. It's not going to be violent. We're going to be silent.*

Adam referred to the "Be water" ethos of the movement, modeled on Bruce Lee's view of kung fu, Eastern philosophy expropriated through a Hollywood lens, anonymity, flexibility, and spontaneity giving them an advantage over police who use more formal tactics and organization. A whole genre of songs, slogans, and artwork had emerged about and around the protests, content also shared online. A culture grew up around a movement gone viral. After summer break, Adam said, the government thought a return to school would stop the protests, but the opposite happened. Students coming back together only added to the momentum as they returned to classrooms eager to participate in this shared identity picked up over the summer.

Everyone in the city who supported the protests contributed what they could. Some people sewed clothes. Others bought bottles of water and set up supply stations behind the protest areas. Others—like the Progressive Lawyers Group—offered professional expertise. The leaders of the Umbrella Movement who had reputations in other countries served as diplomats on behalf of the movement. There was an implicit understanding that different people would go to different lengths, and that was okay. "They know I go to protests," David said of friends and family. "I know a friend who has gas masks. We don't discuss it."

David gave me an example of how this unspoken ethos worked. There had recently been a protest near Hong Kong's legislative council. The police responded with tear gas and water cannons. A canister of tear gas landed right next to David's leg. He ran away with a group of people, but barricades and lines of police blocked their escape. Everyone in his group was wearing a black mask, a sign of a frontline protester. Shops that were closed—owned by people who were losing business because of the protests and may well have disagreed with the tactics used by people who wore masks—opened their doors to let the protesters avoid capture. They closed their gates and covered their windows. David and his friends slipped into the lobby of an upscale hotel, where they were also quietly welcomed. A friend of his fainted from the tear gas exposure and was tended to. They were allowed to pretend to be customers and left unmolested. In this way, the city had become a place of safe houses and collaborators.

I asked about the masks in particular; the authorities had tried to ban them. Was it about concealing identity? "It's about being in defiance," David told me. In Singapore, I'd heard an allegation that had the ring of Chinese propaganda that crates of masks had been shipped into Hong Kong, paid for by rich Taiwanese aided by the CIA. *How do you get the masks,* I asked? "Amazon," he replied.

A brief debate broke out about whether the protests needed a leader—someone who could make decisions, negotiate with the authorities. Adam thought the recent standoffs at universities suggested this was necessary, as students trapped behind the barricades struggled to escape. There was also the larger matter of how to define success. The so-called "five demands" of the protesters represented the clearest statement of objectives. Those five demands were permanent withdrawal of the extradition bill; a call on the authorities to characterize the demonstrations as "protests" and not "riots"; accountability for police violence; the release and exoneration of all protesters detained; and universal suffrage for the people of Hong Kong. The demands were clear, but most of them were about the protests themselves; only the last one began to define a future for Hong Kong.

The demands emanated from the banner of Marco Leung, a protester who jumped to his death from the roof of a shopping mall in the center of the city. Some frontline protesters carried suicide notes with protest demands. Others carried notes indicating that they had *not* committed suicide in the event that they were killed by the authorities. (There's a dark term used when authorities kill someone and call it a suicide: The person is said to be "suicided.") This idea of individuals carrying notes offered a vivid image; to me, the entire city seemed to carry within it a message in a bottle, cast out to the wider world before Hong Kong was swallowed up.

I asked David if he carried a note and he said no. But with a sly smile, he said that he had programmed an "out of office" message for his work email account that would activate if he was gone for a certain period of time, notifying the sender that he'd been detained by the authorities.

"I don't think there's a strategy," Adam said of the movement. "It's a collective of everyone's anger and vision and depression. Within the system, nothing will make a difference." The suggestion was that the protests could at least carve out a temporary space outside the system, a place of refuge for a population who increasingly felt like outsiders in their own city.

"I understand the reasons behind the violence," David said. "We have tried peaceful protests many times, but the government didn't respond." The impulse to fight back became more acute when it was clear that there was no accountability for police abuses. The police didn't even help injured protesters on the streets. One time, an angry taxi driver plowed into a crowd and ran over a girl whose leg was later amputated. The taxi driver was not charged. There were plenty of stories like this going around, fueling the defiance.

The protesters faced a multiheaded opponent that was entrenched and complex. Hong Kong's notorious organized criminal syndicates sided with the government and attacked protesters in their own flash mobs, instigating violence that the authorities wanted so they could cast the protests as riots. The Chinese-state-owned and Party-friendly media then portrayed the protesters as violent rioters, wearing down public opinion in Hong Kong and abroad by invoking the hundreds of billions of dollars at stake for the city's private sector and the inevitable strings that Beijing could pull in the Hong Kong government. "We don't know all that is happening behind the scenes," Adam said, particularly with regard to the relationship between the government and various powerful business interests. I asked about the economic drivers of the protests—the frustration over inequality, over the lack of housing. To David and Adam, those were indistinguishable from questions about democracy. The system is structured to favor certain groups, they said, including mainland Chinese interests and those who backed them.

In the end, the protests were about something bigger than a rigged system, bigger, even, than democracy. "Hong Kong identity has been created during this movement," David told me.

As powerful as that idea was—a community of people who had forged a new identity in opposition to authority—there was still the seeming impossibility of defining what success looks like for a Hong Kong that is, after all, still a part of China. Can a distinct Hong Kong identity be preserved? Or would China itself have to change in order for Hong Kongers to have their own identity? And how long would that take?

"It does scare the shit out of me," Adam said, referring to a future in which Hong Kong has been fully swallowed up by China, the idea of one country, two systems rendered an eccentric historical footnote. "If we don't win this movement, it could be in a few years, it could be now, it could be in 2047—it will happen. When we look at Xinjiang, this dystopia is happening to millions of people. I don't want people to go through that." Adam was composed, intelligent, articulate—the kind of person who would likely succeed at whatever he chooses to do. He was deeply invested in the movement, yet over the course of our conversation, I couldn't help but notice contradictions—between his awe at what the protests had accomplished and his awareness that they hadn't changed any of the fundamentals at work; between his belief in the world as it should be, and his recognition of the world as it is.

For David, these contradictions were beside the point. The rightness of the movement was all that mattered. He said, matter-of-factly, that he understood he might end up getting imprisoned. "I'm prepared for it. I will not think what I've done is wrong." What was also clear is how much the movement was about more than just democracy; it was about Hong Kong identity. In the act of protest, this identity had been forged. A community had come together through their recognition of where things were going, and they had found themselves in their effort to stop it. Through that action, they'd discovered the extent of their own agency in the world, and its limits. But they'd also discovered who they were, and *that* couldn't be taken away.

IN A WORLD increasingly defined by identity politics, Hong Kong raised distinct questions. What does it mean to be a Hong Konger in a place that was passed from colonial British rule to the Chinese Communist Party? If your ethnicity aligns with the very power that is encroaching on your sense of identity, how do you think of yourself? If your identity is in opposition to the forces steadily swallowing up your community, what do you do with it?

To get at these questions, I wanted to meet young people who weren't particularly active in politics but were struggling to make sense of it all. I reached out to a friend named John, a perpetually sunny millennial who prided himself on knowing people across Hong Kong's political spectrum. One afternoon, we went to a local bar and met with two young people named Charles and Lorraine, both around thirty years old. The sound system churned out a steady stream of American rock hits from the 1980s, the music of my childhood, the dusk of the Cold War, the long tail of American influence: Def Leppard's "Pour Some Sugar on Me" and Journey's "Don't Stop Believin'."

I asked them to go back to the handover to give me a sense of how things had changed. Lorraine explained what "one country, two systems" meant by quoting a Chinese proverb famously used by the former Chinese Communist Party leader Jiang Zemin: "The river water does not intrude into the well water." For her, as a child, the change in sovereignty had been almost imperceptible; she started to learn more about China in school, and that was about it. Many people were proud of their Chinese identity and the end of colonialism.

By 2012, she said, things had changed. Lorraine remembered being conscious of a particular aspect of this shift during the London Olympics. When a Hong Kong pop singer cheered on Hong Kong athletes as a distinct unit, she was trolled by millions of people on Weibo. The message was clear: If Hong Kong pop stars wanted to sell music to the vastly larger mainland audience, they had to toe a Chinese nationalist line. This wasn't politics in the form of laws or elections, it was the sense of politics changing your culture, your sense of identity. "The river water," Lorraine recalled, "started to invade the well water."

The Communist Party's version of truth also seeped into Hong Kong society. Lorraine described the more extreme manifestation of the new reality. "It's like pointing at a deer and saying it's a horse." The methods for compelling self-censorship became more blunt. An arts group, for instance, was denied a venue to stage performances critical of the Communist Party. Topics like Tiananmen and Tibet became increasingly off-limits. The word "national" was removed from the name of Taiwanese institutions in Hong Kong, suiting Beijing's preference. Lorraine, who liked to punctuate her points with proverbs, explained the feeling by telling me that she thought there was an American proverb that captured the process: "boiling the frog."

Charles told me that this process accelerated around the time that Xi Jinping ascended to power. That's when a new curriculum was launched in schools aimed at making children feel like they were a part of China. But the move backfired. By pushing propaganda on kids—forcing them to learn about the Party's history and requiring them to sing the national anthem—the government only fueled a burgeoning sense of Hong Kong identity in the city's young people. The authorities were, Charles said, "trying to brainwash the next generation but ended up promoting a sense of Hong Kong independence." Not necessarily a desire for political independence, but more that desire Wilson talked about: to be left alone. Like so many young people, those in Hong Kong were figuring out who they were by figuring out first who they did not want to be.

Around this time, Charles worked as a civil servant in Hong Kong's government. He was required to attend multiweek trainings in Beijing that included classes on social and political science in line with Communist Party orthodoxy. But this indoctrination came with enticements. There were rooms in newly built five-star hotels. There were sumptuous meals. The message was not lost on Charles or his colleagues: There were rewards on offer for those who embraced the orthodoxy that was being drilled into them.

When the Umbrella Movement took hold in 2014, many Hong Kongers were sympathetic to the protesters, though they were careful about expressing support. In homes and offices, many people put stickers with movement slogans inside their books, even as they stayed quiet in public. People started creating different personas on Facebook, thinking that it would be safer to express political views under a different name. When the Umbrella Movement ended, there was a sense of deflation. "It was quite disappointing," Lorraine recalled, "that after all those days, nothing happened."

She said a turning point in the latest protests came when commuters, including a group of protesters, were attacked by a pro-government mob in a railway station, the police clearly doing nothing to stop it. Suddenly, the uprising wasn't just against Beijing or the extradition law, it was about what some Hong Kongers were doing to their own people. "People trusted the police," she said, "but that trust was broken." During the entirety of the Umbrella Movement, the government fired fewer than one hundred rounds of tear gas into the crowds. In the current protests, they have used more than ten thousand rounds. It was this sense of persecution that had created a new sense of solidarity—for instance, the shop owners who would let protesters slip inside their doors to evade detention. Lorraine also suggested that the leaderless nature of the movement made a point beyond avoiding decapitation; having no leaders, she said, "contrasted with the centralized discourse of China." In this way, aspects of the identity formed in protest weren't just against Beijing; they represented Beijing's opposite.

It was striking that these somewhat less politically active people had seen the warning signs as cultural—a singer being trolled, a new curriculum in school, colleagues self-censoring. The amorphous protest movement encompassed the pent-up frustrations of everyone who had lived in a society that was being encroached upon, like an organism reshaping itself to resist a much larger predator coming into its realm, who can see a future coming inexorably into view. I asked what the Chinese wanted. "They want George Orwell's regime in their own space," Lorraine replied.

Job interviews now came with the question of whether the applicant would be willing to travel to the mainland. How strange, I thought, to be asked whether you'd travel to a part of your own country as part of your employment. Charles told me that the last time he was in China, he felt as if he was living in *1984*. "I didn't hate China," he said. He still found the people friendly. He still liked them. But he knew he didn't want to go back to the mainland.

Charles told me that some Hong Kongers were involved in nation building, though he was quick to add that this wasn't the same as independence. China might swallow up Hong Kong, but it was also possible that at some point China would spit it out—as Singapore broke off from Malaysia, he said hopefully. Drawing a different analogy for a less optimistic scenario, he saw a lesson from the Jewish people, wandering in exile, carrying with them the idea of a community with a shared language and culture. This was ultimately a battle between Chinese nationalism and Hong Kong localism, and young Hong Kongers could go to Britain, Europe, America, or Taiwan to preserve their sense of identity. Perhaps in the next several decades, the world would change, allowing them to come home. And perhaps, in that time, Hong Kongers could help change the world.

The understanding that the world would have to change in order for Hong Kong to be the place that its young people wanted it to be had become more prevalent. Protesters embraced the universal rights that China was violating and found solidarity with movements around the globe protesting everything from corruption to climate change, both inspiring and being inspired by other movements of young people. Charles said the protests that had been raging against inequality in Chile, literally on the other side of the planet, were closely followed and cheered on from Hong Kong. Later in 2020, when I spoke to protesters from Belarus standing up to a dictator, the Belarusians told me how surprised they were to get a flood of online messages of support from people they'd never met in Hong Kong. Even as the Hong Kong protest movement was about this particular localized identity, the movement was self-consciously globalizing, a vessel for opposing the generalized sense among the world's young people that the world they grew up in was being ravaged by authoritarianism, inequality, the abuse of technology, and the looming danger of climate change.

This sense of being connected to the broader trends at work in the world came naturally to Hong Kong, a place that had been shaped by larger forces beyond its control—from negotiations between colonial Britain and the Chinese Communist Party, to the way that the Party's successful hack of global capitalism increased its leverage over Hong Kong. Perhaps, with time, the tables would turn. Perhaps people would look back and see that the movement in Hong Kong failed to change Beijing's posture in the short term, but helped set something in motion in the wider world, something that could change those larger forces in the longer term.

"What's happening is shaping how I think about the future and a vision for myself," Lorraine told me. "Suddenly, all this is happening and my priorities are much clearer." For her, that meant studying international law and conflict studies—a mind being shaped for the world that lay ahead. Lorraine now harked back to a different slogan, this one from the student demonstrations of 1968 in Paris: *"Sous les paves, la plage!"*—"Under the paving stones, the beach!"—the idea that you need to tear something up to find something beautiful underneath. I asked her what the beach represented to her. "A better future," she responded, "though I will likely not see it in my lifetime."

20

Power Doesn't Give Up Without a Fight

WHEN YOU'RE A speechwriter, you notice when your boss ad-libs a line that wasn't in the text. Late in the 2008 campaign, as victory appeared increasingly within reach, Barack Obama started adding a line to the stump speech that he gave over and over again: "Power doesn't give up without a fight." It was a heady time, a period of American progressive political ascent unlike any in my lifetime (not least of all because the candidate was Black). The Obama campaign had become a cultural force complete with its own songs, slogans, and artwork. *Yes we can. We are the ones we've been waiting for. Hope.* And yet I realized that Obama's line "Power doesn't give up without a fight" was a warning that reflected the other side of that coin. It was a simple idea, but it also situated Obama—ironically, because he was about to be elected president—among the outsiders and underdogs who are usually repelled by established forces.

Even after we were ensconced in the White House, power never really did give up. The wealthy business elite never took to Obama, even though he didn't castigate or prosecute those who had caused the financial crisis. The military and foreign policy establishment never fully took to Obama, even though he refrained from exorcising all of the demons (and people) who led us into Iraq or participated in the use of torture. America's oil-rich allies in the Gulf never took to Obama, even though he continued to sell them weapons. The Republican Party relentlessly attacked and sought to undermine Obama, even though he came into office determined to work with them. Eight years later we got Trump, a reality star playing a billionaire, committed to cutting taxes for the wealthy, wrapping himself in the trappings of the military, rewarding the oil-rich allies, and tapping the darkest veins of the Republican Party's racism and jingoism through his brand of white identity politics. Don't tell me Trump isn't the establishment.

No, power does not give up without a fight. The power in Hong Kong is the Chinese Communist Party—an entity strong enough to point at a deer and say it is a horse. It is not going to give up without a fight.

On my last day in Hong Kong, that phrase banged around my head as I walked for miles, considering the future that awaited the protest movement. I took the same ferry over to Kowloon that I'd taken in 2002, the same breeze blowing in my face, an even more spectacular skyline receding as I crossed the water. If I could talk to that younger version of myself, how could I explain the two decades that had passed? Would I have believed that I was within six years of entering the inner sanctum of American political power? Would I have believed that the global economy would collapse at the same moment? Would I have believed that America would lose itself in the post-9/11 wars? Would I have laughed at the idea that Donald Trump—a punch line in the New York of my youth—would somehow become president? Would I have been able to picture a Hong Kong—and a world—that was becoming more like China than America?

On the Kowloon side, I started to notice all of the things that could disappear if the Party got its way. Campaign posters still lined many of the walkways, smiling young faces captioned by Chinese characters and English words: THE DEMOCRATIC PARTY. An entire building plastered with the words JESUS IS LORD in both languages, a reminder of the religious freedom that would be impossible on the mainland. Young people staring down at their phones, reading social media posts that could soon be blocked, filtered, or dangerous to access. Clusters of people around small shops offering a dizzying array of newspapers and magazines—certainly with an increasing bias in favor of the Party, but still a degree of choice that you couldn't find on the mainland.

It wasn't hard to imagine all of that gone. Most things would still appear the same: the skyline's reflection would still ripple in the water; the joggers would still be there getting in an evening run along the waterfront. In the last light of the day, children would still play on structures that looked no different from the ones my daughters enjoyed back home, a lab-tested combination of ladders, swings, monkey bars, and slides. Women would still hang clothes out to dry from the balconies of sprawling apartment complexes. Dumpling shops would still be filled with families out for an early Sunday dinner. Along the main thoroughfare, the finest luxury brands would still cater to the tastes of tourists from mainland China. As I walked, the entire city seemed to be built upward, toward the sky, to the point that it was shocking to encounter an empty plot of land—usually a holding space for the next development. This building spree would not change, either, if China had its way. The space would be filled, perhaps with more high-rises with undersized apartments where the pro-Beijing newspapers would be delivered for free, and the people who lived there would know better than to say—or think—certain things.

IT WAS HARD for me not to think about my experience in Shanghai while I was in Hong Kong, the sense of being in a fully developed metropolis where you also assumed that anything you did would be monitored. I told Wilson Leung about this feeling. "When you go to Shanghai," I said, "you see people around our age—thirty to forty-five—who are successful, who travel internationally, and it feels like they're trained not to think about politics, so they don't." I was trying to explain to him a question that had gnawed at me: Are they denied those freedoms, or do they not want them? "To me," I said, "the sense of having no privacy whatsoever is what's so off-putting. I think about it when I come here. Are they in my phone? Are they in my computer?"

Wilson understood what I was saying. "I think that's the fear of what we might see in the coming decades." He stopped and corrected himself. "Or coming years. The increasing use of technology to control what you can say before you say it."

This was the crux of the issue to me. Could a mixture of prosperity and nationalism, authoritarianism and technology, control how human beings think? Could people be highly educated and connected to the wider world, and yet so conditioned by their education, aspiration for wealth, and fear of those with power that they wouldn't want those things that Hong Kong still offered, albeit in shrinking portions: the right to speak your mind and choose your leaders, the space to worship Jesus or any other deity, the freedom to read whatever you want? Could the concept of truth be permanently altered to suit the Communist Party's objectives? Could the deer really become a horse?

It was hard to see how Hong Kong could resist that direction unless China itself changed. I asked Wilson about the split screen that was seen around the world that fall. On one side: Carrie Lam, Hong Kong's chief executive, sitting on a dais with Xi Jinping as they watched a massive military parade to mark China's National Day. On the other screen: black-clad protesters in Hong Kong being chased through the streets. To Wilson, what was happening in Hong Kong wasn't entirely new, even if some of the tactics were. "It's not very unusual," he said. "You often see throughout history these dominant powers, colonial powers, install a local government that basically acts as they want. Colonial governments. Or the Vichy government. Or the Japanese when they installed their puppet government in Manchuria."

From this perspective, the Chinese Communist Party was acting in line with the norms of history, the human condition that has prevailed throughout most of civilization on this planet. The center exerts control over the provinces. The strong control the weak. The Communist Party has been ruthlessly efficient in silencing voices that challenge its right to control, as great powers—including the

United States—have done before. That's why they visited me in the middle of the night in Shanghai to make it uncomfortable for us to visit the Dalai Lama. That's why they bully airlines to change "Taiwan" to "China" in the flight route options that you find online. That's why the flight jackets worn in the sequel to *Top Gun* no longer have the patch of the Taiwanese flag that Tom Cruise wore in the first *Top Gun*. That's why NBA games didn't run on Chinese television for the 2019–20 season after the general manager for the Houston Rockets sent a seven-word tweet from his phone.

When I asked Wilson what America should do about this development, he had a familiar list. Set a better democratic example. Impose sanctions on Chinese officials engaged in repression. Offer asylum to those threatened with arrest in Hong Kong. Work with allies to raise awareness and impose pressure on Beijing. Perhaps most important, Wilson argued that people in the United States should *care* more about these issues, and the actions of the U.S. government should reflect these concerns. He offered an example: "What we see from the UK, Australia, Canada—they issue these really cookie-cutter statements. I'm sure you could have done it in one minute." He laughed. "Basically, just take the previous one and change the name of the country. Call for both sides to show restraint. Everyone should de-escalate. Dialogue. Which China just ignores. It's a signal to them that you're not going to do anything."

I had written some of those statements, sitting at my computer in the basement of the West Wing, and then watched as U.S. allies put out versions of the same statement. On behalf of people in Egypt and Bahrain, Kyrgyzstan and Ukraine, Cote d'Ivoire and Kenya, Tibet and Hong Kong—places most Americans would be unable to find on a map. It was a genre, really, though I had believed the words I was writing—believed them without thinking hard enough about them, believed them because words like "de-escalate" and "dialogue" have a positive connotation and make complete sense from the safe distance of the White House Situation Room. Safe statements, in part because the sources of power in the United States—our military leaders, defense contractors, technology companies, business and banking communities—don't want to see the government rocking the boat too much.

It was, I realized again, the pageantry of caring about something that wasn't the top priority. There was always a good reason. Truman didn't want to go to war to save a Chinese Nationalist government that was falling to the Chinese Communists right after the end of World War II. Nixon wanted the Chinese to help us win the Cold War. Clinton wanted access to a vast Chinese market and lower prices for American consumers. In the first years of the Obama presidency, we couldn't recover from the financial crisis of America's own making without China; then we needed China to take the fight against climate change seriously by remaking their economy, developing clean energy, abandoning coal, spending money. Trump, in his trade war and later in his railing about the "China virus," prioritized not people but Chinese purchases of soybeans, reduction of our trade deficit, the domestic political benefit he could scare up at home. These objectives were divorced from values. They revolved instead around the language of power and money, a language understood by the Chinese Communist Party.

What mattered, I realized, wasn't so much our statements; they served a purpose in demonstrating that the most powerful nation in the world was watching, and reflexively defended certain values—even if tentatively. What mattered was how the context around those statements had changed—that we were no longer clearly the most powerful nation in the world, in part because the values reflected in those statements were receding. As with the Hong Kong protests, for the statements to matter again, the context around them would have to change.

OBAMA AND I had a running debate during his presidency. *Who makes history?* Individuals or movements? Gandhi or the Indian masses? King or those who marched with him? U.S. presidents or the bottom-up pressures that force them to respond? We found ourselves taking different sides of this debate at different times. Obama's view was that movements can provide the spark that initiates change and apply new forms of pressure on those in power; but he insisted that the moral vision and kinetic energy of movements ultimately has to be channeled into the accumulation of power and the reform of institutions—the business of political parties, laws, and programs. Movements that failed to do so risked chaos or the setbacks that come from the reprisals of those in power. My heart was shaded a bit more to movements as the drivers of change, though I was consistently proved wrong by the failures of the Arab Spring, Ukraine's descent into war, the quiet end to the Umbrella Movement. Perhaps, though, even these failed efforts were seeding even bigger movements to come. Hong Kong was a leaderless movement testing this proposition, but the success of that movement would depend on intangible factors that, I have come to realize, go beyond the outlines of our debate: the course of events yet to come, the actions of other world powers, wars yet to be fought, the fallout from a pandemic or changing climate, the strength or fragility of markets, the stories told by popular culture, the emergence of new charismatic leaders or mass movements in other places, the sum total of choices made by billions of people, the momentum of history.

To Bao Pu, the Hong Kong movement could not succeed because it wasn't big enough in its objectives. He was sympathetic to the protesters but wary of their focus. "This Hong Kong thing is about Hong Kong identity," he told me. He assessed that there were probably 3 million Hong Kongers who strongly identified with the movement. "That three million is younger, more educated, and basically—mostly—Western-educated. Not necessarily in the West, but in Hong Kong, through the school system, from what they read, from the songs they listen to, they have nothing to do with Chinese—the mainland Chinese experience of the same age group." I was surprised he wasn't more enthusiastic about what was happening around him in Hong

Kong. "They're going to lose, unless they convince the rest of the world that they're fighting for something bigger. Unless they embrace universal values. *We're going to fight authoritarianism. We're going to fight for the rule of law. We're going to fight for democracy. We're not for Hong Kong identity, we're for democracy for all China.* Unless they make that leap."

Like everyone, he had his own interests. In rejecting Hong Kong's identity politics, Bao Pu was in some way affirming his own focus on mainland China, but he was also making a larger point: that identity-based movements are going to be unable to bring about the scale of change necessary in a world moving rapidly in the wrong direction. "Identity politics is the driving force of the twenty-first century," he said, and not happily. "Identity politics is not based on universal values, because universal values should apply to all human beings. But specific identities are not. Identity is basically rooted in some kind of discrimination, because you have to define yourself versus others."

Wandering the contested yet eerily normal streets of Hong Kong, it occurred to me that Bao Pu was essentially right: In order to get the Chinese Communist Party to change its approach to Hong Kong, the movement would have to contribute to changing the wider world. Change how the world sees the precipice that has been reached. Change how the world evaluates the trade-offs—about what issues other governments prioritize in their relationship with China, about whether companies will keep getting steamrolled by the Chinese Communist Party, about whether individuals are willing to evolve in their own political activism. Change how the world looks at its own future. Make the world see the desperation people feel when they're about to be swallowed up by a nationalist, authoritarian superstate and let the world know that this could be their future as well; be that message in a bottle. To do that, hopefully the people going about their day around me on peaceful Hong Kong streets won't have to sacrifice themselves, inviting a Tiananmen-style crackdown on a city of millions of people in the hope that it could stir something in the rest of the world. But one thing was clear: In order for China to change, the direction of events in the world would have to change.

It was, in a way, selfish of people like me and Bao Pu to put the onus for changing the world upon the people of Hong Kong. They wanted to preserve their identity. Sure, that was tied up with concepts like democracy, liberalism, and the rule of law. But it was also tied to that other universal concept Wilson had talked about: *the desire to be left alone.* And over the coming decades, people were not going to be left alone unless they forged a solidarity with others who felt the same way, like different tributaries feeding into a larger whole, a building wave.

After a full day of walking, I staggered back to the ferry for the colder ride across darkened waters. What else had changed in those nearly two decades since I first took that ferry ride? All around me, people were looking down at smartphones containing an infinite amount of information, and yet it's not as if people had grown any smarter. Young Western couples took selfies with the Hong Kong skyline behind them in the same way that young Chinese couples took selfies on the Staten Island ferry with the Lower Manhattan skyline behind them. I would reach the other side and eat dinner at a dumpling shop that I found on Tripadvisor, where I would have a meal that is now as readily available in most major American cities as it is in Hong Kong. We live in a world that has erased distances—the distance that information can travel, the distances between the lived experiences, meals, and cultures of people in different countries. The Disney movies that my daughters watch are made as much for Chinese kids as for them, drained of democratic values. Technologies created in Silicon Valley become perfect tools of surveillance in Xinjiang. Along the way, the ideological conflicts of the last century were being subsumed by a blend of late-stage capitalism, older nationalism, and China's newer techno-authoritarianism. The only permanence was in the landscape around us and the human beings who moved within it, and the hope that they'd insist on a different direction of events. The ferry reached the dock and I joined an orderly procession of people walking onto the shore.

At the height of the COVID lockdown in the United States, China introduced a national security law that essentially eliminated the legal divisions between mainland China and Hong Kong. Wrapped in the guise of securitized goals like antiterrorism, the laws placed Hong Kong at the whims of their Beijing rulers. Opposition figures and democracy activists were detained. The repression and pandemic kept the street protests to a minimum. Power does not give up without a fight.

In July 2020, I got on a video call with John, Lorraine, and Charles, the young people who had been my guides through the mindset of Hong Kongers. They appeared shell-shocked, like people who had just been given a terrible diagnosis. The new laws took a sweeping view of what could be categorized as foreign interference in Hong Kong's affairs, and it felt eerie that the simple act of a video chat—now the daily rhythm of my lockdown life—had to respect certain vague legal boundaries, lest I be seen as interfering in Hong Kong's internal affairs.

John said some radical protesters in Hong Kong had welcomed the Chinese move as clarifying and more likely to invite greater international pressure on the government. But he also said that the more widespread mentality—the mentality of "the Johns, Lorraines, and Charleses"—was less confident. There was a sense among many in his cohort that people should continue to resist but should also seek an exit option. He described friends looking to move to Canada, Australia, and Britain. The United States, presumably, was not particularly open to Hong Kong migrants under Trump, despite all the anti-China rhetoric. "I think the determination to resist has increased, but there's also a deep sense of pragmatism. Whether this resistance succeeds or not is a different question. But we know that even if it succeeds, that's a long game, and between now and that time, things will get worse before they get better."

His comments reminded me of what Charles and Lorraine had said about enduring some form of exile to preserve their identity, hoping to return to a Hong Kong that has changed at some point in the future. They raised an uncomfortable question in my mind about how it feels not to be able to be yourself where you live—a feeling I had become familiar with in the United States on some days, without anywhere near the same degree of risk.

Lorraine compared her circumstances to the Harry Potter books she loved as a child. After reading the first few books, she had to stop. "I became so attached to the magical world there," she said, "but I could see what was coming. And it was like a big dark cloud looming over the horizon. I knew bad things would happen. And because I was so attached to the world of Harry Potter, I couldn't bear to read the ending. What is happening now often reminds me of Harry Potter. It is that sense of doom, the inevitable dark cloud over the horizon that is coming closer and closer." With Harry Potter, she said, she could refuse to read the last three books in the series to avoid the trauma. "But now I am actually in Hong Kong and it's like a nightmare that I can't wake up from."

Lorraine had endeared herself to me with her proclivity for proverb and parable, and she then turned to a more ancient source of perspective than Harry Potter. She cited the "four kalpas" of Buddhism, which encompass the phases of life—"forming, continuing, decaying, and disintegrating. Basically the cycle of all things." In these four stages, we become attached to the first two—when things form and continue. We often want to reject the last two—when things decay and there is a void. But each of us, in our own life, has to accept that we're going to live through each of these stages, and we shouldn't get attached to any one of them. "The meaning to me," she said, "is that I am very grateful that for the first thirty years of my life, I experienced the better stages in Hong Kong, even though I know the society didn't work for everybody. But for me—as middle class—I think things have worked well, and now I'm more prepared for the next thirty years or the next sixty years where things may go downhill in Hong Kong, when we are in the decaying phase and the emptiness phase. This is a cyclical view of history. But I think that the broader direction of history is still linear. I still think there will be some sort of progress in the longer run. It's just that in this linear progression, there will be these cycles going on, and I don't know when those cycles will end. Will I see something in my lifetime? I still think that in the very long run, things will improve. Maybe."

Maybe.

As she spoke, I remembered an email I sent to Obama on election night in 2016. Like Lorraine, I had been comforting myself with the idea that history moves in cycles but ultimately would move in a positive direction. *Progress doesn't move in a straight line,* I'd written in the middle of the night as I walked home on an empty Washington street. In the days and weeks after the election, Obama repeated a version of the line—"History doesn't move in a straight line, it zigs and zags"—in private and public, over and over again, as though it was a life raft amid the eddying currents of history. It reminded him, he said, of an image from Ralph Ellison of how a crab moves—forward, then backward, then side to side, then forward again.

John wasn't sure how he would respond to the current zig and zag. Perhaps he would emigrate. Perhaps he would leave the concerns of politics behind for a time. Perhaps he would get more involved in Hong Kong politics, even if it meant that he might be branded as part of the opposition. One thing was clear: Even if events had taken a bad turn, there was something invigorating about being in a place where history is happening, as in that Chinese saying about living through interesting times. "I think that part of me recognizes that this is a historic moment in world history, and I have the opportunity to define that chapter." The familiar tug. The desire to step into the currents of history and swim, rather than avoid them or be carried along by them.

This attitude did not come naturally to John. He was by disposition a moderate. But moderation was getting harder as the Chinese Communist Party suffocated Hong Kong identity. "The separation between politics, or what's political, and one's daily life is becoming increasingly blurry," he said. "Now you are forced into picking sides." He related that a taxi driver he'd had a few nights earlier had reflected the fear of this dynamic, the notion that taking any political stand would inevitably anger either the Chinese or the protesters. "I found this immensely interesting," John said. "His idea of apathy, of disengagement, is because of the polarization and the stakes. For those who think that not everything should be political, it's not so much choosing sides as trying to disengage from this suffocating environment."

At this point, John stepped out of the conversation about Hong Kong and asked me what I'd learned in reporting this book about how different authoritarian regimes acted. He was looking for some germ of insight that could be of use. I did my best to give him a brief summary. I described to him how they all made similar efforts to swallow institutions and lubricate their efforts with corruption. How they try to make politics so futile or toxic that people just succumb to apathy, like John's taxi driver. How Putin makes examples of people—killing or poisoning the occasional opposition figure as a message to others. How the Chinese Communist Party exhibited all of these characteristics but also used their economic and technological leverage to try to control not just Hong Kong but the behavior of countries like the United States and individuals as well. How all these leaders wrapped everything up in a nationalist bow to justify their control while their authoritarian repression became steadily more brazen.

Given that reality, John asked, what could be done to restore what he called "normalcy"—where these leaders showed restraint; where, implicitly, China didn't feel compelled to swallow up Hong Kong even if it didn't like Hong Kong's freedoms.

All I could do was speak for what America could do, and I walked him, and maybe myself, through some of the realizations I'd come to in writing this book. How over the last thirty years, American-led globalization, our post-9/11 fixation on national security, and our scaling up of technologies that we didn't fully understand had helped create the authoritarian dynamic that I'd just described. How America had been weakened by the Iraq War and the financial crisis and then gone through our own crisis of identity with Trump, which rendered our moral authority—those statements we issued—less powerful. How that made us, in many ways, a more "normal" country, as dysfunctional as anyone else—one that couldn't go around shaping events in other countries the way we once could. But perhaps that could open a new door to America. It could free us to set a more recognizable and relevant example if we got our act together as a multiethnic democracy. It could free us to use our voice more forcefully and honestly, unencumbered by the notion that we had to be restrained in order to solicit cooperation on other matters as a global hegemon. Perhaps, I said, this pandemic could be an inflection point for America and the world, just as I'd come to see that the 2008 financial crisis was an inflection point.

I found myself verbalizing both the depths that this book had led me to and the strange hope I found there—not just for America, but for the world: the possibility of a new beginning. "Everything blew back on us, right?" I said. "So after 2008, people are like, 'You guys invaded Iraq and then you got us all into this financial crisis, so screw you guys. Maybe the Chinese have this figured out better than you.'" John laughed. "'And maybe democracy as you guys practice it is not that great,'" I continued. "'And you've created this whole globalization thing, which doesn't seem to be working out.' Now some of this is going to blow back on China. And I don't just mean the pandemic—I mean everything. Be careful what you wish for, because if you're the top guy they're going to come for you." I talked about the fact that the global economy was headed into a recession, just as in 2008. I said that if I had my old job, only this time I was advising Xi, I'd advise him against what he was doing in Hong Kong. "You're inviting a backlash," I said, addressing a fictional Xi Jinping or whatever Chinese monitor might have been listening to our conversation. "You're inviting a backlash in Taiwan. You've already got a backlash in Hong Kong. You're going to get a backlash in Southeast Asia. These Belt and Road countries are getting tired of being pushed around."

I was off topic. These people, after all, were just a few days into a Chinese announcement that could transform their lives. Was I projecting my own search for hope onto their predicament?

"My own story says a lot about this," John said. "The fact that a young person like myself who has the means to emigrate but has never seriously considered it has now considered it for the first time. I think that says it all." With that statement, the reality of this one person's life, all my theorizing fell away.

"I feel that the international concern, the headlines, actually underestimate the impact," Charles said. "If this law truly happens in Hong Kong, I'd say the first two years, maybe nothing happens. But gradually, they will definitely put people into jail, go to court, and after a decade, it will be Shanghai."

Was that the future? Or did the resistance in Hong Kong suggest something different?

I'd looked to the people of Hong Kong for hope, but as Lorraine's dark cloud settled over the city, I came to see that what I'd learned from them was that their city's future depended upon the direction of events in the wider world more than on anything that happened there. For China, whatever window had opened around Tiananmen had been slammed shut, and the direction of history since 1989 had led in its own mercurial way to 2020 and its overlapping crises—the moments, as Lorraine also said, when things decay and then disintegrate to emptiness. It was also impossible to ignore that those thirty years encompassed a time when America had more global influence than any other nation—that this is the world we made, through our choices, through the unintended consequences of our actions, and through our own collective embrace of a blend of capitalism, militarism, and technology that somehow bred identity-based polarization. And yet people in Hong Kong still willingly shared their stories with me, and the fact that they would do so was inextricably tied to the fact of my own identity: *American*.

As Bao Pu said, identity politics has come to shape the twenty-first century as ideology did the twentieth. Of course, America still matters to the world because of our sheer size and strength, albeit diminished—the idea that we could fight a war over Taiwan, or sanction other countries, or organize others to stand up to repression. But more important, America matters because our identity is inherently contested. We, more than any other nation, contain multitudes, made up of every strand of humanity, encompassing all of the contradictions, hypocrisies, competitions, fears, and hopes in the stories that people tell themselves about who they are. America cannot arrest the direction of events in the world—the decay, as Lorraine said—simply through one election or even a new set of policies. More fundamentally, we need to figure out who we are—what it means to be American. Can we demonstrate that there is a way to think about ourselves that isn't tied just to the place we live, the tribe we belong to—to forge an identity that is universal so that, as the Hong Kongers told me, each of us can scale the peak in front of us, each in our own way? Isn't that what being American is supposed to be all about?

Looking at the last thirty years, I have learned how much the world could change in a relatively brief period of time, and how many turns that change could take that nobody could have imagined in 1989. But I take comfort in the realization that if the world could change like that, it can change again for the better. Movements can seed other movements. People can learn from their mistakes. Underdogs can win. That, too, is a belief that America has always represented to the world.

ON THAT TRIP with Obama in 2017, after we left Shanghai for New Delhi, the Dalai Lama was older and more frail than when I'd seen him last a few years earlier. He and Obama had a pleasant conversation. At the end, Obama—who rarely shows how the troubles at home have backed up on him—let his guard down. How does one retain hope, he asked, in a world so beset by ugliness, tribalism, and strongmen? I could tell he was genuinely searching. The Dalai Lama just smiled his beatific smile, grasped the sides of Obama's head with his two hands, and said, *You must remember that we are all one, and all capable of love.*

It felt, at the time, like an anodyne dodge from one of the few people on earth who is supposed to have all the answers. But then again, if you do believe that, if you do believe in a sense of common humanity, if you do believe there is irreducible dignity in the identity of every person, then you cannot succumb to a fatalism that human beings are destined to cast aside their own essential nature for a manufactured package of self-serving nationalism and state-controlled prosperity, numbed and monitored by technology. Nor can you restrict your concerns to your own narrow definition of identity. You have to begin from an uncompromising and unshakable belief: *This is not who we are.*

Part IV

WHO WE ARE: BEING AMERICAN

American history is longer, larger, more various, more beautiful, and more terrible than anything anyone has ever said about it.

—JAMES BALDWIN

21

Who We Are

IN LATE FEBRUARY 2020, I sat in Barack Obama's Washington office talking about what had gone so wrong in global politics. COVID-19 was gathering force but had not yet descended upon us like a hurricane. Lockdowns were weeks away. The economic, climate, and racial crises were still hidden underneath the surface brush of American life. The Trump impeachment had predictably passed as inconsequentially as a cable news segment. Obama was grinding away to finish his memoir, having methodically missed self-imposed deadlines.

Obama's office suite is understated in its representation of the figure who works there. A blend of dark, spare furnishings, patriotic photographs, and sports memorabilia exudes a self-contained male confidence. The Secret Service wears casual clothes in accord with Obama's wish for a casual postpresidency, so you have to look directly to see the earpiece on the guy lurking by the entrance. A large framed flag hangs by the couches where you wait for appointments; you have to squint at fine print to see that it was carried on the mission to kill Osama bin Laden. At the end of a long hallway you can see the framed image of the back of a man's head in a black-and-white photograph; you have to draw nearer to determine that it's Dr. Martin Luther King, Jr., speaking at the March on Washington. Look at the encased boxing gloves and you'll notice they're signed by Muhammad Ali. Like the Obama presidency, the radicalism is in the history of those who made it possible and those who hate that it was possible. Obama's own office is relatively modest, and you notice the absence of natural light, not offering a window to someone who might want to kill him.

Talking politics with Obama in the Trump years was a stratified experience, the surface familiarity overlaying the deeper stakes involved. Like the rest of us, on any given day Obama might send an email or text with a link expressing incredulity over this or that thing Trump had said or done—usually some offense to a foreign leader, nation, or region, or a particularly absurd debasement of the office of the presidency. I'd have to remind myself that we weren't just casual observers complaining for sport; these were leaders, nations, or regions that we'd worked with when Obama was president, and the office was something that he'd labored to occupy as scrupulously as he could, carrying the burden of being the first Black person to get there. Trump was a lightning rod, but focusing on him avoided plumbing the depths underneath, the currents that shaped our country. Obama's frustration was more likely to come out in dark humor. *Trump is for a lot of white people what O.J.'s acquittal was to a lot of Black folks—you know it's wrong, but it feels good.* For the next layer down, a shifting and familiar series of subjects could be analyzed that both made Trump possible and circled him like moths to a flame—a radicalized Republican Party, a trivialized news media, a selfish business elite, corrupt foreign leaders. The deeper, unspoken anger was tied up with the country itself, America's multitudes that we were—after all—a part of.

When he'd been president, Obama used a turn of phrase a lot when describing certain offenses, large or specific—widening economic inequality, for instance, or some act of bigotry. *This is not who we are,* he'd say, usually drawing applause for this or that rejection of America's demons, or a proposed policy fix that was blocked by Republicans. But the fact that someone like Trump could even get close to the most powerful office in the history of the world made plain a reality that didn't have to be named in conversation because it was so painfully obvious, hanging over the legacy of the Obama presidency like some toxic cloud: Maybe this *is* who we are.

As we talked, Obama asked me to summarize what I'd learned

in reporting this book. I gave him the same recap that I'd offered the Hong Kongers, including my creeping awareness of how much the world I was investigating was, in many ways, one of America's creation—a reflection of the type of hegemon we had been since the end of the Cold War; how the financial crisis had collapsed global confidence in America, opening the door wider for the nationalists and authoritarians to offer people a different form of belonging from the one we had represented for eight years. I saw him pause before responding, turning things over in his mind to find the right angle between countering or confirming what I'd said.

He began by offering an amendment to my focus on the 2008 financial crisis. "I think you need to recognize the transitory nature of the post–Cold War moment," he said. "There have been two artificial periods in our history when we were the dominant power in the world. The U.S. post–World War II, and post–Cold War." After World War II, he pointed out, we were both exhausted by the experience of war and afraid of the prospect of another one—thus beginning the "elongated reason cycle," that methodical effort to establish an international order of institutions, laws, and norms aimed at preventing another world war. There was no similar dynamic after the Cold War. "It was going to come to an end at some point," he said. "Even before the crisis, Chinese economic power was ascendant and Russia had figured out that it could be a mafia-authoritarian state; 2008 was an accelerant to that process."

We'd had a version of this conversation many times when he was in office, when we'd been trying to manage that reality, to slow down that acceleration, to shape what would emerge from the dusk of America's time as a hegemon. I pointed this out but emphasized the more disturbing reality that the world was basically a reflection of America's post–Cold War identity, our prioritization of money, post-9/11 militarism, and technology.

"The thing is," he said, "I basically agree with Bernie's critique of the system"—that American society had been wired for the benefit of a tiny minority of wealthy and largely white people, and that this was the result of policies from Reagan on, and of the flood of money into politics. "But there's something missing when Bernie talks about it," he added. "A spiritual component, a national identity that's not nationalist." He briefly ticked through the ways in which the other candidates had tried to fuse an adequate critique of what had gone wrong with an affirmative expression of national identity. Some, like Bernie Sanders and Elizabeth Warren, were closer on the critique. Others, like Joe Biden and Pete Buttigieg, were better at offering a vision of national unity without speaking as directly to the dislocation people felt. This was through no fault of their own; it wasn't an easy thing to do. "What Bobby Kennedy was doing," he said, searching for a historical analogy and landing on this brief 1968 campaign, "had that spiritual component."

The conversation was drifting into the angst that had characterized the entire pre-COVID presidential campaign—the gnawing sense that the best candidate would amalgamate the attributes of many of the people running: Biden's experience and core decency, Bernie's indictment of the system, Warren's remedies, Buttigieg's generational change, and so on. The fear that whoever we nominated would lose. Perhaps sensing the futility of this exercise, Obama stopped himself.

"I've been doing something recently with my close friends," he said. "I've been asking them a simple question: What gives you a sense of joy and meaning in life? And in what moments do you feel that?" He mentioned the last person he'd had this conversation with, one of his best friends from high school, who is now a plant manager at a yogurt factory. This guy described a long day in which he worked hard. At the end of the day, he was out in his yard by himself, having a drink and lighting the grill to cook dinner for his family. That's when everything stopped and this guy was alone with his contentment—a feeling of having been useful, connected to a community, and loved by the people he was preparing to feed. In that moment, he felt something about his life coalesce. "You see," Obama said, "politics has to lead people to that moment, to that *feeling*. And there's nothing about American politics today that does that."

I walked out into the Washington dusk, the air a tinge warmer than it was supposed to be in February. The streets were filled with people ignoring one another, glancing down at phones or hurrying to some evening function, with the occasional exception of a member of the city's growing homeless population—most Black, some post-9/11 veterans, some with the dead-eyed blend of world-weariness and generalized hostility that signaled an addict. I walked into a characterless chain bar south of Dupont Circle, the room hitting me at once with that American smell of climate control, craft beer, and Buffalo wing sauce. I glanced around the place at the blend of faces—different races and ethnicities, people who had come to D.C. to serve political agendas of every stripe, identifiable by the clothes they wore and whether their ties remained knotted. A grand experiment in self-determination still unfolding. I scanned the tall tables bolted to the floor looking for my friend as my mind remained stuck on Obama's remark. As I was enveloped by the noise of voices around me, I felt a wave of anxiety, the endpoint to which so much about American life leads us today.

ONCE IN MY life, I had a full panic attack. It was in 2006, around the time I was auditioning for a speechwriting gig with Mark Warner, the former governor of Virginia, who was preparing a run for president. I was driving alone back to D.C. late one Sunday night after a raucous weekend in New York. My mind was turning over the challenges of cracking into the presidential campaign speechwriting game, and I remember someone on the radio talking about Iraq and saying something like *The American people want to win in Iraq, the question is how badly the American people want to win*. I remember considering the hubris of the language soon to be required of me: *The American people don't like XX, the American people have always been XX, the American people want to win*. Who were these "American people"?

I preferred the phrase foreigners use: "the Americans." Neutral and menacing. Appropriately plural.

I passed from the New Jersey Turnpike into Delaware. I always chafed a bit at the fact that the stretch of I-95 that passes through Delaware to Maryland is less than twenty-five miles but you pay two tolls, the price of American infrastructure being shifted onto the backs of drivers. Floodlit billboards compete for your attention, along with a sprawling "Welcome Center" placed in the middle of the freeway to pull you into a dispiriting Sbarro or Cinnabon. Wilmington, a city I'd driven through hundreds of times but never visited, goes by quickly in the middle distance—a local economy tied to the credit card industry that pushed those of us paying tolls deeper into debt, the interplay of individual human desire and profit-driven capital markets that would soon sink the economy of the entire world. As people stopped writing letters and the mail became a catalog of faceless interests competing for your attention, my mailbox often contained envelopes with a Delaware return address.

My mind was turning over the usual reasons I might have felt drained and out of sorts. Drinking, smoking, not sleeping? A longing for the life I'd left behind in New York? Fear of the future? I started to feel a tingling in my left hand, which soon traveled up my arm and into my chest. This led to a growing anxiety that this was somehow linked to the slightly high blood pressure report I'd received in my last doctor's appointment. The familiarity of the drive made it seem possible to continue before stopping, to make it out of Delaware and into Maryland, beyond the halfway point of the drive, always measuring myself against a goal. I switched the radio to FM, which played some familiar eighties anthem. I switched it off. The silence was jarring. *You shouldn't be on the road.* My left hand gripped the wheel. The tingling intensified in my wrist. As I approached the tollbooth that signaled the end of Delaware, I started to swerve, both hands gripping the wheel. I imagined what happened to people who had heart attacks on the highway. I cruised through the toll—*EZ Pass Go!*—moving much slower than the other traffic and onto an off-ramp that curved, conveniently, into one of those ubiquitous American complexes: the gas station, the convenience store, the parking lot. I was sure something was wrong with my heart. I dialed 911 and mumbled my location. I'd never called 911 before. Within what seemed like a minute, an ambulance arrived, and the sight of it sent me spiraling further.

In retrospect, I see the absurdity of the situation. A couple of EMTs approached a bit cautiously and asked me how I felt. I walked in circles, stamping my feet, increasingly short of breath, a tightness in my chest. I was both relieved and outraged that these men didn't seem too concerned. I followed them to the ambulance. The EMTs looked my age, slightly bored, slowly preparing a blood pressure cuff. I looked up at the white roof of the ambulance and felt that the people were moving too slowly as I yelled, "I can't feel my hands!" They moved with only slightly greater urgency, saying something about an IV. I remember thinking, over and over, *I can't be dying, I'm only twenty-eight.* I remember not believing that, barely clinging to consciousness.

Events were a blur as I was admitted to a workmanlike hospital in Elkton, Maryland, lying on a gurney. A nurse with a Nigerian accent checked on me and gave me—literally—a pan to piss in. He was cheerful and upbeat, probably a doctor where he came from. He advised me to focus on exhaling. Then came the doctor, a youthful woman who informed me that I'd had a panic attack. *A panic attack?* That seemed like something reserved for hysterics and pill poppers from the 1950s; just that day, I'd attended a Mets game.

"Did you think you were going to die?" she asked me. She had cut right to the point and I was grateful.

"Yes," I said. "Yes, I did."

"That's a pretty scary thing."

"Yes. It is."

Her eyes were smiling.

"Are you on drugs?"

"No."

"Are you drunk?"

"No."

And so on.

"But I have high blood pressure," I offered.

"Your blood pressure is normal." She ticked through the potential triggers—anxiety, lack of sleep, stress, drinking, allergies, emotional distress—the familiar aspects of the human condition in early-twenty-first-century America.

"Have you had thoughts of harming yourself recently?" she asked.

"No," I said. She let the question hang there. It felt like the pivotal moment in some minidrama, the guy lying on a gurney under white lights, temporarily in the care of others who would have to make a judgment about whether to release him back into the world.

"Well," she said, "it's not uncommon. We get a couple of these every night." She told me to focus on exhaling; people make the mistake of trying to take too much air in, which makes things worse. I thought about all of these people, *a couple a night,* in thousands of emergency rooms across the country taking you in and turning you back into the yawning night: *the American people.*

And just like that, I was a guest overstaying his welcome. I walked out into the hallway to find an emergency room doing modest business. I had no way to get back to my car. The woman at reception told me, without empathy, that cabs stopped running at midnight. It was ten minutes after midnight. My agitation caught the attention of a young white guy in the waiting room. He wore oversized sweats with a Yankees hat on sideways and tattoos twisting up his arms. He volunteered to give me a ride. I followed him silently to a crummy Nissan parked outside, the backseat filled with power tools. He asked me what I was in for, like it was prison, and I said it was an allergic reaction. He told me he was in for his "fucked-up back." He worked construction and his supervisor wouldn't let him come to work until he got a note from a doctor telling him he was okay. Best time to come to the ER, he said, was midnight on a Sunday.

As he turned in to the gas station, I was filled with overwhelming gratitude for everyone involved in this episode—from the 911 operator to the EMTs to the African nurse to the no-bullshit doctor to this tattooed guy next to me. I was grateful to be alive in Elkton, Maryland. *What a name:* Elkton. My car was sitting, not in a parking spot, but next to the gas pump. I stepped out into the darkness and, not knowing what else to do, filled the car with gas.

LOOKING BACK, I think a part of my twenty-eight-year-old self had some cosmic instinct. I sensed that I was barreling down that dark highway from one life into another. Away from the New York City I loved and the people there. Deeper into the world of Washington, D.C., where I never felt entirely at ease amid the valedictorians and student body presidents. Deeper into the business of politics that seemed to require everyone to compromise the reasons that had motivated them to get into it in the first place, a world tinged with duplicity and dishonesty. This was the height of the Iraq War, after all.

Within a year, Obama offered an off-ramp from that feeling. After I went to work for him, the rhetorical flourishes and appeals to American identity no longer felt dishonest. Instead, they felt like a noble entry into the redemptive story of American self-improvement. The campaign office hummed with the energy of a few dozen young people who were dissatisfied with all the other choices and committed to the one we'd made. The story we were telling was about an America where historical sins were confronted, people's differences were celebrated, and there was a positive momentum to the American project. As speechwriters, we felt an ease and—yes—a hubris in expropriating American political language for the purpose of electing a singularly talented Black politician. I'd grab a phrase from the American air and drop it into the text of some Obama speech—*We are the ones we've been waiting for*—and it would interact with the culture as if through osmosis.

The villains in the story were all obviously discredited to our youthful minds—the warmongers, torturers, racists, climate deniers, special interests, and amoral wealthy who always tried to stand in the way of progress. The compromises to political reality—the occasional hawkish language on terrorism, for instance, or the critiques of capitalism that had to be carefully worded to avoid charges of socialism—felt incidental to the larger project. Facebook was a game-changing force for good that allowed enterprising young liberals to organize their own political communities. Hungary, Russia, and China were a million miles away, but on some level they would not be immune to the contagion of hope. There was a sense, as Obama seized the nomination and began his final sprint to the presidency, that we'd moved so fast and with such confidence that we'd caught the forces of entrenched power by surprise, like Jackie Robinson stealing home against the Yankees in the 1955 World Series. Even the financial crisis in the fall of 2008 felt like the universe affirming the rightness of change. This was the moment that Obama's politics led me to, a feeling of forward movement laced with inevitability: *Yes we can*.

And where was politics directing us by February 2020? Each morning I'd wake early and instinctively reach for my phone. I'd open the Twitter app and feel my body flush with a mix of anxiety and anger at whatever debate or outrage cycle I was consuming, a cacophony of noise conducted by an incompetent narcissist in the Oval Office. The media available throughout the day would keep you amped about whatever was most triggering in the nation's ceaseless political combat, steeling your sense of certainty no matter what your perspective. The rest of the world was rendered irrelevant—a solar system of distant planets that revolved around our own political dramas, secondary characters to our own self-obsessions. The leaders of Hungary, Russia, and China were finding solidarity with—or solace in—the brand of leadership in an Oval Office once occupied by men like FDR and Lincoln. The absurd wealth of the richest Americans was like a weight on the rest of the society, evident every time you ordered something on Amazon or logged on to Facebook. Algorithms populated your social media and email accounts with insistent demands for your money or attention tailor-made to be the logical extension of your past choices, your presumed obsessions, the anticipation of your wants and desires.

Still, this endless convenience of consumerism only seemed to highlight the impossibility of acquiring everything you needed, never mind what you wanted. Underneath it all was the gnawing sense that something about America itself was no longer sustainable. But the sum total of American experience seemed to be an insistent affirmation that opting out of this anxiety-inducing reality was an impossibility. *No you can't.*

The only respite for me was the experience of having two daughters, aged three and five, who were not cognizant of the circumstances of the world around them. My older daughter was just becoming aware of the fact that she was American. It was a knowledge that we'd first communicated to her so that she would understand why we were celebrating the Fourth of July; not to relate the history of the day, but to understand why we were watching a parade and eating cotton candy. It was further driven home for her each time she did one of her favorite puzzles in which each of the fifty states was an individual piece, represented by an image that spoke to some well-known and well-worn aspect of their identity: the Alamo in Texas, a covered wagon in Oregon, the Statue of Liberty in New York. In this orderly introduction to national identity, incongruous to the actual moment, each of the pieces fit neatly together into a coherent whole.

22

We Do Big Things

FOR SANDOR LEDERER, that first reveal of political consciousness was tied up with the sense of things changing—from the new products advertised on billboards to the new political parties debating issues on television. For Alexey Navalny, it was the idea of being the Soviet pioneer, citizen of the greatest nation on earth, only to have that feeling taken from him by West German army rations. For Hong Kongers, it was the blending of civic identity with a China that—they hoped—would evolve to become more like their open city. America lurked in the backdrop: the wellspring of the capitalism and democracy that came to Hungary; the hubristic victor that cast a shadow over a privatizing Russia; the global force that suggested that China's rising technology-fueled prosperity would be accompanied by an opening of Chinese society.

My own flickering awareness of being American was tied up with flashing lights and explosions—fireworks to mark the hundredth anniversary of the construction of the Brooklyn Bridge. I remember being a small boy on a promenade packed with people. I was terrified by the crack and boom, the disorienting sensory experience of being a child in an adult world, legs in every direction. But the bridge fascinated me. The feat of engineering that made no sense to a child. The stories from my mother about how they tested the bridge by marching elephants across it. The idea of progress tied up with technology in picture books that showed horses pulling carriages that evolved into cars and trucks. My father hoisting me onto his shoulders to get a better look. It was 1983 and I was five years old, but I sensed that the Brooklyn Bridge was tied up with the idea of America: *We do big things*.

A few years later, in 1986, I was back in the same spot for the same fireworks display marking the hundredth anniversary of the Statue of Liberty. A queen who beckoned the tired, poor, and huddled masses yearning to breathe free. My eight-year-old self assumed that those migrants—including my ancestors—had literally disembarked on the island where the statue stood. I marveled at the idea of crossing an ocean on a boat and then seeing both the Brooklyn Bridge and the Statue of Liberty announcing an undoubtedly bigger and better life. I remember a soundtrack of patriotic songs—from "America the Beautiful" to Lee Greenwood's "God Bless the U.S.A." All of this was tied up with the Reagan era that shaped my political consciousness, the movie star president whose genial certainty assured me that we were the good guys and the Commies were the bad guys. That's what the Statue of Liberty, in some essential way, represented. This was the story we told ourselves. I began to know it in my bones, believed in it deeply, and felt that I lived at the center of the world.

MY FAMILY'S STORY was an American mix of privilege and eccentricity. We lived in a prewar apartment building between Park and Madison avenues with mostly Latino doormen to save us the inconvenience of opening a door. These were the days before the really big money took over the city, though. My father was a partner at an antitrust law firm. My mother took care of us. She'd been a magna cum laude graduate and president of Bryn Mawr College, but her career trajectory as a woman met the 1970s end of being an assistant to a series of men. I was sent to a private all-boys school along with the sons of other lawyers and doctors (today, it would be the sons of hedge fund managers and investment bankers). The school dated back to 1628, a creation of the Dutch who governed what was then New Amsterdam, a piece of trivia that reinforced my connection to some mystical American thread. I wore the prep school uniform of jacket and tie, which assured that—in the rough-edged 1980s New York of street muggings—I had the occasional baseball cap stolen or was chased until I took refuge in a doorman building. The fact that it was almost always Black kids chasing white kids was part of another, unspoken, aspect of American reality; on some level, I just knew, we deserved it.

The eccentricity derived from my origins. My mother's family were quintessential New York Jews. They'd come over at different times from different places—Russia, Poland, and Germany, though no one claimed those nations as part of their heritage. They were Jews, mostly secular, and loved America with the ferocity of converts. They embarked on the generational ascent from the Lower East Side to Brooklyn to the Upper East Side. They joined the right synagogues and went to City College. My great-grandfather had the preposterously American name Daniel Webster Janover, and used to tip his hat to the rabbi when the sermon started and find a nearby park bench to replenish his spirit; when there were fundraising drives for Israel, he told the rabbi that he preferred to direct his charity to Americans. As a child, I didn't go to synagogue or Hebrew school like my friends. For me, being Jewish was tied up with shopping at Zabar's, learning about the Holocaust, and discovering Philip Roth. We observed the rituals of the occasional Jewish holiday—seders in Westport with heavily perfumed great-aunts, liberal politics, and a cacophony of gossip. As the occasionally youngest child, I'd sometimes ask the four questions: *Why is this night different from other nights?* The lesson I took was not religious but political: We got out in time and made it to the promised land.

My father's family came from Texas. As far as I knew, they'd lived there forever, though my grandmother's people were Germans who came over after the European revolutions of 1848 didn't work out. I was raised with stories of my grandfather's ancestors who'd fought with Sam Houston for Texas independence and been granted a parcel of dusty land as a reward. My grandparents had been schoolteachers before my grandfather settled into a lifetime job working on the Exxon refinery in Baytown—then a small town, now a suburb of Houston. My dad raised us with stories of his matriarchal grandmother, a mother of eight boys with names like Clyde and Mac, willing them through the Depression. Then stories of uncles who'd fought in Europe and the Pacific. As a boy, I'd visit the family farm in a tiny central Texas town called Pert. To a New Yorker, it was unimaginably quiet and vast. You'd open a creaky metal gate and follow a dirt road to a mobile home. The annual family reunions featured Methodist prayers, giant glasses of artificially sweetened iced tea, and shooting guns at beer cans. My father had grown up attending segregated Robert E. Lee High School, punched his ticket to Rice University, earned a law degree from the University of Texas, and moved north.

I was formed from these opposites. A Jewish mother from New York and a Christian father from Texas. A liberal Democratic mother who came of age revering the Kennedys and a conservative Republican father who revered Ronald Reagan. A woman of the sixties who dabbled in drugs and protest politics and a man of the fifties who loved Willie Nelson and long drives. An American love story in which each had disappointed their parents by marrying after meeting in Lyndon Johnson's Washington, breaking the unspoken promises of their identities: My mother was supposed to marry a Jewish doctor from New York and my father was supposed to marry a Texas debutante. They have the best marriage of anyone I know, decades of exploring new frontiers of identity in each other and in so doing becoming more alike. A melting pot of two.

Growing up, it wasn't hard to see the strain caused by this American story. Even as a child, I could sense how both sides of the extended family saw the arc of my parents' lives as communicating that they thought they were better than where they came from—my mother for marrying this WASP, my father for leaving Texas for the Upper East Side. During my teenage years, my mother became painfully estranged from her parents. The proxy for this rift was a dispute over a family business that made fillings for cakes. Inexplicably, there were endless lawsuits trying to claim my mother's shares, which hardly amounted to a fortune but carried the larger emotional weight of inheritance. My father drifted further from his Texas roots; the Jimmy he was in Texas became the James he was in New York. At the end of one visit to Baytown, as my teenage self pouted over a barbecue lunch, my kindly grandmother fixed me with smiling eyes and asked if I knew that my father once told a "fib"—he had promised, when he left Texas, that he'd come back. Even then, I knew that this remark was intended for his ears, not mine.

Out of this mix, my brother and I had a relatively happy upbringing that, despite our privilege, somehow placed a chip upon each of our shoulders. Perhaps because we had no clearly defined tribe to fall back upon, and because our parents had become exiles from their own tribes, we both carried a restless ambition—a desire to prove ourselves to some unseen audience, to validate the choices that our own parents had made, to do big things. To me, this explains the strangeness of the career heights we reached in our thirties, when he became the president of CBS News while I was working in the White House.

The fact that we both entered some form of public life is less surprising. In our heterogeneous household, America was the secular religion. Despite their differing perspectives (which my brother and I would end up mirroring, him leaning right while I leaned left), my parents were ferociously patriotic. It wasn't a flag-waving patriotism. It was a sense that America could offer people who might otherwise feel like outsiders a sense of belonging, a story within which to center themselves. We made pilgrimages to Philadelphia's Constitution Hall, George Washington's home at Mount Vernon, and the Alamo. The news was always on and we were expected to have opinions about it. We were raised to see baseball stadiums as cathedrals, rock concerts as rites of passage, blockbuster movies as communal sacraments, and the American literary canon as key to understanding ourselves. We honored the wartime heroics of distant family and the anti–Vietnam War protests of my mother and her friends. We heard the Lost Cause version of Confederate military greatness that was drilled into my father in school, and how my mother had memorized Lincoln's Gettysburg Address as a child. We learned how America had turned away Jews seeking refuge from Nazi Germany, and how Americans had liberated the camps. These contradictions were embedded within the American experiment.

Race was an occasional subject. I could tell my father carried a shame over aspects of his upbringing. His first friend had been Black, a little boy who drowned, but my young father hadn't attended the funeral. With pride, we heard how his family had resisted recruitment into the Klan, the "citizens councils" that sprang up across the South in the first part of the twentieth century; we heard stories of the eccentric uncle who welcomed my Jewish mother to Texas with a stiff drink out of the trunk of a car. My mother had been shaped by the civil rights movement and had a connection to Andrew Goodman, one of the Jewish boys who'd been killed in Mississippi. She'd urged us to read Baldwin, Ellison, and Wright—writers who opened a different window onto America, even as reading them as a white child of the 1980s reinforced an implicit perception of Black people as Other, an experience that could make me feel shame but that I couldn't fully understand. While racism was unequivocally cast as wrong, it was also something that was insidiously permanent in its presence. My father occasionally reminded me of this reality, citing the old truism that compared racism between North and South: in the South, they don't care how close Blacks get as long as they don't get too high in society; in the North, they don't care how high Blacks get as long as they don't get too close.

In retrospect, I see that we were a well-meaning white American family who unwittingly found a sense of selfish virtue in America's narrative of racial progress, which never actually solved structural problems. The secular sainthood of a Dr. Martin Luther King, Jr., or the courtroom heroics of Atticus Finch. It was a subject that we engaged from a position of a privilege that we didn't question. My world growing up was an enclave of Manhattan. I remember that I used to go with my father to park our car in a garage across the Fifty-ninth Street Bridge in Queens. For years, the parking attendant was a kindly older Black man named Booker whose world seemed to be within the confines of that garage—he was always there. He and my father struck up a New York friendship of brief sports conversations and family inquiries, deepened by the impression that Booker shared Southern roots. When Booker died, my father gave his family money for the tombstone. I remember feeling good about this gesture. I don't remember seriously considering how I could square my own sense of America with the factors that separated my family's life from Booker's, a man who worked every day of his life but couldn't afford his own tombstone. There but for the grace of God went I.

IN 1991, WHEN Operation Desert Storm began, my thirteen-year-old self wrote in a journal: "War. War is upon us." In my mind, I was like a British child in the Blitz, my life about to be connected to big and dramatic forces accompanied by a whiff of danger. Instead, the Gulf War was over within weeks.

The whole thing was like one of those blockbuster action movies I'd grown up watching, a concise series of images and special effects with an underlying message about a greater good. Here was Wolf Blitzer narrating green tracer fire like fireworks over Baghdad. Here was Stormin' Norman Schwarzkopf, a modern-day Patton in desert camouflage. Here was unflappable Colin Powell standing in front of maps, symbol of a hypercompetent military and of racial progress. Here were the noble Kuwaitis, liberated from the boot of oppression. And then, a few months later, here *I* was, a young American, watching our heroic troops march down the Canyon of Heroes for a ticker-tape parade just as the Mets had done after they won the '86 World Series.

In my patriotic frenzy, I felt a smug supremacy to the naysayers—the "no blood for oil" crowd, those who had predicted a desert Vietnam. Of course, there was the history that I did not yet see. The plain fact that oil interests *did* motivate our concern over the tiny desert kingdom of Kuwait, and would blind our nation to the looming danger of climate change. Or the fact that the liberated Kuwaitis lived not under a democratic government but under a king. Or the fact that after the quick war, Saddam slaughtered the Iraqi Shias and Kurds whom we had encouraged to rise up against his rule, hardening tensions among Iraq's sectarian groups in ways that would shape my own time in the White House. Or the fact that the stationing of troops in Saudi Arabia, the heart of the Islamic world that I knew nothing about, would trigger Osama bin Laden—a man who had received CIA support during the 1980s—to start a terrorist organization named al-Qaeda that would bring the war to my hometown, creating a peculiar set of circumstances that would lead America back into war in Iraq under the leadership of George H. W. Bush's son. Those were the shadows of things unseen. At the time, there was no reason not to trust the grandfatherly President Bush as he boasted of licking the Vietnam syndrome and building a new world order.

Hadn't that been the lesson of the dizzying array of events that had recently unfolded? The inevitability of history, observed from the comfort of my cocooned childhood. I watched it all on television. When Sandor Lederer's life was transformed by the fall of the Berlin Wall, my parents marveled at the sight of Berliners deconstructing this symbol that had shaped their lives; I saw it simply as the natural order of things, the good guys winning. When Alexey Navalny was watching grim-faced Soviet military men briefly depose the reformer Mikhail Gorbachev in a coup, I had little doubt that they would fail to stop the momentum of history, embodied by the bearish Boris Yeltsin on top of a tank. When Bao Pu was watching his friends get gunned down in Tiananmen Square, I assumed that the Chinese student standing in front of a tank would prevail. *The new world order.*

The 1990s were an anticlimactic Cold War epilogue. A victorious America struggled to figure out where to direct its energy, what it was all about. With the drama of ideological conflict and looming nuclear war lifted, politics shifted to smaller preoccupations like budget deficits, trade agreements, government spending, and the residue of the sixties—debates over draft dodging, abortion, the war on drugs, and hip-hop lyrics. The burgeoning Internet contributed to a sense that technology was the new frontier—the power of personal computing and the rising stock prices of dot-com companies replacing the wonder of going to the moon or the societal reach of businesses that actually built things. A succession of relatively insignificant cultural phenomena consumed national attention—from the O.J. trial to the grunge rock wave, from the death of Princess Diana to Bill Clinton's affair with an intern. The world at large seemed to present a series of loose ends to be tied up from the Balkans to the Middle East, a mop-up effort for the American hegemon. Hungary was safely in the democratic column. The Russians were privatizing their economy, which would inevitably make things better. The Chinese were opening things up, while their uglier authoritarian side was the subject of scolding efforts like the Tibetan Freedom Concert.

At home, my father's life was upended by the policies of the man he had revered. The Reagan-era gutting of antitrust laws put his firm out of business and him out of work, forcing him to scramble to assemble a law practice out of his accumulated knowledge and contacts while big corporations got bigger. This ultimately led him to work for a time on real estate transactions, helping to construct deals that made more money for other people than for him. His focus, like my mother's, remained on ensuring that my brother and I could have opportunities that exceeded his, the ceaseless momentum of the American Dream.

IN POLITICS, THE partisan combat grew bigger as the issues became smaller. The Gingrich Republicans presented themselves as in some civilizational struggle against a competent Clinton administration that accepted a conservative consensus around fiscal austerity, deregulation, free trade, and fighting crime—*The era of big government is over.* It was hard to tell what it was all about. My own politics took a strange journey through this turn-of-the-millennium landscape that can be best understood through two political campaigns that bookended my university years.

In the summer of 1997, after my freshman year in college, I worked on the reelection campaign of Rudy Giuliani. I was indulging a conservative contrarian streak that I'd cultivated against the dogma of my left-wing prep school. Giuliani, after all, was the guy who cleaned up New York City, wiping out crime while splitting the Democratic coalition through his courtship of labor unions—particularly cops and firefighters, the salt of the earth. For a time, I arrived at work early and put together the packet of relevant news stories that would go to the senior campaign staff. I attracted the attention of the communications director, a chain-smoking ex-reporter named Sunny Mindel who affectionately (I think) nicknamed me Little Shit. She set up a desk for me in her office and I got a running education from her alternatively bantering with and cursing out reporters on the phone.

I was put to work as a "tracker"—essentially, I would take the subway to wherever the Democratic candidate, Ruth Messinger, was doing an event. I'd linger in the gaggle of reporters and record her every utterance before taking the subway back to the corporate-style campaign office to transcribe her words in search of a gaffe. It was a campaign designed around the idea that Messinger was a danger to New York's renaissance, a woman who said that sex shops gave Times Square character. What I missed at the time is that the methodical corporate takeover of Times Square may have steamrolled the peep show joints that I'd sneaked into as a teenager, but it also brought with it the relentless pursuit of profits and the same kind of real estate dislocation that had motivated Sandor Lederer and Alexey Navalny half a world away: faceless moneyed interests remaking neighborhoods with no regard to the human beings who lived there.

For me, the bigger lesson of that campaign was the city I discovered. I'd follow Ruth Messinger to the South Bronx, deep Queens, and Staten Island, places I'd rarely visited before, places where people like Booker lived—a collage of bodegas, small parks, railroad bars, housing projects, ethnic food shops, dollar stores, pizza joints, promenades, baseball fields, public libraries, and Democratic clubs. New York was suddenly a diverse tapestry that extended beyond Manhattan, a city where people weren't particularly benefiting from the fact that Manhattan drivers were no longer inconvenienced by squeegee men trying to wash their windows at stoplights. In Giuliani's New York, the better off were less inconvenienced while others were shunted into the shadows of the rising city. By the time I returned to college, turning down an offer to stay in my job through Election Day, seeds of doubt had been planted about the politics of people like Giuliani. This transformation was completed for me when, the following summer, I was fired from a job at City Hall on the morning I was supposed to start work. Someone had discovered that I once got a summons from the New York City police department for urinating on Amsterdam Avenue. I was suddenly cast out, on the wrong side of Giuliani's idea of law and order.

Attending Rice University completed my leftward journey. It wasn't my schooling so much as my surroundings. Like New York, Houston had its share of alluring diversity and Texas eccentricity, but there was also an America I hadn't experienced before: the suffocating sameness of chain restaurants, the towering highway crosses of evangelical Christianity, the racial politics, the isolating reality of the garden-style apartment complexes where I lived. A growing downtown of glass office towers centered on the oil and gas industry, churning out the wealth that sustained the people filling their cars in the city that unfolded in characterless neighborhoods in the flat distance. Something about that America terrified me. It had a sedating quality: television and religion and sports wrapped around a job that made other people money.

Meanwhile, when I went home I saw New York continuing to change as well. Kids just a few years younger than me were being chauffeured around in SUVs that they summoned with cellphones. All this money was being created, but it wasn't at all clear to me what that money was creating. I studied ancient Greece and Rome at school and began to wonder what big things the American empire was building. What monuments and ideals were we creating that would be worthy of study thousands of years hence? Or were those all behind us in that century that spanned from the dedication of the Statue of Liberty to the end of the Cold War?

By 2001, I was back in New York politics, working for the City Council campaign of Diana Reyna, a dynamic young Dominican community organizer. The actual boss was a machine politician named Vito Lopez, a tall and bulky man with a comb-over who worked out of the storefront Democratic club in Bushwick, Brooklyn—one of those neighborhoods on the edge of being colonized by hipsters. Vito was an Italian blessed with a Latino name that allowed him to appeal to the borough's changing demographics. He understood intuitively the link between ethnic neighborhoods, affordable housing units, gentrification, and winning elections for state and city offices. He was obsessed with people showing him "respect," a topic he regularly discussed like a mob boss. If someone had crossed him, he'd talk about "sticking an arm out." A pragmatist, he endorsed Republican governor George Pataki in exchange for one favor or another. He was on his way to becoming the head of the Brooklyn Democratic Party—until his career was capsized by allegations of sexual harassment against his younger, female staff.

I loved that campaign. In my room in a shared apartment in Queens, I was a young graduate student writing short stories, working odd jobs, and getting a master's degree because I didn't know what else to do. My one problem: I was a writer without a subject, accumulating short stories about alienated men living in garden-style apartment complexes in Houston. I'd board the G train and make the ride to Bushwick. Then I'd walk the few blocks to the storefront Democratic club, listening to songs by Radiohead about alienated young men: *A heart that's full up like a landfill, a job that slowly kills you.* Inside, the one constant was usually Vito wearing an oversized and untucked shirt, barking instructions, working the landline, greeting visitors. My friend Karl Camillucci was the twenty-four-year-old campaign manager, and we'd take smoke breaks outside like hardened émigrés to the neighborhood. Diana's sisters came and went, along with a mix of local pols, union guys, precinct captains, the kind of people who could deliver votes to the number. Vito was a genius at counting votes, and I was assigned a rotating series of odd jobs. He'd figured out, for instance, that there was a growing Chinese population in the housing projects, so I would write a letter about the issues that concerned them. Vito had a guy who could translate it into Chinese, and he would slide it under every door that bore a Chinese name, an algorithm that lived in his head and his neighborhood contacts before the tech companies made data harvesting easy. At some point someone would make a run for canned beer and we'd sit there drinking deep into the night, a strange collage of New Yorkers.

I'd lived the two ends of American politics within the span of a few years: the Republican corporate-funded machine of the Giuliani juggernaut, weaponizing fear and grievances and promises of more cops being more aggressive on the streets, and the ethnic equation of the Democratic machine, tallying up a winning number of constituents based on ground-level appeals and bite-sized government programs that didn't alter the structure of things. On some level, I knew this.

Election Day was Tuesday, September 11, 2001—the only election day that mattered in Brooklyn, the Democratic primary. After voting in a Queens school for the local machine politician for mayor, Peter Vallone, I caught the G train to the Democratic club. Then I was deployed to a polling site on the Brooklyn waterfront, with a clear view of the World Trade Center.

Just under ten years later, I'd sit down in the White House with Barack Obama to write his speech announcing that we'd killed Osama bin Laden to avenge what I saw happen next. The point Obama wanted to end with, he said, was the idea that America could do whatever we set our mind to, that *we could do big things*. The previous decade had upended American life, reorienting our national purpose into a global war against a few thousand terrorists, a war that had taken us back into Iraq and further derailed any possible effort to address that creeping sense of alienation in American life, the arguments about small things, the dehumanizing blend of twenty-first-century capitalism and technology, the disregard for whatever was happening to people in places like Hungary and Russia and Hong Kong, never mind Bushwick or Houston.

As an aside, Obama mentioned to me that he really meant it—killing bin Laden was an incredibly complicated, precise, and difficult enterprise that took years of painstaking work. It was like putting a man on the moon. If only, he briefly lamented, we could devote that kind of effort to something bigger than killing someone.

23

Forever War

WHEN I PLAY back the tape of September 11, 2001, in my head, I see the shadows of everything to come—the unraveling of the American empire and our social fabric—in a few interactions.

I was loitering in front of a polling site near the Brooklyn waterfront in the minutes before the attack unfolded, handing out Diana Reyna palm cards and eyeing my counterpart from the rival Democratic machine, when a cop shooed the two of us down to the corner to get legal distance from the voting. My mind was on looming death. Our family dog was scheduled to be put down later that day.

In a matter of minutes, we were back in front of the polling site, staring at the smoke pouring out of the World Trade Center. The cop started to get updates on his radio, which he occasionally relayed to us, our only source of information because cellphones didn't work. A small plane had hit the tower, he told us. Perhaps it had taken off from one of New York's airports. The Fire Department was on the scene in huge numbers. For these brief minutes, I could sense that he (like the rest of us) did not know exactly what he was supposed to do—whether this event implicated him in any direct way, whether the election would still go forward, whether the appropriate thing was to stay at his post or abandon it. We stared at the smoke in silence. We all knew people in Lower Manhattan. Then we saw the second plane plow into the second tower. The cop's eyes opened wider. Soon he was on the way to his car. There'd been a "total recall" of the city's emergency workers. *Get in your car and head to*

Ground Zero. He was a young white guy, probably in his late twenties, handsome in the way cops are. I always wondered what happened to him.

In my mind, this cop is all the people we threw at 9/11—troops doing multiple tours, waving on a screen at halftime of the Super Bowl from Iraq or Afghanistan, wounded warriors with prosthetic limbs or vets returned to militarized police forces.

After the first tower collapsed, I walked away from the polling site. I wandered in no particular direction, with the vague idea that I'd find some store or restaurant with a working TV. An older man stopped me on the street and gestured in the direction of the fire. "This is sabotage," he explained, in a thick French accent. "Sabotage, sabotage," he kept saying, over and over again. I nodded in agreement before moving on, leaving him there, gesturing.

In my mind, this French guy is the rest of the world—trying to warn us against the overreaction they expected from America.

I walked to Bedford Avenue, the heart of hipster Williamsburg, which incubated that mix of detached irony and precise observation that helped shape the popular culture of the 2000s. I had helped friends move there over the last couple of years, unpacking station wagons and SUVs as if it was a second turn at college. I ran into Sarah Heller, a poet in my creative writing graduate program, a kind Jewish girl with an old soul and long black curly hair. She took me into her book-filled apartment where a few of us sat silently watching television together. When I got up to leave, she gave me a long hug and urged me to take care of myself, as if sensing the surreal journey my life was about to take.

In my mind, Sarah is liberal America—highly educated, isolated in our enclaves and groups, searching for meaning.

I wandered down Bedford. The street was full of people who'd come outside to be near one another, crowded in front of bars with names like the Turkey's Nest. People with hands over their mouths. People with dumbstruck looks on their faces. People in long, quiet embraces. Years later, we would have all been inside, glued to Facebook or Twitter, in numbed isolation. I noticed a large SUV parked illegally on the corner. A muscular white guy in a tight T-shirt stood menacingly in the driver's-side door, glaring at everyone and no one in particular. The radio was blasting Howard Stern, who was ranting about reported images of Palestinians celebrating in the streets. Stern's was the first voice I heard demanding vengeance.

In my mind, that guy in the truck is the American right wing, talk radio and Fox News, the momentum of negative impulses that would become less about fighting terrorists and more about rubbing it all in the face of Americans like me and Sarah Heller until it reached its logical expression in the person of Donald J. Trump.

I walked across the bridge connecting Brooklyn to Queens, which offers a panoramic view of Manhattan. A man had set up a camera on a tripod, capturing images of the giant cloud of black smoke and office debris and human remains drifting in the clear blue sky. This was one of the last seismic events that took place before cellphone pictures, so I was forced to consider how the event looked through someone else's camera. It seemed ghoulish, photographing all that death, but I understood that the scene demanded attention. The horrible grandeur of it. The unuttered reality of what the image signified about where the world was headed. There was a before and there would be an after. This was the suspended present.

In my mind, that photographer is the American media, captured by the bigness of a story that offered the elemental aspects of fear and vengeance, good and evil, fetishizing images of terror without trying to understand it, looking away from other aspects of American life in search of something sensational.

Eventually, I found a subway that could take me out to my Queens apartment. The subway car was half full of people riding in silence. A man who appeared to be of Arab descent sat with his legs wide apart, head in hands, overcome by emotion. Nobody sat in the row of spaces on either side of him. He seemed to know that his life in America was about to be transformed. Years later, when I shared this anecdote publicly, my usual collection of right-wing trolls insisted that I'd made up this man, as if it was necessary to refute the obvious fact that someone could have anticipated that the story of 9/11 was anything other than the beginning of a glorious morality play of people donating blood before the nation went off to win a war.

In my mind, that man is every person who has become the Other in post-9/11 America: from Muslims falsely accused, to Sikhs beaten up, to refugees turned away, to Black people assaulted by police in repurposed armored vehicles, to families separated at our southern border.

IN THE SPRING of 2019, I taught a class in presidential speechwriting and U.S. foreign policy at UCLA. One of the speeches we studied was George W. Bush's address to a joint session of Congress a few days after 9/11, in which he seized control of American politics and—for a time—global events. In it, he defined the heroes and villains of our new epoch. On one side: first responders, Rudy Giuliani, the members of Congress who sang "God Bless America," faithful Tony Blair, the soon-to-be-created Department of Homeland Security, the law enforcement personnel and intelligence professionals who would be handed the authorities of the PATRIOT Act, the military preparing to once again fight and win wars, a great nation stirred to action. On the other side: al-Qaeda, a name most Americans were hearing for the first time. "Why do they hate us?" he declared. "They hate what we see right here in this chamber—a democratically elected government."

It was reassuring to have this unfathomable event framed in a way that fit neatly into the American narrative that I'd grown up with, a framing that had little to do with the terrorists and everything to do with us. "Our War on Terror begins with al-Qaeda, but it does not end there," he said. "It will not end until every terrorist group of global reach has been found, stopped, and defeated." America had a new national purpose, on a par with the Cold War—another generational effort to make the world safe for democracy. It was a uniquely effective piece of presidential rhetoric, explaining this horrible thing that had happened in terms that Americans understood intuitively and offering reassurance that the attacks were merely the preface to a story of inevitable triumph. It pointed the nation in a new direction and led inexorably to action.

But the narrative was false. The terrorists hated not so much our government as their own. They hated us for supporting those governments through our foreign and military policies. Defeating every terrorist group of global reach was an impossibility, a recipe for forever war.

My students were just a couple of years younger than I'd been when I was roused by 9/11 and that speech. They responded to these words as if they were from another planet. Had the United States really made its entire national purpose a war against a group of terrorists? From the distance of 2019, it seemed an unfathomable error. I asked them to list what they believed were the most pressing issues facing the country, writing them out on a chalkboard. Climate change topped the list. Economic inequality, structural racism, student debt, education, automation, and a host of other issues filled it out.

Not a single student mentioned terrorism.

PICK A COUNTRY where the War on Terror traveled. Let's say Yemen.

In government, I became familiar with the intricate ways that America learned to kill people in many countries in the decade after 9/11. Cold precision. Pick someone out of the harsh desert and take him out. A vehicle, a camp, some mud-walled compound. All of the intercepted phone calls, data, interrogations, intelligence sources, and patient analysis that led to a missile descending from the endless sky. Another terrorist crossed off a list, to be replaced by another.

The terrorist plots were real, even if their ambitions fell short of the scale of 9/11. Sometimes it was hard to tell whether an attack was actually the responsibility of a terrorist organization, or simply the action of an angry, grievance-fueled individual like the mass shootings that were increasingly common. In 2009, a U.S. Army psychiatrist killed several soldiers at Fort Hood, motivated in part by sermons he'd viewed online by a Yemeni American, Anwar al-Awlaki. Then, more concretely directed by a foreign terrorist organization, a young Nigerian boarded a plane with explosives in his underwear on Christmas Day. No one was harmed. The next year, a printing cartridge filled with explosives was loaded onto a cargo plane, only to be detected and intercepted, thanks to a tip from Saudi intelligence. Both of these failed plots had their point of origin in Yemen, directed in part by Awlaki.

No one was killed in the Christmas Day or printer cartridge plots, but they seemed to spark more political hysteria than the shooting at Fort Hood. Perhaps the shooting fit a more recognizable American scenario, the lone man with a gun. By contrast, there was zero tolerance for even failed attacks if they were elaborate in nature. The news media was comfortable in the cycle of fear, outrage, calls for vengeance, charges from Sunday-show tough guys like Lindsey Graham that the Democratic president was in some unspecified way "weak." Hours of on-air analysts warning hyperbolically of death on a scale that would account for a single day's emergency room toll during COVID-19. Eventually, death would come to Anwar al-Awlaki when a vehicle exploded in the Yemeni desert, destroyed by an American drone.

Al-Qaeda in the Arabian Peninsula. That's what the subsidiary was called. They had an online publication entitled *Inspire*. Published in English, it was a collage of grievances and pro-tips on terrorism. Articles about the American enemy, how-to pieces for making homemade bombs, second-rate religious instruction. I'd sit in endless Situation Room meetings where people would debate options for what to do about this. Could we block its publication? Did we need to refute its arguments? Did we need our own magazine? The use of English was alarming because it was intended to motivate Americans to commit acts of terrorism, but I suspected that English had another purpose as well. The magazine's creators surely knew they had a wide readership in the U.S. government and intelligence community. It was a form of trolling. Samir Khan, the publisher of *Inspire*, wrote, "I am proud to be a traitor to America." Khan himself was killed along with Awlaki. Killing people in Yemen could at times be necessary to protect American lives. But it was also easier than efforts to change gun laws in the United States, which would have saved exponentially more American lives, but which couldn't get through the U.S. Congress. It was also easier than addressing the reality, which extended beyond what any government could do, that too many American men of all ethnicities and religious backgrounds were becoming vulnerable to radicalization: men living in isolation and fear, numbed by unattainable wealth and omnipresent social media that affirmed your grievances. Far more Americans would be killed in the decade from 2010 to 2020 by white Christian Americans with guns motivated by that information flow than would be killed by Muslims.

Throughout Obama's time in office, America's military engagement in Yemen steadily escalated, a smaller war amid America's larger endeavors in Iraq and Afghanistan. I remember one cruise missile strike targeting what were apparently terrorist training camps. Our military had the capacity to monitor air strikes through aerial imagery. One general spoke about the tiny images of people that could be seen fleeing the scene of the explosion. They were called "squirters." The word stuck in my head. Individuals being stripped of humanity, rendered into something analogous to the splattering of paint drops on a desert canvas, something to be subsequently cleaned up one way or another. What happens when a superpower devotes trillions of dollars to killing a certain number of people in multiple countries on the other side of the world? Human life itself is devalued.

There could always be a justification, some intelligence that suggested a danger to Americans at home, serving in embassies and consulates abroad, or stationed in the constellation of military outposts stretching from Iraq to Afghanistan. Intelligence that, if not acted upon, could serve as an indictment for inaction, negative media attention, political scandal in the aftermath of a terrorist attack that claimed lives, or even the ones that didn't. In the American mindset, there was also an enduring justification for our actions rooted in the horror of 9/11. But even that justification obscured the deeper reality that America had built a complex infrastructure in the 1980s to transfer weapons to the mujahideen fighting the Soviets in Afghanistan. That network of supply chains ran through the tribal regions of Pakistan, making use of Pakistani intelligence and Saudi money that facilitated everything from training camps to madrassas for austere religious education. Ronald Reagan welcomed the mujahideen to the White House as freedom fighters, men of God, comparing them to George Washington.

The Soviet Union ultimately buckled and collapsed in part because of the extent to which they'd been overstretched and humiliated in Afghanistan. America ascended to the position of the world's hegemon. Then we would go to war against the same infrastructure that we had built, including some of the same men that we had armed and trained, and others who were radicalized by the Saudi money that funded their rigid religious education and supported by the same Pakistani intelligence service that had been our partner in the 1980s. Drone strikes in those same Pakistani tribal regions. Counterinsurgency warfare against those same mujahideen in Afghanistan. Secondary wars in places like Yemen. Our effort in the 1980s had generated unintended consequences like the birth of al-Qaeda just as our post-9/11 wars have generated all manner of unintended consequences, including the creation of al-Qaeda in Iraq, which became ISIS. In this way, the forever war has actually been a forty-year enterprise at war with itself.

In 2015, Saudi Arabia—the birthplace of Osama bin Laden and fifteen of the 9/11 hijackers, the source of the oil money that fueled decades of radicalization around the world—went to war in Yemen. A Houthi sect that had long been a rival to the Saudis had seized control of the capital. The Houthis were aligned with Iran. The new Saudi defense minister and heir apparent to the throne, Mohamed bin Salman, wanted to send a message that he was an assertive character while using the war to consolidate his control over the kingdom's foreign policy. He was, according to some reports, thirty years old.

Tentatively at first, America participated, providing logistical and targeting support. The Saudis were, after all, our allies, and the machinery of our government was built to support them. Obama was ambivalent, but he was ultimately persuaded that by participating, we could be a moderating force on the Saudis. It was soon apparent that this wasn't the case, and this war would escalate when Donald Trump came to office, offering a full embrace of Mohamed bin Salman. Hundreds of thousands of people would be killed, displaced, put at risk of famine. Al-Qaeda in the Arabian Peninsula was fighting the same Houthi enemy as the Saudis were. So the United States, nearly two decades after 9/11, was fighting on the same side as al-Qaeda and Saudi Arabia in Yemen. Such was the logic of the forever war.

THE UNINTENDED CONSEQUENCES of our forever war go far beyond the creation of more terrorists and perpetuation of more war. This enterprise has also set a particular kind of example while defining America anew in the eyes of the world—an example that has been a gift to the forces of authoritarianism and nationalism, and an albatross around the neck of values that America is supposed to represent.

Ching Cheong, the Chinese journalist who was once imprisoned, compared the beginning of the War on Terror to that moment in the 1990s when the Chinese Communist Party embraced nationalism as a source of legitimacy and control. "The moment I could tell that the U.S. was going to be tied to a more nationalistic approach is the PATRIOT Act," he told me.

To people around the world, he said, the United States that many wanted to believe in was a pluralistic haven that embraced universal values, from the equal administration of justice to the sanctity of civil liberties. "But the PATRIOT Act itself violated the spirit of your

Founding Fathers," he argued. The American consul general in Hong Kong was unhappy when Ching Cheong shared this view in an interview at the time, but Ching Cheong refused to meet with a U.S. government representative. In his mind, America had already set a new nationalist, authoritarian course for itself.

The PATRIOT Act was one of many American laws and measures put in place after 9/11 under the guise of antiterrorism. Some of this infrastructure was surely necessary to prevent terrorist attacks going forward. But these measures set in motion sweeping powers—to conduct surveillance, to restrict immigration, to detain people without trial, to torture people in the custody of the American government, to kill people in other countries. Some of these excesses were curbed or reformed in the years that followed, and Americans could defend individual measures at a given time, as I often did in government—from the use of drone strikes to the surveillance of telecommunications. But the sum total of this apparatus remained a sprawling, securitized enterprise, and sent a signal to other nationalist, authoritarian leaders who were more than happy to draw the same conclusion as Ching Cheong. Those same powers could be used to restrict immigration, target political opposition, shut down civil society, control the media, and expand the power of the state, all under the guise of antiterrorism.

The securitization of society. The demonization of the Other. Far-reaching laws of social control branded as counterterrorism.

These would prove potent tools. Vladimir Putin had already been waging a brutal war in Chechnya before 9/11. But when he used security and antiterrorism laws to transform Russia into an authoritarian cabal where he controlled all aspects of Russian politics, he could nestle these measures under the wing of the American hegemon and its shared commitment to fighting a global War on Terror, while bristling at America's moral standing to criticize him.

Xi Jinping also embraced the American War on Terror as a template and a justification. The Chinese Communist Party built an infrastructure of mass surveillance that took the PATRIOT Act to the next logical step of making maximum use of all that reach into the lives of their citizens. In 2014, after Uighur attacks took dozens of lives in Xinjiang Province, China's media began to refer to "China's 9/11." Xi set in motion the crackdown that would lead to a million Uighurs being thrown in concentration camps by calling for a "struggle against terrorism, infiltration, and separatism." China, he said, should show "absolutely no mercy." According to secret documents that were leaked, Xi urged the Chinese Communist Party to learn from how America waged the War on Terror after the 9/11 attacks. The Chinese called their own effort the People's War on Terror.

Several Uighurs were held in the prison at Guantanamo Bay. None of them were found to pose a serious danger to the United States. Instead, they were among many people detained after 9/11 in Afghanistan largely for the crime of being there. After Obama took office, as he tried to close Gitmo, there was a plan to release a few Uighurs within the United States. It was necessary to show that we would do our part, as we were also urging many countries around the world to repatriate detainees who had been cleared for release, people who could not be convicted of any crime. It was also not safe for them to be sent home to China.

The proposal was met with political and media hysteria. Lindsey Graham and Joe Lieberman led this charge from the Senate, declaring jointly that the Uighurs "have radical religious views which make it difficult for them to assimilate into our population." The uproar led to legislation prohibiting the transfer of any Guantanamo detainees to the United States, even to supermax American prisons from which no human being has ever escaped. This made it impossible for Obama to close the prison at Guantanamo Bay. Today, the Chinese government uses essentially the same argument as Graham and Lieberman to justify genocide against the Uighurs. *They have radical religious views which make it difficult for them to assimilate into our population.*

Americans may find it uncomfortable to be compared to dictatorships that brutally kill their own people. But Americans also like to think of our country as the world's leader, a shining city on a hill that sets an example to the world. Why would we think it is okay for our country to kill people, torture people, and demonize immigrants and refugees, then be surprised when other countries emulate those actions, build upon them, or use them to justify their own repression? How would history have been different if America's response to 9/11 had not been framed as a global war, with the mass securitization and reorganization of our government at home and extrajudicial detentions of individuals and the invasion of Iraq abroad?

PICK ONE PERSON'S experience of the forever war: Mohamed Soltan.

In 2011, Mohamed was a twenty-three-year-old finishing up a degree at Ohio State. He'd grown up in Michigan and Kansas, sporadically interested in politics—an Egyptian American, but by his account more American than Egyptian because of the gulf in lived experience between the two countries. "For a long time," he told me, "I struggled between the Egyptian part of my identity and the American part of my identity." The struggle was tied to the absence of basic freedoms in Egypt, a country ruled by the iron fist of President Hosni Mubarak. Mubarak was a military man, the second-largest recipient of American assistance in the world on account of Egypt's peace treaty with Israel, a staunch ally of the Gulf monarchies Saudi Arabia and the United Arab Emirates. "I had this far-fetched dream," Mohamed said, "that someday the Egyptian side of my identity could enjoy the same freedoms and liberties as the American side. And that dream became more and more far-fetched until 2011 when I'm sitting there at Ohio State University watching the protests break out on my iPhone."

Mohamed flew to Egypt and joined the protesters in Cairo's Tahrir Square. He stayed for days, finding solidarity with other Egyptians who wanted their identity to be wedded to those same freedoms that Mohamed had lived in America. He was there when Mubarak stepped down in the face of the protests. He joined the chants—*Raise your head up high*—and for the first time he felt the American and Egyptian parts of his identity converging. February 11, 2011. It was the last time I felt a sense of unbridled idealism about the Middle East in the White House because I knew that this was a moment that signaled Obama was different from other presidents, different from the big names in the administration—Joe Biden, Hillary Clinton, Bob Gates—who wanted to back Mubarak. Ordinary people had toppled a dictator, backed by an American president, making use of American technology platforms like Twitter and Facebook for the purpose of mass mobilization.

Mohamed stayed in Cairo to be a part of the new Egypt and to care for his mother, who had cancer. Then things went wrong. The young people who'd protested lacked any political experience. The interim military government that was supposed to manage a transition to democracy cracked down on the secular activists, a familiar target and one that clarified the choice for the nation: the military or the Islamists. The Muslim Brotherhood emerged as the only viable opposition, sweeping to victory in the parliamentary and presidential elections. The new president, Mohamed Morsi, began to steer the country in an Islamist direction. The U.S. government, through muscle memory, was engaging with the military and intelligence contacts it knew best while trying to find ways to nudge the Brotherhood in a more pragmatic direction. Then the Saudis and Emiratis started pouring money into the country—paying protesters against the Morsi government, funding disinformation campaigns against the United States, casting America as a dangerous ally of the Islamists.

In July 2013, Morsi was ousted in a coup led by General Abdel Fattah el-Sisi. In one of the most demoralizing experiences of my time in government, Obama decided against calling it a coup, which would have put that assistance relationship at risk. Parts of the U.S. government had never been comfortable with Morsi anyway, even if Obama himself had welcomed his election and tried to work with him. The U.S. intelligence community doesn't like an upended status quo. The U.S. military didn't want a rift with Gulf Arab allies. The U.S. Congress was deferential to an increasingly autocratic Israeli government, which saw Muslim autocrats as preferable to and more predictable than the Muslim public. By the time of the coup, Obama himself seemed resigned to the reality of a hard world. In two short years, the tide had turned from popular mobilization to authoritarian mobilization, from revolution to counterrevolution. Even the technologies that had seemed so promising were reverse engineered and turned into means of disinformation and suppression.

Mohamed went back into the streets to protest. "I didn't mind if Morsi left through a democratic mechanism," he said. "But I definitely wanted it to be through a democratic mechanism and not a coup." He started talking to Western reporters. He wanted, he said, "to let them know, 'Hey, I'm this American kid who is here, I don't believe in this mumbo-jumbo sharia stuff, but the military coming back in this way is not right. This is against everything I've been raised to know.'" Mohamed speaks hurriedly, as if eager to get to the next point, perhaps—I couldn't help but think—the habit of a man who had been brutally imprisoned for a time, who once never knew if he could indulge in conversation again.

On August 14, 2013, Mohamed joined a mass demonstration in Cairo's Rabaa Square. The crowd was intent on staying in the square to protest the authoritarian turn of the new military government, repeating the tactics of Tahrir Square. This time there would be no restraint. The security forces were sent in to clear the square, and Mohamed was shot in the arm as he live-tweeted a crackdown that killed more than a thousand people. Eleven days later, he was arrested in his house. The Egyptian authorities took his American passport and used it to mock him—*You think this is going to save you, it's not.* Mohamed was taken to prison. He was beaten on his bullet wound. He asked to be taken to a doctor to operate on his arm. Instead, he was forced to lie on a dirty mat while a fellow inmate operated on him with pliers and a straight razor. There was no sterilization or anesthesia. Other prisoners had to hold him down.

He was held in an underground cell, unable to see sunlight. He was beaten with whips, batons, and belts. He did months in solitary confinement. He spent much of his time on hunger strikes, protesting unjust detention, seeking the attention of the wider world, reaffirming the power of nonviolent resistance that had drawn him to Egypt in the first place. He lost a hundred fifty pounds. He developed an embolism in his right lung. He was warned that he could die. He was wheeled into court to appear in front of judges who sentenced him to life in prison.

They tried to break him, to erase even his impulse for nonviolent resistance. They told him they were torturing his father, who had worked with the Brotherhood. Some days, the guards would slip razor blades under his cell door and tell him to cut vertically, not horizontally. *You can end it faster that way*, they'd say. They threw a terminal cancer patient into Mohamed's cell and left the man there to die. Once he did, they left his corpse there.

Even on his worst days, Mohamed held on to his belief in that story that had brought him back to Egypt in the first place, the idea that there are universal values and dignity in every human being. He believed that both the pathway of oppression and terrorist violence were dead ends, different sides of the same coin. His American upbringing had taught him that. The stability promised by Sisi was a fiction. The lure of violent opposition was a similar betrayal of his values. Yet his government was supporting a Sisi dictatorship that was clearly going to radicalize many young men who would succumb to the lure of violent opposition. "Tora prison is the same exact prison where the Islamic jihad movements gave birth to al-Qaeda, that grandfathered ISIS, those were the breeding grounds for those kinds of movements," he said, and he was right. Both al-Qaeda and ISIS have roots in the torture chambers of Egyptian prisons. Egyptian prisons. Saudi money. That's how we got al-Qaeda. "But guess what," Mohamed added, "back then in the sixties and seventies there were much better conditions than we have today and a lot less people in there."

While Mohamed was on a hunger strike, his jailors let ISIS recruiters in the prison, content to have their prisoners radicalized into the terrorists that the government claimed they were. "They were actively allowing ISIS recruiters to float around the prison, whether it is to recruit or just to walk around with this victorious air that their methodology of might makes right is the only one that the world understands or pays attention to, that these nonviolent means for change simply don't work, that world powers are going to stand by authoritarian regimes regardless of what's going to happen, that they will never be on the side of the people and that people have to take matters into their own hands."

This same story about the futility of nonviolent change was told by both the torturers of the Egyptian regime and ISIS. Both of these totalitarian systems need each other as enemies, to justify what they do.

At one point, an ISIS recruiter was put into Mohamed's cell and the door was locked. And so Mohamed Soltan, a kid from Ohio, found himself in the absurd, dystopian scenario of arguing with an ISIS recruiter who was enabled by an authoritarian regime that was ostensibly at war with ISIS, a regime that received billions of dollars in weapons from Mohamed's own American government based on the idea that it was an ally in the War on Terror. The two of them debated, there in the cell, whether Mohamed's hunger strike was futile. "My rebuttal to him was they're not all the same," he said, referring to the diversity of Americans. "It's not all the same. It's not that easy. It's not that simple." Mohamed told the ISIS recruiter about statements from American leaders—from the White House, from John McCain, from others—calling for his release. "What kept the balance of good and evil in my head was that this wasn't my existence, that there were good people who'd never met me and out of the goodness of their heart—their steadfast belief in values and principles—they advocated for me."

Mohamed faced down the ISIS recruiters and the Egyptian regime through fidelity to an insight that he had about America, and about human beings in general: "There's this perpetual cycle of good, just like there's a perpetual cycle of evil, so then I became more resilient." Statements of support from America that found their way to him helped water that seed and forestall the process of radicalization. "Rhetoric slows down that process because it allows people to say 'Not everyone is the same, there's good people out there, maybe we should be a little more patient.'"

Mohamed refused to give in to his jailers. "I knew they wanted to break me, and I was not going to allow that to happen." On May 30, 2015, he was finally released from prison and allowed to return to America. "All of that happened to me and I'm an *American citizen.* You can imagine what sixty thousand political prisoners in Egypt are going through right now just for daring to have the same dream that I had: the most basic universal right to self-determination, to a dignified life." As a condition of his release, he had to relinquish his Egyptian citizenship, a part of his identity ripped away.

The Egyptian government has a peace treaty with Israel. It is backed by the oil-rich Saudis. It casts itself as an ally in the War on Terror. In return, the United States provides those billions of dollars in arms that are actually payments to job-creating American defense contractors who then turn over the weapons to the Egyptian government. To America, all of those interests have been more significant than the interests of those sixty thousand prisoners, or the absurdity of that same Egyptian government's trying to radicalize their own opponents to create terrorists in order to justify those billions of dollars in assistance. Such is the logic of our forever war.

It is a logic tied to the reality that America's chief allies in the Middle East since 9/11 have become more authoritarian: from Saudi Arabia to Egypt, from Turkey to the United Arab Emirates. If I were a Muslim living in one of those countries, I would think that George W. Bush's stirring post-9/11 words could apply in reverse. What does America hate? It hates the idea of a democratic government in any of these countries. As an American, I find more hope in Mohamed's resistance than in Bush's words. He was more willing to put himself on the line for what America is supposed to be than America itself. How powerful that is; how hopeful.

EIGHT YEARS IN government taught me a lot about the fallacy of control. I would sit in Situation Room meetings that were predicated on the idea that America had control over certain world events. The idea that if we continued to provide weapons systems to a guy like Sisi, we could exert control over his actions. The idea that if we armed a certain proxy group in Syria, we could obtain some lever of influence and manipulate events inside a chaotic civil war like a mathematical equation. The idea that if we bombed a suspected terrorist hideout in Yemen, it would lead would-be terrorists in other countries to make different choices. The truth is that we controlled only our part of the transaction. If we provided weapons systems to a guy like Sisi, he would have those weapons. If we armed a certain proxy group in Syria, they would fight with those weapons. If we bombed a suspected terrorist hideout in Yemen, we could kill those terrorists. Obscured in those calculations was the wider impact of what we were doing. What example did it set for the world's governments and people if the United States gave billions of dollars' worth of weapons to an autocrat, armed proxy groups in a civil war, and killed people in other countries?

On one of my last days in the White House, I took a walk with Mohamed Soltan. We had struck up a friendship, and as I considered who I wanted to spend some of my final time in government with, I set aside an hour to meet with him. He'd been on something of an emotional roller coaster, and he wanted to channel his energy into pursuing structural change: He wanted to know how to reorient American policy away from the absurdity that put him in that prison cell with an ISIS recruiter. As we walked past the characterless eight-story office buildings of Pennsylvania Avenue, the law firms and lobbying shops that made money trying to influence the direction of government, we talked about the influence that Israel, Saudi Arabia, and the United Arab Emirates had on American policy. How they poured money into lobbying efforts, courtship of influential media, and the interests of powerful defense contractors who held sway on Capitol Hill and at the Pentagon. How the Republican Party had turned itself into a convenient domestic vessel for any hawkish, anti-Obama view that legitimized the pursuit of more war, more support for authoritarianism. More fundamentally, how they deftly aligned their interests with the post-9/11 American orientation that was hardwired in the direction of fear; how America had been primed to be influenced to believe that more force against the terrorists, more confrontation with Iran, was the only logical course.

Mohamed understood this mindset intuitively. He'd lived it. He referred to what I was talking about as a "hypersecuritized narrative." In my own experience, this narrative wasn't just flawed because of the unintended consequences it wrought. With Iran, we'd just successfully controlled something—Iran's nuclear program—by making a transaction in which Iran had to abide by restrictions on its nuclear program. But that effort ran counter to the post-9/11 American view of the world. So despite its measurable success, the Iran Deal proved to be far more controversial than the routinized aspects of the War on Terror, the cycle of conflict and American-supported autocracy, the tens of thousands of prisoners in Egypt ripening for radicalization, the proxy war between Saudi Arabia and Iran that was endangering millions of lives in Yemen.

How do you change this narrative, Mohamed wanted to know.

Part of it, I reasoned, was money. Investments needed to be made in supporting an alternative narrative with respect to our foreign policy, one that prioritized diplomacy and actual democracy. More fundamentally, we had to change something about ourselves. The hypersecuritized narrative, after all, wasn't just restricted to our foreign policy. It was the mindset where citizens had spent more than a decade taking their shoes off to board an airplane, where immigrants were regarded as security threats instead of potential contributors to society, where four American hostages murdered by ISIS received exponentially more media attention than a seismic shift in global influence toward China. An America where Donald Trump had been elected president. To change that narrative, we'd have to reckon with some truths about ourselves that run far deeper than any single foreign policy.

24

The Ocean Liner

OBAMA USED TO refer to the U.S. government as an ocean liner—a massive, lumbering structure that is hard to turn around once it's pointed in a certain direction, encumbered by the limitations imposed by Congress, the courts, state and local governments, media chatter, world events. This, he'd say, cut both ways. The genius of the system was that it limited the damage any one president could do. Trump, for instance, could rewrite Obama-era climate regulations, but those efforts would get tangled up in the courts; meanwhile, Trump couldn't unravel all the changes that had been made over the previous eight years at the state and local levels or in the private sector. But the other side of that coin was what made government frustrating: Even with two terms, it's hard to do more than point the ocean liner in a particular direction, hoping that some future government will reach the destination.

Eight years felt like a long time in the span of my relatively young life, but it was just a blip in time for the journey of the American ocean liner. After 9/11, Bush had pointed the ship in a new direction and generated an enormous amount of momentum. Wars launched, troops deployed, sweeping powers granted to the executive branch, vast new bureaucracies established—the Department of Homeland Security, the National Counter Terrorism Center, Immigration and Customs Enforcement—organizational charts erased and redrawn, trillions of dollars spent, the entire apparatus of the national security state focused on this new mission of fighting terrorism. More fundamentally, the construction of that hypersecuritized national narrative. "Our War on Terror begins with al-Qaeda, but it does not end there."

Despite the impersonal nature of the ocean liner, it takes human beings to make it run. I gravitated to the people lower down the chain of command, in their thirties, nearly all of whom had signed up in one capacity or another because of the attacks I witnessed in New York. The 9/11 generation. It was comforting to meet well-meaning people operating the machinery of the U.S. government even if we were all uncomfortable with some of the things that machinery did. The foreign service officer who'd been kidnapped in Colombia and nearly killed by mortar fire in Baghdad, who'd developed a deep affinity for the minority groups in Iraq caught in the crossfire of the sectarian war that America had unleashed—Christians, Shabaks, Yazidis. The intelligence analyst who'd once infiltrated white supremacist groups in the United States and showed me pictures of himself posing in the living room of a prominent white nationalist. The Special Forces soldier who never talked about his deployments and asked to be assigned to D.C. to finally be around his family and work on programs that benefited the young people from places where he'd participated in wars.

There was a particular blend of idealism and disillusionment among this 9/11 generation. It was interesting to me that these younger diplomats, soldiers, analysts, and intelligence operatives had all developed a deep skepticism about some of the tasks they'd been assigned. Nearly all of them believed that the Iraq War had been a mistake even though many of them had spent years of their lives contributing to it, and most knew someone (American or Iraqi) who'd died there. Those who had served overseas had developed an appreciation for America's limited capacity to shape events inside other countries, even as they also understood how large America loomed in the imaginations of foreign publics who experienced us as the unseen hand behind events, the shaper of markets, the provider of loans, the inventor of new technologies, the representatives of values we regularly betrayed, the narrator of what was happening in their lives.

In Washington, this 9/11 generation was often out of step with the more established sources of power—the cabinet secretaries, generals, prominent columnists, and senior members of Congress who were too far along in their own journeys, too evolved in their worldview, too invested in the series of decisions that America had made to question the fundamentals. Mostly men who'd supported the wars, ignored the risks, and couldn't change their minds because doing so would necessitate acknowledging how profoundly wrong they'd been. About, for instance, why we were engaged in a multitrillion-dollar global war against a constantly replenishing series of terrorist organizations that was eroding our democracy at home and sending all the wrong messages abroad. Many of these older people had been shaped by the end of the Cold War and the 1990s, when it did seem that America could do anything it wanted in the world, when it felt as if we had control.

Yet there was a persistent idealism among the 9/11 generation, a commitment to make whatever difference you could wherever you could. Resettling refugees who'd been displaced by America's wars. Negotiating a nuclear agreement with the Iranian government to avoid another war in the Middle East. Trying to catch up to the danger of climate change that was bearing down on us like a massive hurricane swelling off the coast. Negotiating an opening with Cuba to begin untangling sixty years of punishing sanctions and conflict with a small island nation. Or less prominent efforts to help individuals trapped in the stifling circumstances of the wider world. Programs to assist civil society in forgotten places. Initiatives to get assistance to populations made vulnerable by famine or disease, sometimes on the fringes of the places where we participated in wars. Advocacy to free people like Mohamed Soltan. America encompassed these contradictions, a force that broke things and tried to put them back together.

I had access to all manner of secrets for eight years, but the longer

I was in government, the less important that information became. Inhabiting a paper flow of terrorist plots, intercepted conversations among government officials, and clinical reports on the political stability of this or that country increasingly felt like a view of the world through a particular securitized window—one that tended to reinforce whatever it was that America was already doing. This wasn't the fault of those who gathered and analyzed the intelligence. It was the muscle memory created by the direction they'd been given for decades—budgets, reporting requirements to Congress, political pressures imposed on the executive branch. If you're asked to provide information on threats, you construct a narrative of threats.

I increasingly sought out foreign voices that could give us a clearer sense of ourselves. In Europe, I met civil society activists who were warning of creeping nationalism well before the refugee crisis of 2015, rooted in the post-financial-crisis austerity of the European Union. Russian writers like Maria Stepanova could explain to me how Vladimir Putin had weaponized information against his own opposition in ways that foreshadowed what he would do to us. In Laos, a group of young civic leaders took me to the top of a monument in the heart of their capital city, an Asianized version of the Arc de Triomphe befitting their French colonial heritage. In the distance, I saw a complex of office buildings rising above the surrounding structures. When I asked about it, one of the Lao said—with a tinge of anger—that it was a Chinese zone. You couldn't enter without a Chinese passport even though it was in the heart of Laos. An image that said more than an intelligence report could.

Despite my growing alarm about what America had done in the world, these warning signs cautioned against succumbing to the reflexive leftism that sees America as doomed to do *no* good in the world. If we were absent, then it would be only the Putins and Xis aiming to direct events. What would become of the European activists, the Russian writers, the Asians living in China's growing totalitarian shadow, Mohamed Soltan in an Egyptian prison cell, if America ceased to even try to be its better self?

Sometimes, though, it felt as if we were spending all of our time trying to clean up the messes left in the wake of our own ocean liner. Meanwhile, others around the world were riding the currents of global events: Orban demonizing immigrants, Russian trolls sowing social discord, Chinese officials going to work in neocolonial outposts.

OVER THE SPRING and summer of 2011, we began to have meetings in the Obama White House about how to bring the 9/11 era to a close. All U.S. troops were slated to be out of Iraq by the end of that year, and the drawdown of troops in Afghanistan had begun. Obama started to use the expression "the tide of war is receding," which sought to signal a direction without being definitive. We were, after all, still at war. What was interesting to me at the time is that the very use of that expression drew the ire of the American right and elements of the establishment. To suggest that these wars should end short of the victories that had been promised at the outset was to acknowledge that the whole enterprise had been a mistake of almost unimaginable proportions. It also threatened the many interests that wanted to see the 9/11 era perpetuated, from American defense contractors to Gulf monarchies to Republican hawks whose political identity was tied up in the passions generated by a mindset of war against "Radical Islam."

Obama's second term would become a tug-of-war between his desire to move beyond the 9/11 era and a constellation of forces—some real, some manufactured—attempting to pull him back. By 2016, the number of American troops in Iraq and Afghanistan fell to roughly 15,000 from the 150,000 who were there in 2009, but the infrastructure of the War on Terror remained hardwired into America's overseas footprint. The Iran Deal avoided another nuclear-armed nation or war in the Middle East, but the hyperbolic opposition at home contributed to the sense that we had to compensate for it by demonstrating our support for dissatisfied allies in Israel and Saudi Arabia. Climate change was made a leading priority in nearly all our foreign relations in order to get the Paris Agreement done, but the infrastructure of government supporting those efforts was minuscule compared to the machinery dedicated to fighting terrorists who posed far less danger to the planet. And then there were the tides that pulled us back into war. The rise of ISIS and the murder of four American hostages, which drew American troops back into Iraq. The pointless Saudi war in Yemen that could operate only with American support. These actions were most vociferously criticized not by those who thought we were doing too much, but rather by those who complained that we weren't doing enough.

These substantive debates were, in retrospect, the less important aspects of how 9/11 was evolving in the American mind. The American people had been promised military victory in the aftermath of the 9/11 attacks. In Bush's words in that speech to Congress, the terrorists "follow in the path of fascism, Nazism and totalitarianism. And they will follow that path all the way to where it ends in history's unmarked grave of lies." If you watched Fox News or consumed right-wing talk radio for most of the Bush years, you were always told we were on the brink of this victory, as surely as the Nazis were defeated and the Berlin Wall fell. But by the time the first decade after 9/11 reached a close, it was clear that America was not going to win these wars.

What happens when great powers fail to win wars? Inevitably there is a search for an enemy within, the force that stabbed the great power in the back or lacked resolve. This has been fertile ground for the emerging strongman, from Hitler after World War I to Putin after the loss of the Soviet Union. And so just as Obama was talking about the tide of war receding, the Republican Party was driving much of the political and media conversation into a toxic stew of issues that were simmered in the stock of post-9/11 fears and grievances. The charge that Muslims wanted to spread sharia law in America. Obama's refusal to declare war on "Radical Islam." The antipathy toward immigrants seeking asylum at our southern border. The ceaseless outrage over Benghazi, a word that came to signify everything from a lack of diplomatic security in Libya to Hillary Clinton's use of a private email server. This orientation spilled over into specious establishment debates seeking to pin the blame for the chaos wrought by America's War on Terror on Obama's incremental efforts to end it rather than the decision to begin it. If only we'd left ten thousand troops in Iraq after 2011, there would have been no ISIS. If only we'd kept sanctioning the Iranian government, they would have capitulated. If only we'd launched some cruise missiles at Syria after a chemical weapons attack, the sectarian Pandora's box of the Syrian civil war would have been shut. If only Obama more forcefully declared an unbridled American exceptionalism, the world would accept it.

These currents merged and ultimately snowballed into a vast Other that could be blamed for America's post-9/11 humiliations as surely as Putin blamed a constellation of domestic opponents for Russia's post-Soviet humiliation. This vast Other could be interchangeably comprised of a Black president, brown-skinned immigrants, Muslim refugees, and a shifting cast of targets. Generals like Michael Flynn and James Mattis, both of whom were fired by Obama, became symbols of the betrayed military men who could have defeated America's enemies if not for the weakness of liberal politicians. With the movement for Black lives and advocacy for immigrant rights, the promise of white supremacy itself was implicitly cast as being at risk in a country with changing demographics. Propaganda outlets like Fox drove the overarching narrative. Social media mainlined pieces of it relentlessly into people's news feeds. Trump himself paid lip service to ending the overseas wars but doubled down on the mindset of war—it was America First, and America's security obsession would be unleashed on this shifting assortment of villains at home.

Despite all of these headwinds, by the end of the Obama years, I believed that the ocean liner had been pointed in a new direction. The wars were winding down. Climate change was being embedded into our domestic and foreign policies. Diplomatic initiatives from Iran to Latin America to Asia were coming online. Obama's personal popularity was high, which indicated majority American support for a different orientation abroad and a more liberal culture at home. The 9/11 generation was poised to ascend to positions of greater influence, drawing on the lessons of the previous fifteen years. But while we had steered America in a different direction, we had been unable to repair structural damage to the ocean liner itself. We were moving in a better direction, but we were taking on water.

IN THE SECOND year of the Trump presidency, I attended a dinner of American hedge funders in Hong Kong. I was there as a guest speaker, to survey the usual assortment of global hot spots. A thematic question emerged from the group—was the "Pax Americana" over? There was a period of familiar cross-talk about whether Trump was a calamitous force unraveling the international order or merely an impolitic Republican politician advancing a conventional agenda. I kept interjecting that Trump was ushering in a new era—one of rising nationalist competition that could lead to war and unchecked climate change, to the implosion of American democracy and the accelerated rise of a China that would impose its own rules on the world. Finally, one of the men at the table interrupted with some frustration. He demanded a show of hands—how many around the table had voted for Trump, attracted by the promise of tax cuts and deregulation? After some hesitation, hand after hand went up, until I was looking at a majority of raised hands.

The tally surprised me. Sure, I understood the allure of tax cuts and deregulation to a group like that. But these were also people who clearly understood the dangers that Trump posed to American democracy and international order. The experience suggested that even that ambiguous term "Pax Americana" was subordinate to the profit motive that informed seemingly every aspect of the American machinery. I'd come to know the term as a shorthand for America's sprawling global influence, and how—on balance—the Pax Americana offered some stability amid political upheavals, some scaffolding around the private dramas of billions of individual lives. From the vantage point of these bankers, the Pax Americana protected their stake in international capital markets while allowing for enough risk—wars, coups, shifting energy markets, new technologies—so that they could place profitable bets on the direction of events. Trump was a bet. He'd make it easier for them to do their business and allow them to keep more of their winnings, but he was erratic and hired incompetent people—so much so that he might put the whole enterprise at risk. But it was a bet that enough Americans were willing to make, including those who knew better.

From the perspective of financial markets, I had just finished eight years in middle management, as a security official doing his small part to keep the profit-generating ocean liner moving. The debates of seemingly enormous consequence—about the conduct of wars, the nature of national identity, and the fates of many millions of human beings—were incidental to the broader enterprise of wealth being created. The War on Terror was fine for business, so long as oil-rich states like Iran and Saudi Arabia fought their wars through proxies instead of directly, so long as the terrorist attacks by radicalized individuals utilized car bombs instead of nuclear ones. The rise of China was good for business, so long as gains from access to Chinese money and markets outweighed losses from Chinese theft of intellectual property. Trump himself could be good for business, doing away with taxes and burdensome regulations. There was a logic, I supposed, to seeing the world through this narrow window; part of it was turning a blind eye to the populist radicalization of the American right that was necessary to elect someone who would continue to do something as unpopular as cutting more regulations and taxes for the wealthy.

IN THE SPRING of 2008, I had to write a speech for Obama about the economy. The purpose was to walk through the deregulation of the Clinton years to demonstrate that the structural problems in our economy had roots that predated the Bush administration's own spree of tax cuts and deregulation. The avuncular economist Austan Goolsbee walked me through a brief history, focusing on the Clinton-era repeal of the Glass-Steagall Act, which had regulated commercial banking separately from investment banking, an effort that was fueled by $300 million worth of lobbying and that facilitated more corporate mergers, more risky bets, and more wealth concentrated among those who could reap the benefits. The growth of hedge funds and nonbank financial companies had then allowed the wealthiest to find new ways to get wealthier through schemes that were unavailable to and not at all understood by the vast majority of Americans. The Bush tax cuts then transferred more than a trillion dollars to the already wealthy while creating deficits that Republican politicians could use to justify efforts to slash government spending. And of course the unregulated subprime mortgage lending that was about to drag the global economy over a cliff, in which banks bet money they didn't have by packaging mortgages that Americans couldn't afford.

As someone who worked primarily on national security, I remember being struck by how closely the excesses of American economic and fiscal policy paralleled the excesses in our foreign policy. As a country, we'd spent nearly thirty years methodically designing a system that allowed people who were already rich to get exponentially richer. To what end? For what purpose? How had those in power not stopped to question the myriad consequences? When the bottom fell out in 2008, it helped propel Obama into the White House, but it also ensured that his presidency would be dedicated to cleaning up another mess in the ocean liner's wake.

We lived a split-screen reality at the end of 2008—the explosion of hope that greeted Obama's election paired with the free fall of the American economy, charts with lines pointing straight down, job losses over half a million per month. It was as if the fates had aligned to present Obama with an impossible choice before he even set foot in the Oval Office: Let the economy collapse so it could be rebuilt differently, or rescue it while preserving its fundamentally unequal structure. Obama chose the latter. Between the bank bailout he inherited, the actions of the Federal Reserve, and the stimulus he passed, trillions of dollars were pumped into the American economy to slow and reverse the fall. This helped avert at home the more painful and extended reality of the crisis that gripped Europe and other parts of the world, beginning an unprecedented stretch of economic growth and job creation in the United States. But it also preserved the inequality multiplying like a virus within our system.

We would have only two years with Democratic control of Congress. During that time, Obama took frenetic action to point the ocean liner in a new direction. Obamacare to enlarge the social safety net and give more people access to health services. A package to save the American auto industry. Competent management of the bailout to recover the public's money. Stimulus funding to plug holes in infrastructure and seed clean energy industries. Increased regulation of Wall Street to avoid further crises. Consumer protections. It was the most active two years of progressive legislating since the Great Society, cast as radical socialism by a rabid Republican Party, but it didn't change the fundamental nature of the ocean liner, the gap between the first-class cabin and the accommodations for everyone else on board. In 2010, turbocharged by the unlimited money that Citizens United introduced into our politics and the unguided missile of racialized right-wing populism, Obama would lose his Democratic majority in the House—and with it any chance for structural reform.

As the ocean liner moved beyond the rough waters of the financial crisis, inequality was the most glaring aspect of the global economy that America itself had done more than anyone else to design. Around the world, leaders on the center left seemed incapable of solving it; leaders on the populist right at least offered an intoxicating cocktail of grievances and nationalism. If the whole game was rigged, then better to at least *feel* like a winner.

In the years that followed my meeting with the hedge funders in

Hong Kong, I found that people who worked in finance were often the ones who saw the risks in this money-centered dynamic most clearly. All this wealth, they'd say—it's just on computer screens, it doesn't exist in the world, not even in the promise of production and sales that corporations used to offer. Like the 9/11 generation I'd worked with in government, some of the younger people I met seemed conflicted about the system that they were a part of but incapable of imagining how to change it. Wake up with the markets. Move money around the screens. Look for a slight advantage here or there. Hit your marks. Create return for investors. Make a living in the world as it is.

A SENIOR ASSET manager I met in Asia seemed to have arrived at a similar set of conclusions to mine through his own perspective of watching all that wealth move around computer screens over the years, albeit from a very different vantage point. We kept in touch, and he summed up how he viewed the trajectory of the last thirty years.

There were, he said, three "dividends" after the end of the Cold War: a peace dividend, as the disciplining risk of nuclear war was lifted; an ideology dividend, as democratic capitalism vanquished Soviet Communism as a competitor; and a technology dividend, as the Internet expanded the boundaries of what was possible in the spread of commerce and information. Financial markets had gorged on these dividends, he noted, structurally blind to the inequality it was creating, the risks that were being taken, or the disruptions that lay on the horizon.

When the bottom fell out in 2008, the steps necessary to rescue the global economy made it impossible to overhaul the global economy because it required pumping an enormous amount of money into the hands of the very same people who had spent down those dividends. As if to reassure me that there was little that could have been done very differently during my time in government, he pointed to the example of "quantitative easing"—a monetary policy designed by the Federal Reserve and a practice that I'd occasionally have to defend at international summits.

To stave off a global collapse after 2008, central banks—particularly in the United States—pumped money into the organs of the global economy to keep the body from dying. Trillions of dollars were transferred in part to the same big banks (Goldman Sachs and the rest) that caused the crisis so that they could become a source of lending and investment. It worked. It helped prevent a depression and promote economic growth, but it also perpetuated the same structural flaws and inequities—the short-term pursuit of profit that ignores looming clouds on the horizon. Once again, there was an enormous amount of money sloshing around financial markets. Once again, the small portion of the population that was rich enough to have their wealth invested in markets also got richer, but for everyone else, the cost of everything from education to rent crept higher. The glass towers in New York went up, the old apartment buildings came down.

With so much money funneled into the economy, there was excess capital—money that had to go somewhere because it made no sense for it to sit still. A lot of new technologies and platforms became a natural destination for this excess capital, whether that money was pumped into Silicon Valley start-ups or China's burgeoning tech sector. New economies were developed to service those with means in ever-changing ways, from Uber to Amazon Prime. Unburdened by antitrust laws that had been gutted, the monopolistic technology companies swallowed up their competition and in-person retailers. This helped tech companies grow faster than our understanding of what their technologies would do. There was an acceleration of the ways that technology changed how we consumed information, destroying traditional news media and replacing them with ubiquitous social media that vacuumed up the advertising revenue that used to flow to newspapers, magazines, and television networks. There was an explosion of data available to the technology giants who had billions of users, giving a few companies a degree of power that used to be available only to nation-states. They now held a vast blueprint of immense value to anyone who wanted to sell something or shape how people thought—from advertisers to propagandists.

Meanwhile, people increasingly lived in self-contained bubbles of information designed to make them buy certain things or believe certain narratives. Swimming in profits, the tech companies moved to the next frontier, Artificial Intelligence, which will only accelerate the disruptions to industries, the displacement of workers, and the capacity to control what information reaches people—and what faceless corporations or authoritarian governments can know about them. The impact on human beings is almost impossible to wrap your mind around, but to this guy, the logic of how markets work suggests that the societal disruptions will only grow. Will China have the best model for the future, asserting more and more centralized control to manage disruption? Or can the United States find a way to manage the disruptions that markets are accelerating through our democracy? Or is it a problem without a solution, one that could culminate in war or revolution?

I REMEMBERED ONE of the last meetings I attended with Obama overseas. We were in Lima, Peru, for a summit of Asia Pacific nations less than three weeks after Trump's election. Before doing a town hall with a few hundred young people, Obama met briefly with Mark Zuckerberg. Facebook was a corporate partner of the summit we were attending. In the weeks since the U.S. election, it had become clear just how symbiotic Facebook's model was to Trump's victory. Cannibalizing traditional media that dealt in facts by posting unverified stories for free (and selling ads). Elevating conspiracy theories and partisan vitriol that traveled faster and farther through its algorithm (and selling ads). Serving as an open vessel for Russian disinformation that tore down Clinton and elevated Trump (and selling ads). Collecting massive amounts of users' data, which was in turn used to build a more efficient grievance-based campaign shaped around the likes and dislikes of users (and helping to elect Trump).

We entered the room with the normal pomp and circumstance. Surrounded by a phalanx of armed Secret Service agents and advance staffers, you felt a bit like gangsters strolling into a room—in this case, a fairly pedestrian gymnasium. But apart from Obama's entourage and cultural cachet, we were already yesterday. Zuckerberg stood somewhat sheepishly waiting for Obama alongside his aide, Joel Kaplan. He greeted Obama nervously, the two of them standing as Susan Rice and I looked on from a slight distance. It wasn't a formal meeting, just a chance to catch up on the margins of a global summit, in this case Obama's last.

Zuckerberg had made waves by saying that Facebook had had no impact on the election result and expressing no regret for it. I listened as he backtracked, slightly, in his comments to Obama, making vague commitments to try to understand what they could do better. In a kind of paternal way, Obama encouraged him to do so. Then he started to offer specific suggestions. Could Facebook do more to verify the sources of information on their platform? Even Wikipedia managed to have an open platform while flagging what information could be verified and what couldn't. As Obama talked, you could sense Zuckerberg and Kaplan reverting back to safer, more familiar ground: Zuckerberg spouting talking points about the openness of his platform and how it connected human beings, Kaplan trying to steer the conversation toward some future process they'd undertake internally—wary of regulation that was to me the only logical fix, while Obama prodded and offered to have his people share more information. It went on like that for a few minutes before both men had to get on with their schedules. "I hope he gets it," Obama remarked to us, walking away.

I looked back at Zuckerberg, who appeared relieved the exchange was over, awaiting the debrief with his staff, the well-compensated people who had every incentive to prevent him from questioning his own assumptions—the wildly out-of-date language about connecting people and an open Internet. This reflexively defensive guy was a thirty-four-year-old worth $44 billion, the world's fastest-growing billionaire and CEO of a company that was remaking the global economy, media, and politics for the worse, and he was accountable only on the basis of the wealth his company accumulated. There's something wrong with a society that produces that.

WHEN YOU LEAVE the White House, you have a lot of lunches. Because you haven't had lunch in eight years. Because you have no idea what to do with yourself. Because you need advice and people want to give it. In 2017, these lunches were set against the absurdist backdrop of the onset of the Trump presidency and his nascent efforts to take an ax to everything Obama had done. In these early months, I was just beginning to use whatever voice I had to rail against Trump and the forces that he represented. Nothing of great consequence—tweets, television appearances, podcasts, tiny pieces of real estate in the vast wasteland of American discourse.

Don't be too critical of Trump, I was advised. *You'll be taken less seriously by the shapers of conventional opinion. You'll narrow your options for future employment—in government or the private sector. You'll attract negative attention from the Republicans who control the White House and Congress and seem willing to use their power to punish their political opponents.* The fact that there was a logic to it made the advice more chilling. Even with a fascistic lunatic running the country, self-censorship was expected in how one talked about it.

Be critical of Obama, I was advised. *You need to demonstrate your independence, to reinvent yourself as something other than Obama's guy.* I was familiar with this formula, as it had been followed by some of my former colleagues, including all of Obama's former secretaries of defense. But why was it helpful to criticize my former boss when the fascist lunatic running the country was blaming him for everything? I knew the litany of points that people wanted me to hit. We should have gone to war in Syria. We should have kept those ten thousand troops in Iraq after 2011. We should have been more robust in confronting Putin in proxy wars from Syria to Ukraine. I did have my list of things we'd done wrong—for instance, supporting the Saudi-led war in Yemen, surging troops to Afghanistan, or failing to more forcefully confront the Republican Party's efforts to undermine democracy. But these, I knew, were not the criticisms that most of the people I was meeting with expected to hear. To appear more honest publicly, I was being advised to be dishonest.

I was struck, in those early Trump years, by the incentive structure of the American establishment, particularly in national security. If I wanted a future in government, I was better off keeping my head down and going to work for an investment bank or consulting company than having a podcast in which I heaped criticism on the Republican Party. Even though Trump was an existentially disruptive force, there was still a whole system set up for people to paint within a particular set of lines that had no relevance to an administration that respected no lines.

This whole dynamic was reinforced when Mohamed bin Salman traveled across the United States in early 2018. By that time, it was clear that he was a brutal dictator—imprisoning his own family at home, waging an increasingly out-of-control war in Yemen, briefly kidnapping the prime minister of Lebanon, lavishly supporting autocrats across the Middle East. Yet he was fully embraced—not just by Trump, but by every element of the American establishment (to his credit, not by Obama). He arrived to puff pieces from leading American columnists about how he was a reformer and a modernizer. Here he was at the New York Stock Exchange or having coffee with Mike Bloomberg. There he was meeting with bipartisan leaders in Congress. Here he was meeting with Big Tech executives in Silicon Valley. There he was meeting with the heads of Hollywood studios. He may have been a brutal dictator, but he had bottomless cash and supported the War on Terror. Those were America's preeminent interests. It's no wonder he felt a sense of impunity. A few months later, Jamal Khashoggi—an outspoken critic of Mohamed bin Salman and a journalist for *The Washington Post*—would be chopped up at the Saudi consulate in Istanbul.

Of course, there was also validity to all the advice I received. The more I moved into the lane of being yet another voice criticizing Trump, the more I slid into a chorus that predictably responded to his daily offerings of outrage, another anti-Trump grifter profiting off the reality show. It was also true that I could fall into the trap of becoming a mirror image of the Republicans I criticized, a tribal voice that assigns all blame to the other side. There *was* a legitimate need to wrestle with the errors of the Obama administration, particularly given that it ended in the Trump presidency. I was asked about this repeatedly and pointedly when my memoir came out, particularly in Europe, where journalists were trying to make sense of an America they thought they knew. Shouldn't Obama have bombed Syria after his "red line" was crossed on chemical weapons? Did Obama do enough to appeal to white working-class voters in West Virginia? I understood the impulse, but I had a hard time seeing how these arguments arrived at the core of what was at stake in America and the wider world. The white voters in West Virginia hadn't voted Democratic in decades, and by the end of the Obama presidency we literally couldn't penetrate the right-wing information ecosystem they lived in; if we'd gone into Syria, Trump would have used that against us to great effect.

I could see the structural issues that went unaddressed in the Obama administration, particularly on the three issues that loom so large throughout this book. We didn't change the fundamental nature of the American economy and the inequality it produces. We didn't do more to end a War on Terror that radicalized American foreign policy and politics. We couldn't control the accelerating disruptions emanating from social media platforms that were killing traditional media, spreading disinformation, and hermetically sealing Americans inside information ecosystems. But I found it hard to see what Obama could have done to achieve fundamental change—particularly in the absence of any Republican support after we lost control of Congress. He could steer the ocean liner, but he couldn't rebuild it.

More fundamentally, when it came to Trump and his election, the focus on Obama obscured—to me—the radicalization of the Republican Party that has been under way since the end of the Cold War and that accelerated under Obama, a party that could find common cause with the likes of Viktor Orban and Vladimir Putin by the end of our administration. Obama had not governed as a radical; indeed, the things I wish he might have done differently are mainly policies that would have been further to the left and further antagonizing to the right. This, to me, cast a harsh light on a fundamental truth, one that is as uncomfortable as it is obvious.

At one book event, I was politely grilled by an audience of Germans about Obama's responsibility for Trump. The red line and the West Virginia voter both made appearances. I reiterated that Obama came to office preaching national unity and bipartisanship. He extended olive branches far beyond the point when he had any reason to expect them to be accepted. His policies were more moderate than the progressive wing of the party wanted. He enjoyed broad support from a majority of Americans and would have beaten Trump if he could have run again.

Finally, as one man kept insisting that Obama should have done more to stop the Republican Party's drift in the direction of Trump, I snapped. My voice rising just a sliver, I said that the thing that was most triggering to many Americans, that helped fuel the Republican Party's radicalization into Trumpian excess, that rendered necessary structural change impossible, was the fact that Obama was Black. And there wasn't a damn thing he could do about that.

25

Fight the Smears

WHEN I WAS in my midtwenties, part of my job at the Wilson Center was to answer Lee Hamilton's mail. This mundane task introduced me to darker strains of American culture, conspiracy theories about everything from global governance to extraterrestrial visitations. During his thirty-four years in Congress, Hamilton had chaired the House Intelligence Committee and the Iran-Contra hearings, which made him the recipient of the occasionally eccentric piece of mail. Usually these dealt with some dark aspect of the Cold War. In letters that ran ten or twenty pages, often in meticulous handwritten script, people would detail the miseries of their own lives—jobs lost, marriages collapsed, children estranged—and connect them to a suspicion that they had been the subject of some extraordinary plot. The individual stepping into history. In the quiet boredom of a slow day, I'd find it tempting to go down a rabbit hole imagining one of these letters to be true, the early-twenty-first-century Internet already offering all manner of destinations to capture my American mind with investigations of the CIA's experimentation with mind control and LSD, explanations for Area 51, plots hatched by the secret societies of powerful men. The Internet was the perfect host for conspiracy theories, offering a bottomless well of distraction from the minutiae of life, a community of believers, explanations for events beyond our control. What religion used to do.

After the 9/11 Commission's work was done, I was an occasional contributor to an obscure foreign policy blog to which my email was linked. I almost never heard any feedback on my earnest musings, which tended to be concerned about wonky matters like NATO, nuclear weapons, and the efficacy of congressional oversight. Then I wrote a piece with a degree of snark about 9/11 conspiracy theorists, people who thought the attacks were an inside job. I linked to studies that debunked some of the more common allegations—that the World Trade Center had been dynamited, or that the Pentagon was hit with a missile instead of a plane. Within a few days, I received hundreds of email messages. People calling me a fascist, a murderer, a lackey for a shadowy cabal. I was shaken, having never before been the subject of that flavor of vitriol. It was my first personal experience with the sinister empowerment that the Internet provides, the way it offers meaning and mobilization to lost souls—something to believe in, someone to hate.

Early in the first Obama campaign, we confronted this swelling ecosystem through a phenomenon of forwarded emails and shared social media posts—missives that reached tens of thousands of people alleging that Obama was a secret Muslim, that he wasn't born in the United States, that his book had actually been authored by Bill Ayers, a member of the Weather Underground. It seemed a comical diversion at first, not unlike the strange letters I used to read in Lee Hamilton's office. But the reach of these missives was so extensive that we started to arm our large network of field organizers with talking points debunking them. We called the effort Fight the Smears—a nascent defense against what we assumed to be the fringes of American thought.

As Obama started to win primaries, the smears migrated to more mainstream platforms—right-wing websites, talk radio, and ultimately Fox News. It was as if the ascendance of a Black man up the ladder of American political power was an unthinkable phenomenon, something that couldn't be explained by the simple fact that he was a talented politician winning an election, something that suggested more sinister forces in play. Something else must have been afoot. By the time Sarah Palin was on the Republican ticket, these fringe views had become the subject of dog whistles and pronouncements by a major party candidate for vice president of the United States. Obama "pals around with terrorists." Obama's not a "real American."

In retrospect, it's possible to see the perfect storm that was building. The way the inexplicable nature of an Iraq War based on a false premise and the collapse of the financial system hinted at some darker explanation, the innate corruption of elites. The way that the election of Barack Hussein Obama was similarly unfathomable to whatever vast swath of the population had been raised to believe in the inferiority of those who were Black or of Muslim heritage. The way social media platforms prioritized the spread of content that captured people's attention and held it, organizing them into enclaves of the like-minded who believed they were discovering something essential and evil about whoever comprised the Other. The way this became mainstreamed in the American right wing after Obama's election, as Fox's leading prime time personality became Glenn Beck—a raving lunatic who offered nightly explanations of nefarious and un-American plots being hatched by the administration that I was serving. Death panels to render judgment on the elderly. Sharia law that would be imposed on unwitting American communities. Puppet masters like Soros pulling the strings.

During the Obama years, a virus of conspiracy theories was unleashed on the American populace that spread with the ruthless precision of a social media algorithm and the support of the country's leading conservative politicians, the heirs to American icons like Ronald Reagan, vested with the legitimacy of elected office. Conspiracy theories offered an explanation for the seeming unfairness of a system that was felt to be rigged. They offered belonging in a community of fellow believers who shared the same sense of discovery about the shocking truth behind things the elites don't want you to know. The identity of the nation itself was something that could only be defended against an ever-changing cast of villains through a baptism in a rising ocean of conspiracy theories.

Donald Trump immersed himself in this ocean, a deeply flawed human being vested with the credibility conferred by those essential American calling cards: He was rich and famous for being rich and famous. When he emerged as a leading voice on behalf of conspiracy theories about everything from Obama's birth certificate to his college transcripts, Trump was simply the avatar of an American ecosystem of often racist right-wing conspiracy theories that was already mutating in more extremist directions, a mirror image of the ecosystem that Putin was building in Russia. America seemed to have few antibodies to fight off this disease. Mainstream media couldn't resist Trump, offering him a microphone whenever he wanted it. Political reporters felt obligated to cover pseudoscandals simply because Republicans were talking about them.

In the first Obama campaign, I'd written speech after speech about the need for Americans to come together. This idea was embedded in the DNA of Obama's political ascent, the idea that we're not a collection of red states and blue states but rather a United States of America—a country where people of goodwill solve problems together. *We do big things*. But many of my frustrations during the Obama administration would be rooted in the impossibility of finding common ground with Republicans on everything from taxes to immigration to foreign policy, in ways that put a ceiling on our efforts to reduce inequality, welcome immigrants, or wind down wars. Despite the obvious racism of things like birtherism, the self-censorship of America's political and media elite rendered it impossible to find the language to describe what was happening. A relentless, well-funded effort to confine a large chunk of the country in an extremist and conspiracy-theory-based information ecosystem was normalized with lamentations about "political polarization." It was like the force of gravity—the idea that both political parties were to blame, or that everyone in politics was somehow responsible.

How strange it was, in the later Obama years, to write presidential speeches that had no chance of reaching some 40 percent of the country because the words would be filtered through the fun-house mirrors of the right-wing information ecosystem. How disconcerting it was to become a subject of a seemingly incalculable number of conspiracy theories myself—the Svengali behind a Benghazi cover-up or support for the Muslim Brotherhood and the Iranian regime. How doubly enraging it was to have so little capacity to stop the Russian attack on our 2016 election, only to be charged with pursuing a relentless campaign to fabricate that Russian attack and undermine the incoming Trump administration.

When Trump and his people moved into the same offices where I'd worked for eight years of my life, I wasn't just replaced by people who disagreed with me—I was replaced by people who sought to erase the very objective reality that I lived in and to use the massive machinery of the U.S. government to amplify a chorus of conspiracy theories that would once have existed only in the isolation of handwritten letters or forwarded emails.

WHEN I WANTED to escape from Washington, I'd make the ninety-minute drive to Harpers Ferry, West Virginia. The town is built on a hill that descends to the junction of the Potomac and Shenandoah rivers, ringed by mountains. A railroad bridge over the rivers, the brick buildings, and the church steeples give the place the feel of nineteenth-century America, a landscape that you might glimpse in a painting hung in the American wing of an art museum. This was also, of course, the place where the Civil War began; where the radical abolitionist John Brown seized the local arsenal in the hopes of sparking a mass slave uprising; where Brown was detained by the leadership of Colonel Robert E. Lee and hanged for his crimes under the watchful eyes of a young spectator named John Wilkes Booth. I'd often hike up in the mountains across from the town, secluded places where Confederate and Union troops once forged camps, fought battles, and traded control of territory. You are aware, up in those mountains, that the whole tableau looks the same as it did through those soldiers' eyes. A quiet American place filled with American ghosts.

In the winter of 2018, I drove out to Harpers Ferry to finish writing my White House memoir. The town was going to be cold and empty and that's precisely what I wanted. I stayed in a drafty bed-and-breakfast on the main road, an old house with antique furniture and a deep quiet other than the creaky stairs. I was the only guest, so for the bulk of my day and through the night I'd be alone in this house reviewing pages that told the story of the last decade of my life. I spent my first night there giving careful attention to the chapter that dealt with the Benghazi attacks, aware that it would be combed over by right-wing trolls who'd used my every utterance about Benghazi over the years to advance the projection that I was a villainous liar spreading disinformation.

In the morning, a cheerful middle-aged woman who made breakfast and looked after the place for the owners was intent on making conversation. I stood in the kitchen drinking coffee as she cleaned up after breakfast and peppered me with questions. What did I do? I was a writer. What was I writing? A memoir. What was the memoir about? My time serving in government. What did I do in government? I worked on international issues. When was I in the government? I was in the Obama administration.

Once the subject was broached, the woman was quick to volunteer, in the friendliest possible way, that she was a Trump supporter. She talked about how she'd moved to West Virginia from Florida, where her grown daughter was in law enforcement. She had become upset by illegal immigration, she said. She had no problem with immigrants, and she had long been okay with the influx of Latinos. But it had just gotten to be too much in their Florida community, and it was contributing to the crime that her daughter had to deal with professionally. She took out her phone and showed me a picture of her daughter, smiling, in a photo with Trump during a recent trip to Mar-a-Lago.

I was, I realized, having the proverbial conversation with a West Virginia Trump voter—one of the white working-class voters who had abandoned the Democratic Party and elevated a New York reality television show star to the presidency on a promise of keeping immigrants out. It felt like a useful conversation, two citizens with earnestly different opinions about how to fix our immigration system, but it obscured the more insidious aspects of the president. I inquired gently about how she felt about Trump's character. She laughed. "Of course I know he lies," she said, "but that's just what he did as a businessman. It's how he does business."

I could see her perspective. Her concern about immigration wasn't without legitimacy, even if I didn't share it. Her world-weary acceptance of Trump's lying indicated a belief that she was in on the joke and I wasn't; that Trump's crass politics was simply the natural way to get things done, particularly when the task was upending a failed political establishment to which I belonged. She even volunteered that she'd voted twice for Barack Obama. "Barack," she said, claiming a first-name basis, "was cool." But in her view, Obama's time was simply done and Trump was what the times required. So she was also one of those prized "Obama-Trump" voters. I recalled Obama telling me about focus groups that were done with these voters by the Democratic Party after the 2016 election. Nearly all of them could enumerate Trump's personal failings—his dishonesty, his treatment of women, his rude and vulgar manner. But they reserved deeper scorn for the Clintons and the corruption they seemed to represent—the profiting from power, the condescension, the membership in an elite that didn't care about them. I could see this woman fitting easily into those groups.

Then she started to tell me about the "research" she'd been doing. This entailed looking further into the "true story" of what was going on—deep reading online and watching documentary films. I could sense her moving into precisely the kind of space that I'd come to Harpers Ferry to avoid. Did I know, she asked, that "George Soros is the devil." She said it more as an assertion than a question, with an intensity that made me wonder whether the assertion was meant literally or metaphorically. Then she asked me if I knew about Benghazi.

It was as if time suddenly stopped, the universe conspiring to place me there in West Virginia, standing in an old kitchen clutching the handle of a coffee mug on a winter's morning. It was, I realized, the first time I'd met one of the tens of millions of people who had likely consumed some volume of content about my role in a terrible conspiracy without the person's knowing my identity. My name was written in the register, all of that information one Google search away. This was a transitory moment. I could retreat from the room, or explore where this could lead.

I'd be curious, I told her, *if you could tell me what you think happened in Benghazi.*

She said she'd be happy to, and we moved into the adjacent room, which—given the age of the house—felt as if it should be called a parlor. She started right in with the "talking points," the idea that Susan Rice had knowingly lied on the Sunday talk shows by spinning a fake story about the attacks in Benghazi being caused by a video. I was tempted to share what I'd been reliving the previous night. How there was an offensive movie about the Prophet Muhammad that had prompted violent attacks at U.S. embassies and facilities across the Muslim world. People killed and black flags raised over our embassy in Tunis. Masses of people rushing our embassy in Khartoum. Flames rising up from the ruins of less conventional targets like a Hardee's in Lebanon. But that, I felt, would be a bridge too far, starting an impossible argument in which we could never agree upon even basic facts.

What if, I said to her, the people working in government were not lying, but just trying their best at the given time; that they were people, just like us, conveying what they believed to be true? That had, in fact, been the essential finding of the many investigations that had taken place.

She considered the possibility, before moving on to other aspects of the conspiracy. The lack of security at the facility in Benghazi. The so-called "stand down" order that denied military support to the heroic Americans stranded under attack. Darker insinuations about the Obama administration's shady reluctance to confront "Radical Islam." The implicit accusation that, for some terrible reason, we'd let those Americans die there and then lied to cover it up. I tried to counter pieces of this, pointing out that the facility in Benghazi had not been an embassy, with all the security measures that embassies come with. That there had been no stand-down order, but instead an effort to mobilize the appropriate military resources to get to the scene. That the whole thing was just a tragic attack that sometimes happens in this world, a situation in which people did their best and it wasn't good enough. More than once, I felt compelled to tell her that I was actually a character in this story. "If you knew who I was," I said, "you wouldn't like me." The thought seemed inconceivable to her.

"But you're so nice," she said, waving my concerns away.

Soon we reached the end of the conversation. It was time for me to go back upstairs to work on my own history of these events. As if playing her final card, she asked me why—if nothing had gone wrong—all of these former military and Special Forces officers on Fox News said otherwise. I couldn't help but think of Michael Flynn, the man who'd gone from serving alongside Hillary Clinton in the Obama administration to chanting, *Lock her up.*

Sitting there, I considered the gulf that existed between me and this woman, the different worlds we inhabited. We'd both lived with the same presidents, experienced the same cultural moments, and likely made the same watercooler small talk about Super Bowls and celebrity breakups. We shared the trappings of a national identity that could stitch together disparate states, people of different backgrounds and religions. The national anthem. The Pledge of Allegiance. Memorial and Veterans Days to pay homage to the military. Familiarity with the Civil War that had started right there in Harpers Ferry. Pride in winning World Wars and the Cold War. Familiarity with the phrases inscribed on parchment: *We the People.* And yet her understanding of the course of recent events was entirely different from mine. It wasn't simply the question of immigration policy.

Basic facts—objective reality itself—were different, whether the subject was what happened on a chaotic night in Benghazi, Libya, or the motivations of people like me.

As she got up to leave for the day, she returned to her affinity for Trump. "What I like about him," she said, "is that he just brushes away these narratives." She held her hand in the air, waving it back and forth as if she was batting away flies.

I woke later than usual the next morning, having stayed up late working and finishing off a bottle of wine. I could hear her arranging breakfast on the table downstairs. I took my time getting dressed, nervous about the reception that I'd get, hoping that perhaps she'd just leave the breakfast and go on with her day. Maybe I was embarrassed about who I was and what I would look like through her eyes. When I came down the stairs, she greeted me with a mixture of flushed embarrassment and generous enthusiasm. *I had no idea who you were,* she exclaimed. She went on about how she never would have said those things had she known. I told her not to worry, that it was interesting to hear her perspective, which I'd never gotten to fully hear before. We did the earnest and relieving work of trying to reassure each other that it was okay, that our conversation had been positive, that we'd listened to and learned from each other. She told me that her sister followed me on Twitter because she's a big liberal. We took a selfie together using her phone. She kept repeating a version of what she'd said the day before, as if needing to repeat it to underscore a surprising discovery: *But you're so nice.* I assured her, genuinely, that she was as well.

I left the conversation with a mixture of relief and despair. Relief over this happy ending to the interaction, the human connection that people can forge even when they've been living in those different realities. Despair over the certainty that the same woman I'd just embraced had believed that I was someone entirely different before she met me. *It wasn't her fault.* This was the conspiracy theory I believed: that the vast infrastructure responsible for creating that alternative Ben Rhodes was fueled by unseen forces that shaped the politics of people like this woman—the cocktail of outrage and suspicion that was served up on Fox; the algorithms that filled news feeds with increasingly dire content and conspiracies in order to generate clicks; the wealthy interests that lubricated the machine to achieve more predictable ends like lower taxes and less regulation; the toxins of white supremacy that sometimes explicitly, sometimes implicitly infected the whole project. I had no doubt that she had a long list of legitimate grievances about the variety of disappointments that accompanied American life over the last several decades, just as she felt a sense of pride and likely believed her American identity to be a blessing. In our own ways, we all felt that. But we no longer had a common set of facts that could be agreed upon other than fleeting interactions that are increasingly rare in our individual lives or national experience.

I walked through the chill of empty Harpers Ferry streets, where unseen ghosts reminded me that the story of what is happening in America has always been contested, always connected to larger questions about who gets to be fully American, who profits from those determinations, and how the rest of us understand those realities and live within them.

IN THE FALL of 2017, I had to appear before the Republican-led House Intelligence Committee. They were ostensibly investigating Russian interference in the 2016 election, but the main purpose of their effort was to demonstrate that the whole thing was a hoax concocted by the Obama administration. Central to this narrative was the charge that former Obama officials had "unmasked" the names of Trump associates which should have remained secret in U.S. intelligence reports and leaked the information to the media. Susan Rice and I were the two White House people who featured most prominently in this story, which was the subject of endless right-wing media attention. As I watched this play out, one particular fact was most maddening: I had not unmasked a single Trump associate.

The entire exercise felt like a play in which we performed our parts. We filed into a secure conference room, the pageantry of lawyers present and documents signed. The odious Trey Gowdy led the questioning for the Republican side, marrying a friendly country lawyer's demeanor with the zeal of a Fox News prosecutor. For an hour, he grilled me to establish that I had no personal knowledge of the Trump campaign's efforts to "collude, coordinate, or conspire" with Russia. I patiently answered, alluding to the extensive knowledge I had of Russia's intervention in the election and making it clear that I would have no way of knowing whether the Trump campaign was directly involved because the Obama White House didn't meddle in domestic law enforcement or counterintelligence matters. Then he pivoted to the topic of unmasking, and as he started in, I noted the absurdity of the situation. He had spent the first half of the session establishing that I had no knowledge of Trump associates colluding, coordinating, or conspiring with Russia. Now he had turned to a conspiracy theory that the Obama White House had invented the Russia scandal by leaking reports to the media about Trump associates colluding, coordinating, or conspiring with Russia.

Here was a smart man seeking to ram together two puzzle pieces of a conspiracy theory that he hadn't even bothered to align. There were any number of things that his political party could have been doing, given that it controlled all three branches of the United States government. Instead, they were deploying that power to lend a veneer of legitimacy to the invented reality of an incompetent and egomaniacal leader. It didn't matter whether the effort succeeded, just that it be made. The mere fact of an "investigation" could give Trey Gowdy and collaborators like him the opportunity to go on Fox News and rant about a Deep State conspiring to take down Donald Trump. And the mere fact that Trump and people like Gowdy ranted ensured that the charge of an Obama Deep State Hoax would be similarly covered, debated, fact-checked, and earnestly addressed by the rest of the political media. The fact of this mainstream coverage lent the whole thing legitimacy, a resemblance to the normal scandal cycle of politics, something that obscured the reality that America's governing political party and its base were stewing in the juices of an irrational broth of lies. How corrosive that is to a society.

Did people like Gowdy actually believe these things? I assume not. That was definitely the impression I got in the room that day, as something in his eyes suggested that he appreciated the inconvenience of my being there to play along with the joke. But then there would be the seemingly more fervent acts of believers. In the coming months, I'd learn of a leaked Trump White House memo that cast me as the leader of a conspiracy to take down the president—"likely the brain behind this operation," the memo read, flatteringly.

Sometimes conspiracy theories are the darker musings of those kept out of power in a society. Sometimes they are fueled by those in power to keep a society distracted. But the Trump years went beyond even that—conspiracy theories were a driving force behind the government itself, connecting to the most potent grievances of those who felt excluded even though their guy had won, shaping the subject matter of the national discourse and radicalizing individuals inclined to prejudice. Once people choose to exist in an entirely separate reality, it is no easy task to bring them back, especially when every turn of national events can be framed as a validation of their grievances. We will be living with the residue of that radicalization for a long time.

AS I TRAVELED outside the country, I saw how what was happening at home was leading others to reassess America itself. Shortly before my session with the House Intelligence Committee, I traveled to Tokyo to give a talk on foreign policy. I sat in a windowless room in the hotel's conference area, flanked at a horseshoe arrangement of tables by the vice presidents of major Japanese corporations. Tensions were particularly high with Japan's nuclear-armed neighbor, North Korea, so I expected their questions to be about that. Instead, they asked what had happened that summer in Charlottesville, Virginia. Who were these people marching through the streets? Why had Trump said there were good people on both sides? What they were really asking, I sensed, was a more fundamental question: Is that you? Is that America?

I offered the usual explanations for the 2016 election, the combination of criticisms of the Clinton campaign, the news media, and the bizarre twists that coalesced to elevate Trump; the fact that there had been no massive shift in public opinion to the right, but rather a radicalization on the right. I watched them listen skeptically. These men lived in cold reality, numbers on the balance sheet. They couldn't indulge an America that was experimenting with insanity. Their entire lives had been shaped by American power. We provided for Japan's defense and nuclear deterrent. We implicitly steered its foreign policy. We wrote the rules of global capitalism that had allowed them to thrive. We developed the technologies that were reshaping how their companies managed information. We shaped the culture of international business that led us to be sitting there, wearing business suits, in a hotel conference room that could have been anywhere. They could tolerate acts of temporary insanity—the invasion of Iraq, for instance. They could weather the results of our excesses—the financial crisis, for instance. But they couldn't gamble on a country that had elevated someone like Trump, who praised fascists marching in the streets and steered the national discourse into the depths of conspiracy theory. That was more dangerous than North Korea, and nothing I could say was going to convince them otherwise. For the first time in my life, I had the acute awareness of living in a time when America was no longer viewed as a leader of the world, free or otherwise.

As I traveled throughout the Trump years, I'd continue to have this sense of being in a world that was trying to figure out what this shift meant. I could feel how America had instigated so much of the momentum that shaped the trends at work everywhere. That nagging question. *Is this what we had done with our years of post–Cold War dominance?*

Yet I also found America's DNA in the people and movements

opposing these trends. In Hungary, the young, English-speaking activists and politicians who used American methods of community organizing to push back while holding on to Hungary's association with the European Union. In Russia, where Navalny's organization worked assiduously on Mac laptops and posted their videos on YouTube, while Zhanna Nemtsova attended the renaming of the street across from the Russian embassy in Washington to Boris Nemtsov Plaza. In Hong Kong, where the protest movement painted slogans taken from American popular culture—"Fuck da Police" and "If we burn, you burn with us"—while Bao Pu insisted that the movement should connect to the set of universal values that America had represented (imperfectly) throughout the Cold War. The world contained our multitudes.

By the time I left Hong Kong in December 2019, I was anchored in a belief that all of these movements somehow needed to coalesce. At the time, I was teaching a class in global authoritarianism at the University of Southern California. As I walked the class through a syllabus based upon country after country that had drifted to the nationalist, authoritarian right—Hungary, Turkey, Russia, China, India, Brazil—it was glaringly obvious how interconnected these right-wing nationalists were. They used common tactics, common narratives, and common conspiracy theories to legitimize their rule; many of them shared common sources of financing, corruption, and political consultants. Isolated, the resistance movements that gave me hope would likely fail. But if they were connected, perhaps some of them could succeed. That would require an America that came to its senses while recognizing how much had gone wrong.

America had helped shape the world we lived in before descending into the cesspool of the Trump years. We now had a government that was busy radicalizing a huge swath of American society, with pockets of the country turning to violent white supremacy or a QAnon conspiracy theory positing that America is secretly run by a cabal of child sex traffickers. At precisely the time that progressive forces around the world were under siege, America absented itself from the defense of the most basic propositions that had once defined it in the eyes of the world: The idea that individuals are entitled to a basic set of freedoms that should be applied equally to all people. The idea that democratic governance will compel a society to organize itself around a common set of facts. The idea that people of different races, religions, and ethnicities can peacefully coexist by forging a common sense of identity. The lifelines offered to those who struggled for those things in their own spaces, people like Mohamed Soltan, validated by the results that America itself could produce. We did big things.

Over the past thirty years, we had lost our grip on that lifeline.

OBAMA AND TRUMP perfectly encapsulate two separate Americas, two different stories about where we need to go. In their own ways, these two opposing stories reach back into the recesses of American history—back to Harpers Ferry, where John Brown insisted that slavery was irreconcilable with union; back to the nation's founding, when the author of a Declaration of Independence that stated that all men are equal owned slaves.

To have any capacity to help fix what has gone wrong in the world, we have to begin fixing what has gone wrong with ourselves. The end of the Cold War removed the demon that needed to be faced down abroad, the competing empire that compelled a certain sense of national unity and purpose. But we never did settle on a new national purpose after the Cold War, a sense of what it meant to be American in the world. Instead, after 9/11 we made the mistake of going abroad to look for new demons to confront.

The Cold War that needs to be won is now at home, a battle between people who live in the reality of the world as it is and people who are choosing to live in a false reality made up of base white supremacist grievances and irrational conspiracy theories—and seeking to impose it on the rest of us.

26

After the Fall

AFTER JUST A few weeks of lockdown, my three- and five-year-old daughters had become accustomed to not being around their friends, not going to school, not seeing grandparents. They started wearing pink masks decorated with stars. When we went out for walks through the neighborhood, if they saw someone coming they'd call out "Human!" and move into the street. They had school via Zoom, upending our efforts to slow their addiction to screens. Death was a lurking presence, something that suddenly merited further explanation. You'd think a society would do everything it could to limit the time that children are forced to live inside a disaster movie, wary of the impact. But not America. Not *this* version of America.

COVID exposed all of our most profound failings. Rarely in recent history has the collapse of a superpower been so quick, so complete, and so self-evidently connected to that phrase—*who we are.* We are a country that killed hundreds of thousands of people through our own unique blend of incompetence and irrationality; a place where we condemned our children to a much lengthier period of trauma from their distorted and disorienting reality.

A few months into the pandemic, a police officer in Minneapolis killed a forty-six-year-old Black man named George Floyd by kneeling on his neck for over eight minutes. Protests started to pick up around us. The COVID-shuttered shops on the main artery of our Venice neighborhood were boarded up. People painted murals and tributes on the shops, pictures of Black people who'd been killed by the police—George Floyd, Breonna Taylor, Tamir Rice, Michael Brown, Trayvon Martin. I walked by the pictures with my masked daughters. My older daughter asked who the people were. I explained that they were innocent people killed by the police because they were Black. I reminded her about Dr. King, the man she learned about in school; how he had fought against this kind of injustice, and how we had to as well. She reminded me that Dr. King had also been killed.

Helicopters circled overhead for days. It lent the feeling of a war zone, the experience of countries that I used to attend meetings about in the Situation Room. We went for another walk one morning and found that the National Guard had been deployed around the corner from our house. An armored vehicle was parked across from the local ice cream shop, perhaps repurposed from past experience patrolling the streets of Iraqi and Afghan cities. A handful of troops loitered on the sidewalk, guns strapped around their shoulders and pointed casually toward the ground.

"Why are there soldiers, Dada?" my daughter asked.

I moved them past the scene, into the empty street to keep six feet away. "They're here to protect us," I said.

"Protect us from what?"

"Well, they're here because they're American, the American Army," I said, not knowing what else to say, how to possibly answer the depths and dimensions embedded in that question.

I saw her studying them as we rounded the corner. "Why do they have guns?" I heard concern creeping into her voice, the sense of an image that she would be turning over in her head the rest of the day, maybe longer.

"Because they're soldiers, and soldiers have guns," I said. "But it's nothing to worry about."

As we came home, the anxiety of the past few months filled my chest. I had a feeling of unutterable rage. We couldn't leave the television on when the president spoke if our children were around because we were afraid of what he might say. I couldn't visit my aging parents in New York City, who'd spent a terrifying spring listening to the sirens outside their windows at all hours of the day. There were portraits of people murdered for being Black in my neighborhood, which was now occupied by soldiers. As tempting as it was to chalk it up to some bizarre coincidence of events, the truth was the opposite. *Of course* this was happening. America had evolved to an entirely logical circumstance, an endpoint that was preordained, the natural result of choices Americans had made—the decisions of voters, preferences of consumers, prejudices of masses of people, the momentum of economic and foreign policies that had run the ship of the American state aground. It felt, in that moment, as if I had completed some transformation that had been taking place over the last few years, a brief flicker of experience for a privileged person like me to learn what it feels like to hate the country where they live.

The next day, I heard shouts outside my house and wandered in the direction of the same street where the soldiers had been. A march for Black lives was moving slowly, chanting the names of Breonna Taylor and George Floyd.

As I fell into the crowd, I felt my identity being subsumed into a collective, voices chanting in unison. I looked at the Black faces in the crowd, people who had far more reason than I did to be angry, to feel hatred when it came to America. *What an extraordinary thing it is,* I thought, that they are not simply giving up on this place. How much of what is good about America, even the capacity for America to better itself, comes from an African American community that has given so much of itself. How I used to marvel at Obama's patience with America, the way he could weather bizarre slights at home and defend its exceptionalism abroad from a position of pragmatism—maintaining that even a flawed America still offers the world a unique opportunity, an example of how citizens of a multiethnic, multiracial democracy can change things for the better. How that movement could make a place for someone like me, even if I didn't share an identity beyond that contested word which could, after all, apply to someone who came from anywhere: *American.*

The crowd reached the end of the street and everyone went down to one knee. I felt the same sense of flickering empowerment, that intuitive sense of solidarity with other people—strangers who believe that something is deeply wrong but can be righted—that Katalin Cseh must have felt in her first mass rally in Budapest; that Alexey Navalny must have felt looking out at a crowd of Muscovites standing up to Putin; that the Hong Kongers must have felt attending a flash protest at lunchtime. The American element of this global movement against the forces that are crushing individuals around the world is rooted in opposition to American racism. But, after all, white supremacy is one particularly virulent manifestation of all the other ways around the world that the few claim supremacy over the many, where individual dignity is subjugated to the pursuit of power and money.

To simply hate America would mean succumbing to the apathy that bigots and autocrats always seek to evoke, to quit on what's best about other people, to confirm that America is the worst version of itself when in fact it is a multitude of very different human beings—and therefore contains the good and the evil, the selfishness and selflessness, of which human beings are capable.

I closed my eyes and listened to the crowd chant for justice. I thought about the odyssey I'd been on for the last four years, from an office in the West Wing to this street in Los Angeles, anonymous in a crowd of people from all kinds of backgrounds, a middle-aged guy wearing a mask. And I felt that I understood something that had never been entirely clear to me about the Black American struggle that I'd so admired, and in some tiny way served for eight years: You have to look squarely at the darkest aspects of what America is in order to fully, truly love what America is supposed to be.

EARLY IN THE pandemic, Viktor Orban granted himself emergency powers, including the capacity to imprison whomever he wanted. I emailed Sandor Lederer to see how he was doing. "To be frank," he wrote, "I'm more worried for the U.S. than for Hungary at the moment, horrifying news keeps coming every day. Please do share if you have any optimistic scenario for America."

I had thought my email a gesture of earnest concern. Even after all that had happened the last few years, I was still unaccustomed to the fact that things in America looked worse than what was happening in Hungary. I considered what America looked like from abroad, the authoritarian pageantry of Trump's buffoonish press briefings, the militiamen in the streets, the conspiracy theories mushrooming, the curve measuring the sick and the dead going up like a rocket. Like the last days of some dying empire.

When I FaceTimed with John, Charles, and Lorraine in Hong Kong that spring, they also inquired nervously about the upcoming U.S. election. The Chinese Communist Party had moved to seize the initiative through those national security laws and its COVID response. The government whose totalitarian nature led it to waste the precious early days of the outbreak, to lie and obfuscate about the severity of what was happening in Wuhan, had just as quickly snapped into collective action. Mass lockdowns. Mass production of masks and other health equipment. Mass propaganda campaigns. But even locked within that reality, these young people were closely watching everything that was happening in America.

In August, Barack Obama addressed the Democratic National Convention, imploring people to stand strong. "Do not let them take your power away," he warned. Later that night, after I learned that Alexey Navalny had been poisoned in Russia and was in a coma, I couldn't shake the sense that the timing wasn't coincidental. Not to Obama's speech, but to the broader context—the early phase of a pandemic that was going to reverberate across global politics like an earthquake. I checked the record of the last thing that Navalny said to me. "When I feel demotivated and disappointed," he had said, "it's absolutely one hundred percent that within the next five hours the authorities will do something absolutely stupid and illegal and against my country and my people and all my motivations come back." Now the stupid and illegal thing that his government had done had put him in a coma, and the American president didn't have a word to say about it.

Please do share if you have any optimistic scenario, Sandor had written.

We'd reached a moment when history really did seem to be at some kind of hinge point. Everything was on the table everywhere, and it was increasingly apparent that people sensed this intuitively. The authoritarians I'd set out to understand clearly sensed this, around the world and here in America. At the same time, opposition movements continued to swell. Katalin Cseh joined mass protests throughout 2020 in the streets of Budapest. Protests ticked up across Russia, challenging Putin's dominance and enhancing Navalny's standing; in neighboring Belarus, an explosion of popular mobilization refused to accept the results of the plainly fraudulent reelection of the Putin-affiliated dictator Alexander Lukashenko. Even the Chinese Communist Party was forced to reckon with the fact that the pro-independence candidate in Taiwan had won their 2020 presidential election by twenty points, powered by support for the Hong Kong protests and a backlash to Beijing's repressive response. The demonstrations for Black lives in the United States had sparked similar protests for racial justice globally. Something was stirring. You could feel it. Could all that energy connect in some way, transcending the narrower identity politics that concerned Bao Pu? Could we redirect those currents of history that put us in such harsh waters, gasping for air?

I thought about what Maria Stepanova had told me about COVID, why it might prove to be a circuit breaker to the spread of nationalism and its inexorable march toward violence. "It is a war without an enemy," she'd said, "without the language of hate or the necessity to fight." As much as the nationalists sought to mobilize the language of hate in response to the pandemic, enough people around the world could plainly see that what was required was a response based on science and reason, on facts and the very idea of objective reality that had come under assault. Meanwhile, the economic fallout from

COVID was casting an even harsher light on the fundamental corruption of those in power—their personal wealth and the offensive inequality of the systems that they presided over.

If the nationalist authoritarians had struck the first blows, made the first moves, this was nowhere near the end of the story. We were at the beginning of a new reality that was going to reshape global politics as surely as 9/11 and the financial crisis did. I found myself thinking of Viktor Orban's words, his demarcation of moments of global regime change, those times when "it was clear to everybody from practically one day to the next that from now on they would be living in a different world from the one they had been living in until then." This feels like one of those moments. Perhaps we are all collectively like a swimmer who has plunged into the depths, about to finally touch the bottom and push back toward the surface and the promise of fresh oxygen. Once we are able to breathe again, there will be the chance to start anew.

BECAUSE OF COVID, this was a question to consider in isolation. At home. Through the portal of a Zoom screen, I spoke to people from Botswana and Belarus; Budapest and Hong Kong; Kuala Lumpur and London. Everyone had this one thing in common, this experience of COVID, this primal interest in survival. There was also a common understanding that people everywhere had been somehow wronged by the governments that had failed to get things under control when it could have made a difference, that we were all paying for the selfish preoccupations of the people in charge. What would happen when all of these people could leave their homes again?

I ran on the beach, watching the sun glistening off the surface of the Pacific, attentive to how the patterns of light changed at different times of the day. The edge of America. On some days, the sky filled with smoke, the drifting residue of wildfires burning out of control up and down the California coast. The harbinger of further disruptions to come. I watched basketball games with crowds full of digitized fans. Before the games, the players knelt in protest during the national anthem. I took my daughters to socially distanced ballet classes during which they had to wear masks. The heartbreaking efforts to instill a sense of normality. Culture passed down through generations, across borders, manifest in the pointing of a young girl's toes. At the end of a good day, lighting the grill to cook dinner for my kids, I'd feel a sense of meaning and belonging, just another person trying their best in trying times. Driving on an empty freeway at night, my headlights shone on billboards whose advertisements had been replaced by messages placed by the city government. In giant letters: #AloneTogether.

The U.S. election would take place in these circumstances. It was both entirely familiar and unfamiliar. Familiar because the array of people on the Democratic side were the same people I had served with in the Obama years, from Joe Biden on down. Like a team that has retooled after losing a star player to early retirement, assembling the pieces to make another run. Unfamiliar because it did not resemble any campaign in American history, the communal and collective effort of politics pushed into a virtual space, people organizing and expressing themselves through whatever safe mechanism they could find. Alone together.

Underneath that was the building realization that the election was about everything. Whether America was in fact a democracy. What America stood for. Who was American. What being American means.

It was disorienting to the point of being terrifying that nearly half the country could assess the American carnage of the Trump years and determine that it was worth re-upping for another four. But it made sad sense. Once you've taken the step of believing that two plus two equals five, of—as Lorraine said of the Chinese Communist Party—looking at a deer and believing someone who tells you that it is a horse, there is no easy return. What that alternative reality offers is an elevated sense of belonging, one that floats above even truth itself: America is for you and not the Others; and that sense brings consequences for everything from the exercise of political power to the conduct of your daily life. No matter what happens to you, even if you lose your job, or get COVID because you refused to wear a mask, you have this intangible sense of belonging. The obvious mediocrity and mendacity of Trump and the Republicans make turning back even harder, because doing so requires you to acknowledge that you were taken for a ride by such people: People always lie most frenetically, to themselves and others, when they know they've done something wrong.

Yet it was also heartening to see how plain the stakes were to a larger number of Americans in those weeks leading up to the election. Biden's own flaws as a candidate only made this realization more profound. Here was a fundamentally decent man whose main message, distilled, was a repeated assertion that America was better than this; a message that he clearly believed, deeply, against all evidence to the contrary. But because there was no Obama, no charismatic savior to embody a movement, removing Trump was going to take a collective effort by many tens of millions of people. While Trump and Republicans across the country bombarded the body politic with disinformation and tried to make it more difficult to vote through myriad means, with tactics that too many Americans refuse to see as the common machinery of extremist autocracy and not mere politics, the effort required by some people to vote—particularly Americans pushed to the margins of society—bespoke a fierce defiance. Biden was a good guy, but it wasn't about him. It was about us. *We do big things,* and what could be bigger than ousting an autocrat?

For all of America's mistakes over the last thirty years, I was struck by the unease, expressions of concern, and constant requests for predictions about the election's result that I got from people around the world. By any measure, we had fallen from our position of hegemony, a superpower humbled by its own failings. And yet the question of what America was still mattered to people. They were watching—intently. What a strange and sprawling America they saw.

How fitting it was that the election should take place in this transitory moment of global lockdowns, the pause for an extended breath before the world resumed its routines. Yes, things were going to be different on the back end of COVID, and the American election was going to be an early indicator of which way things would go. I felt I could see why that might matter. It was because America had become an unexceptional country in many ways—the flawed construction of its own excesses, ruled by the corrupt autocrat with the son-in-law down the hall. Because America was like everyone else, made up of people from everywhere, the nation America chose to be might tell people around the world something about what direction events might take everywhere.

WHEN I OFFERED Obama that brief summary of what I'd found while working on this book, he argued against seeing too much uniqueness in the moment. He was a man who lived in history's longer view. "Keep in mind that this isn't unusual," he said. "Every generation has a version of the same competition."

He's right. To me, though, the cyclical nature of the competition—between autocracy and democracy, the powerful and the oppressed, corrupted systems and the uncorrupted masses—only reinforced its weight. When lost, the competition can lead to the murderous mayhem of world war, the brutal logic of the lash, or the chaos of an angry mob. Not every person in Nazi Germany or the antebellum South was bad, just as those who lived in more enlightened periods and places weren't all good. What alchemy was it—what combination of political maneuvering and mass mobilization—that allowed human beings to enter an elongated reason cycle, a period that allowed for more peace among nations, more rights within them, as the arc of the moral universe bent toward justice? Was this the work of individual leaders—great men and women? Or the amorphous accomplishment of movements—the faceless crowd?

I was raised to believe that America had solved this equation, that progress was preordained. Obama's own election seemed to reinforce that belief. But just as Bao Pu came to realize that he had to be deprogrammed in order to see things more clearly, weaned off the nationalist stories of his youth, so it was with me. This was the most obvious and terrifying truth that I'd come to see these last few years: that there was nothing inherent in America that made us immune to the viruses that had consumed all manner of societies in the past, and that we were capable of spreading those viruses to other countries. Things that I once thought unimaginable could happen here, in America. Just voting Trump out was not going to do anything to change that reality, and might even provoke those who supported him to become more radicalized, just as each of Obama's two elections did. The election of Joe Biden could prevent us from drowning, but it didn't assure that our feet touched the bottom; that would require more collective effort, the work of a generation in the cyclical fight over what it means to be American.

Like all human beings, we are fallen, able to do both good and evil. Recognizing that truth, however, only reinforces our agency for events. There is no predetermined reason that the unbridled capitalism we've championed needs to fuel rampant inequality and climate change around the world. There is no reason that the United States has to organize its national security state into a machine that wages an endless and self-corrupting war against the unconquerable fact of terrorism. There is no reason that technological platforms created by human beings need to run on algorithms that reinforce our darker and more destructive aspects. Moreover, the system that has been set up over more than two hundred years of American history *does* offer each generation an opportunity to think twice before committing irreversible damage, and to use democratic mechanisms to redirect and even reconstruct the ocean liner of the American experience.

American democracy doesn't offer us immunity from human fallibility, but it does offer second chances. There was something eerie in the way that events forced us to confront this reality in 2020. How COVID arrived in the final year of Trump's term, the cold truth of biology. How climate change became more apparent, evidence of human-caused global warming in our midst. How America's own legacy of racism exploded in our streets, the ghosts of our worst history. How tenuous the election itself seemed, the flagrant efforts to suppress the vote taken from playbooks shared with the likes of Orban and Putin, shadows from a future in which we could have little or no democracy at all. The cycle of history, the generational competition of which Obama spoke, seemed to pause for a moment—allowing at least those of us who lived in objective reality to see the picture in front of us more clearly.

IN MARCH 2015, Obama was preparing to travel to Selma to mark the fiftieth anniversary of the civil rights march there. He wanted to frame the drama of that moment as a metaphor for the larger arc of America, the way that the generational competition has played out. A simple image. On one side of the bridge stood John Lewis and a collection of protesters for racial justice with a simple aspiration: to march across. On the other side stood the avatars of white supremacy, racist police or police who served the cause of racism, with an equally simple aspiration: to stop them from marching across. A moment that had been repeated in one form or another so many times, the two competing stories that wound their way through America's history like interlocking threads of our DNA.

My friend Cody Keenan was the speechwriter. At one point in the process, Obama came back to him with an idea for how to expand the ambition of the exercise. He'd recently watched Rudy Giuliani on television. Giuliani had been praising the leadership of Vladimir Putin while putting down Obama. To Obama, it was a sign of how far the Republican Party had fallen, the idea that Republicans found more solidarity with a nationalist authoritarian from Russia than an American president. It also tapped into years of frustration that his insistence on a progressive story of an America that constantly sought to better itself, to correct what was wrong about the country, was seen as his being an apologist for America itself when in fact it was the opposite.

This gave Obama an idea. Come up with a list of those underdogs who had made America better through the ages, the people who had marched across bridges. *Don't hold back,* he'd said. So Cody asked me to set aside some time to brainstorm together. I was on my way up to New York. As my wife drove, I sat wedged uncomfortably in the back next to the car seat where my daughter slept. Cody and I went back and forth, constructing our list of American heroes. Sojourner Truth and Fannie Lou Hamer. Holocaust survivors and Soviet defectors. The slaves who built the White House and the American economy, and the strivers who crossed the Rio Grande. Tuskegee Airmen and the Japanese who fought for America while their families were interned back home. Writers and poets. The creators of jazz and blues, of bluegrass and country, of hip-hop and rock and roll. Langston Hughes and Ralph Waldo Emerson. John Lewis.

The exercise had a delirious quality to it. As it proceeded, I saw the simple radicalism of what Obama wanted to do. We were creating a new American canon, our own hall of secular saints, the mirror image of autocrats who build monuments to a particular view of power. Orban and his remaking of Budapest's statues. Putin and his narrative of grievance-fueled Russian greatness. The Chinese Communist Party's elevation of a particular version of Confucius in imposing monuments. The American landscape dotted with statues of the Confederate war dead, my father's own high school named for Robert E. Lee. Every nation is a story. To lay claim to the American future, Obama had sent us in pursuit of the better story of America's past.

In those moments, I didn't feel like a national security official in his seventh year of government service. I was aligning myself once again in some small way with that quintessential cast of American characters: the underdogs, the risk takers, the doers of big things. It felt more important than any Situation Room meeting I'd attended, any decision or diplomatic initiative to which I'd contributed. This was the more immeasurable work of contesting American identity through the assembling of the cast of characters who represented the American Us, a colossal force that could ripple out, for better or worse, around the globe.

I offered Cody the image of Jackie Robinson, an imperfect man who'd endured pitches thrown at his head and abuse hurled his way from the grandstand, stealing home in the 1955 World Series. What an American thing to do! What combination of brazenness, composure, and luck. How subversive, this thing that was allowed by the rules but not by the logic of the game. How many currents of American history informed that act? How many anonymous baseball games played under the American sun—segregated fields, Negro League ball, players forgotten to history—added up to the set of skills and cunning that Jackie had acquired by the time he got to third base that day and sized up the pitcher's delivery against the distance home, marking American time. Obama, I thought, was much more akin to Jackie Robinson than to John Lewis—the barrier breaker who played by the established rules and looked for the occasional opening within the rules to dash home.

Of course, the mere assertion of this identity doesn't make it so. When John Lewis crossed the bridge that day, he was beaten, his skull fractured. The push and pull of history. So it was fitting to await an election in which Obama's own vice president made another effort to cross. Perhaps the lived experience of the Trump presidency would shock America into some form of progress, in the same way that John Lewis being beaten before the eyes of the world helped advance the cause of civil rights, bending the arc ever so slightly in the right direction. No one person could do that for us. It was something that required a mass of human beings deciding that enough was enough and heading for the bridge.

WHEN THE BERLIN WALL came down, America ascended to a position of power in the world that has few—if any—precedents in human history. Perhaps it was inevitable that any nation which acquires that degree of dominance will ultimately misuse it.

There is something innate in human beings that resists unchecked power. America was supposed to be the idea that solved that problem—by distributing power so as to prevent its misuse, by at least paying lip service to the fundamentally subversive idea of equality, by offering a collection of outsiders and underdogs the opportunity to do big things. Yet power corrupts, and when America reached its post–Cold War heights, we were unmoored from our innate resistance to unchecked power. It was too easy to acquire as much wealth as possible, concentrated in the hands of a few winners, without regard to the anger that that could engender—from Russians watching their dignity debased by the ascent of a class of 1990s oligarchs to Hungarians and Americans who concluded that the entire system was rigged. It was too easy to launch invasions of other countries and stir up nationalist sentiment through a war that seemed to offer a clear enemy, the Other of Islamists, without anticipating how that could normalize a hypersecuritized politics of Us versus Them—the Uighurs in concentration camps, or the refugees subjected to inhumane treatment on Hungary's borders, or the ban on travel to the United States from majority Muslim countries. It was too easy to imagine that our technological innovations were ushering us into a utopian age of connectivity without anticipating what else those technologies could do—the flood of Russian disinformation on American social media, the totalitarianism of China's social credit system, or the conspiracy theories that could make masses of Americans believe just about anything, no matter how irrational or dangerous.

America is no longer a hegemon. There is opportunity in that. To recover ourselves; to claim the mentality of the nation of outsiders, comprising every strand of humanity. To make capitalism about something more than money, to make national security about something other than subjugation, to make technology work better as a tool for human enlightenment, to make our embrace of multiracial identity a reality beyond rhetoric. To learn from others around the world instead of thinking that it is always we who have something to teach them. To learn from young Hungarians like Katalin Cseh who are working to construct a politics of belonging that joins a sense of local identity with a set of values that are universal. To learn from Russians like Alexey Navalny who are courageously insisting that the corruption of those in power in the world today be revealed, creating an undeniable logic that the system itself must be upended. To learn from Hong Kongers who offer a warning about where the inexorable logic of politics and capitalism in our world is leading today: to the streets in which the sanctity of an individual's agency to determine who they are and how they think must be defended. To learn how they went about building a movement—*Each of us can scale the peak in front of us, each in our own way.* Alone together.

We live in a time when the world is emerging into a single history, and you can feel the currents of that history moving in the wrong direction. You can see it in the transformation of Viktor Orban from young liberal to aging autocrat, the poisoning of Alexey Navalny, the knock on the door of a Hong Kong activist, or the smoke-filled California air. But the fact is that most people around the world can see it too, close enough to touch. America is not an exception to reality. We are a part of it, and we can offer the solidarity of a people who came from everywhere: *the American people.* Existing structures and inexhaustible grievances will present their own barriers, but there remains the opportunity afforded by each cycle of history: to carefully watch the windup of a pitcher slowed by complacency and a sense of supremacy; to pause for a moment and feel the sum total of experience and brazen belief that propels the underdog's dash toward home.

Acknowledgments

THIS BOOK TOOK me to several continents over the course of four years and was completed during a global pandemic. It evolved substantially from when I started interviewing people who became its leading characters, as the world continued to change at an accelerating pace. Suffice to say, I could not have finished *After the Fall* without support and advice from many people in my life.

First, I am filled with gratitude for my family. My wife, Ann, heroically bore the burden of shepherding our children—and our lives—through my bouts of travel and through a year of lockdown while I disappeared into the storage attic to write. My daughters, Ella and Chloe, developed an understanding that their dad had to write when he should have been playing, and managed to find new adventures every day during lockdowns that robbed them of far too many childhood experiences. My wonderful and supportive parents, James and Jane Rhodes, were careful and generous readers of these drafts through a period of difficult isolation when travel to my beloved New York City became impossible.

Second, I was blessed with an extraordinary editorial team. At Random House, Andy Ward's intelligence, patience, sharp eye, and perceptive guidance made this an exponentially better book than I could have ever hoped to write on my own. My brilliant and tireless literary agent, Elyse Cheney, was similarly by my side throughout this entire process as a friend, editor, and partner through every draft. I'm also grateful to the entire team at Random House for their support and confidence, including Marie Pantojan, Kaeli Subberwal, London King, Ayelet Gruenspecht, and Allison Schuster.

Third, Nimita Uberoi was my indispensable aide throughout the time that I was reporting and writing this book—scheduling travel, finding people for me to interview, researching each country, and reviewing drafts. I could not have done this work without Nimi, and I hope it contains something of her intelligence and optimism.

Fourth, all of my colleagues enriched this work through our collaboration these last four years. The team at the Obama Foundation built an extraordinary network of young leaders, some of whom are profiled in these pages. The team at National Security Action thought deeply and seriously about American foreign policy (and most are now trying to put those ideas into practice in the Biden-Harris administration). My Crooked Media, *Pod Save the World,* and *Missing America* family imbued analysis with a spirit of activism, and you Worldos made me feel like part of a community that cares about what's happening around the globe. MSNBC kept pace with the insanity of American politics and offered me a platform to try to make sense of it in real time. My students at UCLA and USC taught me more than I taught them by letting me see the world through smart, restless, youthful eyes intent on changing the world; I hope you do.

Fifth, each of the people who spoke to me for this book has my eternal gratitude and admiration. With characteristic generosity, enduring friendship, and incomparable intellect, Barack Obama continued a conversation that we've been having for over a decade, which infuses this book and has made me a far better citizen of the world. Above all, I want to thank the activists, oppositionists, writers, and ordinary people who spoke to me from Hungary, Russia, China, and Hong Kong. You inspire me with your courage, decency, tenacity, and innovation. In a world that offers so much cause for concern, you fill me with an abiding hope. Given the risks you take in circumstances more difficult than my own, your example compels me—and, I hope, some readers of this book—to never stop working for the world as it *should* be. Each of us, in our own way.

Index

About the Author

BEN RHODES is the author of the *New York Times* bestseller *The World as It Is;* the co-host of *Pod Save the World;* a contributor for NBC News and MSNBC; and an adviser to former president Barack Obama. From 2009 to 2017, he served as a speechwriter and deputy national security adviser to President Obama. A native New Yorker, he lives in Los Angeles.

Twitter: @brhodes

About the Type

THIS BOOK was set in Dante, a typeface designed by Giovanni Mardersteig (1892–1977). Conceived as a private type for the Officina Bodoni in Verona, Italy, Dante was originally cut only for hand composition by Charles Malin, the famous Parisian punch cutter, between 1946 and 1952. Its first use was in an edition of Boccaccio's *Trattatello in laude di Dante* that appeared in 1954. The Monotype Corporation's version of Dante followed in 1957. Though modeled on the Aldine type used for Pietro Cardinal Bembo's treatise *De Aetna* in 1495, Dante is a thoroughly modern interpretation of that venerable face.